RISE
from the Ashes

Volume 1: The New Inquisition

LYNARE PIPITONE

Trilogy Christian Publishers
A Wholly Owned Subsidiary of Trinity Broadcasting Network
2442 Michelle Drive
Tustin, CA 92780
Copyright © 2020 by Lynare Pipitone
All Scripture quotations, unless otherwise noted, taken from THE HOLY BIBLE, KING JAMES VERSION®, KJV® Copyright © 1973, 1978, 1984, 2011 by Biblica, Inc.® Used by permission. All rights reserved worldwide.
All rights reserved, including the right to reproduce this book or portions thereof in any form whatsoever.
For information, address Trilogy Christian Publishing
Rights Department, 2442 Michelle Drive, Tustin, Ca 92780.
Trilogy Christian Publishing/ TBN and colophon are trademarks of Trinity Broadcasting Network.
For information about special discounts for bulk purchases, please contact Trilogy Christian Publishing.
Manufactured in the United States of America

Trilogy Disclaimer: The views and content expressed in this book are those of the author and may not necessarily reflect the views and doctrine of Trilogy Christian Publishing or the Trinity Broadcasting Network.

Illustrations by: Joseph Carrasco

10 9 8 7 6 5 4 3 2 1
Library of Congress Cataloging-in-Publication Data is available.
ISBN 978-1-64088-471-7
ISBN 978-1-64088-472-4

To Jay Pipitone. Thank you, Jay, for being my sounding board who listened patiently to my vision while I was writing this book, just so you could remind me your ideas were bigger and better than mine.
Touché!

Behind Enemy Lines

Dear reader,

Although Rise from the Ashes is fiction, I wrote it to sound an alarm. The world is changing. Christianity is under siege.

Like the characters in the book, we are all equipped with special gifts and abilities to use in our own personal war zones as we engage in this spiritual battle. We are not carrying physical weapons like guns and grenades and we don't wear the uniform of a soldier or engage the enemy on a physical battlefield, but we are part of a mighty army. The weapons we carry are spiritual and powerful.

Why do you need weapons? We have an enemy who wants to kill, steal, and destroy our lives.

Be assured, my friend, spiritual warfare is a reality in the life of everyone; and like it or not, you are a target. Satan is our enemy. He is not going to walk up to you on the street, looking like a character out of a movie; he is much more subtle. Instead he manipulates our thoughts, filling us with false information that pulls us away from the Word of God. Satan is the father of lies, and the battle begins in our minds. Everything we believe or don't believe will set the stage for our future.

There is only one way to fight this war. God's way.

In order to stay one step ahead of our attacker, we need to know what God says in the Bible—our basic training manual.

Study it. Memorize verses and surround yourself with other believers.

Take a hard look at the battlefield. This is a call to arms!

> For we do not wrestle against flesh and blood, but against principalities, against powers, against the rulers of the darkness of this age, against spiritual hosts of wickedness in the heavenly places. Therefore, put on the whole armor of God, that you may be able to withstand in the evil day, and having done all, to stand. (Ephesians 6: 12–13)

Let me be the first to commend each reader who decides to put on the full armor of God and join the fight to stand up for the Gospel of Jesus Christ.

Lynare

Acknowledgments

Special thanks to my husband, Nate, who read my drafts (over and over) with a respectfully small amount of criticism. He was brave enough to give me honest advice on the content as well as helping me nail down the loose ends while pushing me to finish strong. My hero.

With love to my daughter Lynare who, from day one, made me believe the book is epic. Her siblings on the other hand, Nate and Felice, kept it real. They hate to read, so they really don't know what to think.

I am especially grateful to my prayer partners who believed in the project and continued to pray for the book's completion over the many years of writing and rewriting.

Finally, and most importantly, this story is for the next generation of warriors: Noel, Dom, Brianna, Brittany, Jay, Brooklyn, Nick, and Beaudyn.

LYNARE PIPITONE

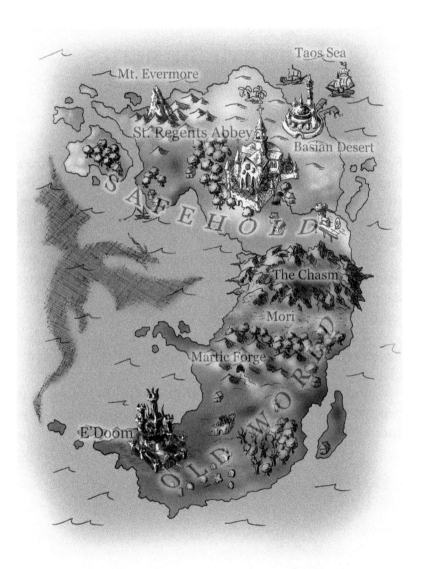

Prologue

In the twelfth month of the centuries' old war, during the age of Nehushtan, two stars appeared in the sky. One star, a glowing red nova with a massively long tail, spilled its seed upon all creation as it flew across the heavens. This germ impregnated the universe with evil, ushering into the kingdom of man chaos, fear, and destruction. The star of death wreaked havoc on the earth, changing her face through famine, earthquake, and plague. The star looked like a red dragon, flying through the constellations, weaving a shroud of evil to blanket the planet.

A new star appeared out of the East. It was pure and white, a beautiful diadem shining in a black barren galaxy. The phenomenon was neither nova nor planet nor comet gracing the cold winter sky. Most inhabitants of the earth took little notice of the light that was unfamiliar to the human eye. The radiant and brilliant celestial event had the appearance of a man. He held a sickle in his powerful hands, ready to sweep across the nations, gathering a harvest of souls. The earth's crop was fully ripe.

These were the years of war and hardship. People lived lives full of fear and terror. Many of Old World's leaders, great men and women, had given into temptation exchanging devotion for prosperity. Those in authority gave themselves over to all manner of lust. They indulged and feasted with the deceiver who ruled the nations. No one stood up to this beast that set himself on the throne, encouraging humans to slaughter their own kind. There seemed to be no one able to maintain the rights of the afflicted.

Many lost hope in the Redeemer's return. Young and old alike questioned the reality of the words in the Book of Life. Who were those heroes, the warriors of old? Were they only stories from the Book of the Ancients? Were there no more soldiers willing to fight the good fight? The world had fallen into the darkness of complacent satisfaction, oblivious to the tribulation that lurked in the bowels of creation.

Unbelief left humanity sterile, impotent against the onslaught of the enemy. Anarchy sprang up from the seeds of corruption. Even as the earth imploded upon itself, a tiny speck of light from heaven warmed the dry parched earth below, creating the right conditions for reaping an eternal harvest.

Table of Contents

CHAPTER 1 Hope for the Future 1

CHAPTER 2 Alex 13

CHAPTER 3 Catherine and John 25

CHAPTER 4 Beryl 35

CHAPTER 5 Beryl and Brother John 45

CHAPTER 6 Nyla 51

CHAPTER 7 Seraphine and Temperance 65

CHAPTER 8 Reverend Mother and Alex 85

CHAPTER 9 No Turning Back 91

CHAPTER 10 Holy of Holies 107

CHAPTER 11 The King of Old World 117

CHAPTER 12 The War Zone 129

CHAPTER 13 The Back Roads 141

CHAPTER 14	The Border	149
CHAPTER 15	Soul-Sifters	163
CHAPTER 16	The Chasm	171
CHAPTER 17	Feast on Souls	193
CHAPTER 18	Tribe of the Remnant	203
CHAPTER 19	Dispensary	211
CHAPTER 20	Friends and Enemies	227
CHAPTER 21	Shaken or Proven	241
CHAPTER 22	Temptation	245
CHAPTER 23	Never Alone	259
CHAPTER 24	Not Ashamed	277
CHAPTER 25	Fellowship	285
CHAPTER 26	Seeds of Deception	305
CHAPTER 27	The Prince of Darkness	315
CHAPTER 28	Treason	329
CHAPTER 29	Refining Fire	347
CHAPTER 30	Road to Destruction	359
CHAPTER 31	Rise from the Ashes	369
About the Author		377

PART 1

St. Regents Abbey

CHAPTER 1

Hope for the Future

Shedim perched on the rooftop of St. Regents Cathedral. His demonic shape blended into the night, along with the stone gargoyles that stalked the facade of the Basilica. The unclean spirit hid within the flying buttress to scan the commune, invisible to an unbelieving eye. High up in the spires, he could see, for miles, in all directions and scan the expansive countryside of Safehold.

This impressive jewel of the empire was given to him by Lord Danjal, the supreme commander, under the authority of King Apollyon. Few cities in the province could boast of a monastery, abbey, and military academy within the same enclave.

The demon puffed out his chest as he thought of Lord Danjal's words. *"You, Shadim, are a true patriot. Your influence over the human mind has led multitudes down the path of enlightenment. King Apollyon wants to honor your success with a promotion. Our king gives you authority to destroy the entire Kingdom of Safehold. You will manipulate the ideas and belief system of everyone within the province, starting with the pontiff. At all costs, you and your soldiers must be certain the church's fall from grace is complete. If you fail, you will reap their fate."*

Shadim remembered the moment like it just happened. The title rang in his ears like thunder. *General* Shadim. He, an angel in the realm of the powers would command a large militia of soldiers, intent on turning hearts of faith into vessel of indifference for the master's pleasure.

His heart skipped a beat as he recalled the one stipulation to his elevated title. *If you fail you will reap their fate.*

Shedim shifted his focus and scaled the cathedral's peaks and pinnacles searching the grounds for infidels. The challenge invigorated him. His strength propelled him through the air as he jumped from one pediment to the next, in an effortless show of skill despite the cumbersome size of his hands and feet.

He smiled and inhaled the scent of lust, avarice, and murder that leaked into the air from within the boundaries of the holy city. *Tonight,* he mused, *after decades of corruption, the crown jewel of the empire will become an unsuspecting prisoner of darkness.*

Over time, the faithful followers of the Word began to crave another kind of power. A power only the root of all evil could supply. He laughed to himself, remembering how the city was once a threat to his Lord's kingdom. The Kingdom of E'Doom.

Looking toward the walled perimeter of the compound, he was grateful to see no torches glowing on the miles of battlements circling the ancient seat of power. He whispered into the ear of a stone angel representing a heavenly warrior. "A good sign, don't you think?"

The ten-foot image stood among sculpted memorials of saints and demons that decorated the outside walls of the cathedral. He wrapped his arm over the stone angel's shoulder. "Year after year, I've watched St. Regent's watchmen become lukewarm. They act like beaten dogs, afraid to bark." He clicked his forked tongue and shook his head. "The sentries guarding these gates sat idle and allowed unbelief to creep in and steal the message of salvation."

He laughed. "Christendom is a beaten warrior. The light

of her truth snuffed out. The holy city has been poisoned by deceit." In a mocking gesture, he kissed the statue on the cheek.

"By the way, which guardian are you?" He looked at the image as if for the first time. He had never noticed the powerful sword the stone angel held in his hands or the breastplate over his heart or the shield of faith he carried. He scanned the monument, looking for a nameplate. "Michael the archangel; a warrior, commander, and protector of the people."

Shadim felt his soul prickle.

He crawled across the outer wall of the cathedral, like a spider moving over massive stained glass windows and past images of devils interspersed with saints until he came to the next stone paragon of virtue—seven in all.

Gabriel. God's messenger. "You don't look so tough."

He moved down the row, reading the angelic warriors' names: *Raphael, Uriel, Seroquel, Raquel, and Ramiel.*

"I guess God's magnificent seven have lost their power," he mocked.

The demon suddenly felt nauseated and moved far down the row to an image of a satanic spirit. The gruesome statue was stuffing a human into its wide open mouth, and with numerous arms, it held other men and women, waiting to be devoured. Shadim regained a sense of power and addressed the archangels. "Don't you care that the flock of Christ is asleep? Maybe you have no authority on earth anymore."

Something about the statues tonight bothered him. There was a strange smell in the air. "Faith is dead within these walls," he told himself. "I made sure any real devotion to God was slaughtered. The sheep are scattered, helpless, and vulnerable, ripe for my master's table."

He jumped down the steep wall to the ground, an impossible maneuver for man or beast, but not for a demon of his caliber. His keen sense of smell led him toward the east entrance of the compound. The unmistakable scent of a believer moved Shadim into action.

"An infidel."

A lone shadow slipped soundlessly through the corridors of the quiet abbey. The formless shape, like a wraith, crept passed the convent cells where the Sisters of Faith slept. Each large oak door, lined up one after the other against white-washed walls, were locked from the inside. The dark form pressed an ear against one bolted door. Nothing stirred within the room. The women of the abbey hid in fear of attracting evil to their cell.

The shadow crept forward using a gloved hand, fingertips touching the walls, as a guide in the darkness. The quiet patter of feet on the cold stone floors was no louder than a moth fluttering around a lit candle. The shadow reached the outer door leading to the east entrance of the abbey and stopped to listen. The only sound audible was her own heartbeat.

Satisfied that no one was watching, she slipped outside into the cool night air. She pulled her cape tightly about her shoulders, confident that her black habit would blend into the dark shadows. She hurried past the empty chapter house, praying the clergy had no fraternity meeting at this late hour. She snuck past the Sacristy knowing the priests were still asleep and would not be preparing for mass. Her heart skipped a beat as she paused and sniffed the air, making sure no one was preparing meals inside the Monks Fraters. The short journey through the darkness felt like an eternity until she came to the heavy steel door that led to the undercroft, the underground storage room on the east side of the Garth.

Reverend Mother pushed the door open, just enough to squeeze inside. A burst of cold damp air jumped at her like a wild spirit. She made the sign of the cross against evil. The stone staircase that led into the underground catacombs was barely lit, making the descent hazardous to navigate.

A solitary torch flickered on the wall, spreading just

enough light on the basement floor so she did not lose her footing. Looking around the familiar space, she tried to see in the darkness. Mother visited the cellarium regularly. Part of her job as supervisor was to make sure the monastery had plenty of wine for the daily liturgical services as well as keeping some in reserve for visiting clergy during the church's many feast days.

During the harvest season, the large room glowed with many torches, exposing the high-vaulted ceilings, rough-hewn shelves, and wooden barrels that lined the walls. There were many caverns underground, causing an unfamiliar visitor to lose their way in the vast labyrinth.

Harvesting the grapes and preparations for the new wine were over for the season, making the vault a perfect place for a secret meeting. Mother knew the layout of the wine cellar like the back of her hand; but tonight, with only a single torch, every tunnel seemed to be a threat, an enemy lurking in the shadows. She began to pace around the dimly lit room as she waited for her accomplice. The rosary beads hanging from her apron made a soft clicking sound as she silently padded across the dirt floor, lost in thought.

When she felt secure that she was alone in the cellar, she sat on a wine barrel near the sputtering torch. Her hands shook as she took a sheet of parchment, with the papal seal from her pocket, and spread the note onto her lap. The message she received from the Supreme Pontiff changed everything. Her heart fluttered in her chest.

Her thoughts fled from the note to her champion. "Alex."

Reverend Mother whispered the girl's name aloud into the surrounding darkness. The sound of her voice echoed in the large cellarium. "Alex," she said again, and the name burned on the woman's tongue like a spark of fire blown stronger by the wind.

"Alex is a rare girl," she mumbled aloud, rubbing her

hands together. "She is an unusual child."

Mother felt a wave of heat rush over her body, and she dropped to her knees in prayer. "Have I waited too long to tell her the truth of her lineage, Lord God? I don't want her to hate me," she uttered the question as a prayer. "This child conceived in sin… chosen." She covered her face with her hands. "Was I wrong to keep her mother's secret all these years? The cardinals would never have believed me," she argued aloud with her God. "If I confessed such a crime as rape by men of the cloth, they would have killed the baby." Her eyes stung with tears. "I could not imagine anyone would listen when I told them the archbishop and the inquisitor left our sister for dead."

The heavy door at the top of the stairs opened, taking Mother by surprise.

Sister Seraphine, Mother's right hand, silently made her way down the steps and appeared in the doorway. She carried a small fragment of wax with the faintest glow of light that made her look like a ghost under the pure-white wimple surrounding her face and head.

Reverend Mother quickly stood up and steadied herself. "Where have you been?" Her words rasped as she tried to catch her breath.

Seraphine pulled a small elderly monk into the room behind her. "The sun is ready to rise, Mother. I had to wait for Brother John to be sure we were not followed."

The portly elder pushed the gray hood of his robe off his head and cleared his throat. "God be with you, Reverend Mother." He bowed in submission to her authority before he continued to speak. "There is evil within the walls of St. Regents. The holy city has many ungodly eyes and ears."

Mother lowered her voice. "All the more reason to keep our project secret."

Shedim slithered through the streets of the compound

like a snake, following the smell of believers until he heard voices. He shifted his shape into a fine mist and bled under the heavy steel door that led to the undercroft. The vaporous shadow hovered like fog on the ceiling, above the three conspirators.

Mother fidgeted with her hands, wringing her rosary beads between her fingers. "Our enemies suspect the identity of our warrior." She dabbed at beads of water that collected on her forehead. "I fear they will arrest and question Alex before we get her out of St. Regents and into Old World."

Seraphine shrugged her shoulders. "They have no proof. If we stay true to our story, the secret dies with us."

Mother snickered. "Have you looked at her? With each birth year, she becomes the living image of Cecilia. A face not quickly forgotten."

John's sandals scraped across the dirt floor as he shuffled about the room. "Our secret has been safe for sixteen years. A few more weeks should not matter."

Reverend Mother stiffened. "His Eminence has ordered us to stop all deployment of warriors and envoys into Old World." She passed the note to her companions to read.

Seraphine finished reading and protested, "He said the door has closed to send soldiers into the war zone. The idea is ridiculous." She crossed her arms over her chest. "St. Regents has trained and equipped soldiers for decades to keep the faith alive in the war zone." Her eyes searched Mother's face. "This must be a mistake. The letter said the church made peace with King Apollyon." She paced the room. "The pontiff said he can no longer sanction our ambassadors."

Brother John grabbed the note from her hand and held it close to the flame, reading the words slowly until the full realization hit him. "The archbishop has begun a new inquisition to stop the Baptism of Fire among believers. If he finds out we are sending a team outside the compound, we will be tried as heretics. For that matter, if we refuse these orders, they can burn us at the stake as traitors to the crown."

Mother moved slowly across the room. "The war in Old World is closing in on our borders. Already the watchmen extinguish our lights, and soon, our doors will close on outsiders seeking protection. Our hostel is full to overflowing with war casualties, and before long we will run out of room for the refugees fleeing persecution." She absently crossed herself. "We must have a devoted soldier ready to lead a team into the war zone. Our men and women in the field are weary of the fight, and many are giving in to the new order of rule."

Mother kissed the crucifix she held in her hand. "Evil has entered our world and someone needs to stop the spread of this plague." She looked at her friends with a spark of defiance in her eyes. "If we decide to obey God rather than those in authority, we must act quickly. This team will be a small regiment of three. We cannot put an entire army in danger. If either of you decide to abandon the cause, you have my blessing."

Brother John folded the note and considered Mother's eyes. "I am committed to the Gospel of Jesus Christ."

Seraphine lowered herself onto a barrel on the opposite side of the room. "Alex is our logical choice as the leader of this crusade."

"Impertinent," Mother interjected.

Seraphine ignored her remark. "She is smart and fearless—"

"Disobedient," Mother interrupted.

Seraphine continued despite her superior's negativity, "She can be unruly, bossy, and arrogant at times but—"

Reverend Mother cut her off with a wave of her hand. "She is chosen but is she ready? I fear her arrogance is fueled by insecurity." Her hands balled into tight fists. "She is a citadel of obstinacy."

Sister Seraphine protested, "She is just fifteen. In time,

she will learn to overcome her weakness."

Mother folded her arms and tucked her hands within the large sleeves of her gown. "We both sense the powerful presence of God growing within her, but how soon before she is a yielded weapon in the hand of our heavenly King?"

Seraphine stood next to her friend and placed her hand on the woman's arm. "This was a difficult choice, Catherine." She used her friend's name on rare occasions. "All of us who hold the secret in our heart have come to love Alex as our own flesh." Seraphine rubbed Mother's hand affectionately. "I am certain she is the right warrior for this mission. Despite her dark background, she is clearly a child of promise."

Catherine wiped a rogue tear from her face. "I am aware of her strengths and weaknesses." She cleared her throat. "The truth is I fear for her safety. There is no protection for her anymore within the convent, and the dangers in Old World have accelerated with the new inquisition."

Mother pulled a handkerchief from her sleeve and wiped her brow. "The faster we prepare our team, the better for Alex. If they send for the inquisitor and she is found out…" Her voice dropped and the rest of her thought stopped on her tongue. "I will not even speak of the consequences."

Mother turned her attention to Brother John. "Is your prophet ready? I hear he is albino. Some say a bit odd, spending much of his time alone in the wilderness."

John watched the statuesque woman square her shoulders and look down on him with a raised brow. He smiled politely. "Let us say he is…unusual." The monk wiped his hands on his robe. "A boy who spends his days with scorpions and jackals is an oddity. But like your warrior, he is young, just sixteen yet growing into a mighty man of courage and faith."

Mother frowned. "Half-baked," she mumbled as she stalked the room like a caged lion. "And the healer promised by Queen Ra'ashad, our benefactress. Is he ready?"

Brother John faked a cough. "This is a problem, Reverend Mother. The queen's own daughter, Nyla, they call her, took temporary vows and became a Beguine, a new order of sisters that are free to live the celibate life for a short time in order to travel."

Mother wrung her hands. "I am aware of this hypocrisy." She clenched her fists. "Has the queen no influence over her own offspring? The very word *beguine* means heretic. That being said," she scoffed, "what does this Nyla have to do with our team?"

Brother John rubbed his bald head. "The girl disobeyed the queen's wishes to marry a foreign prince and become heir to the throne." His small brown eyes darted from one woman's face to the other. "Instead she chooses to go into the war zone as part of *our* team."

He watched Mother's eyes blink rapidly as if she was having trouble comprehending his words.

"Get to the point," she demanded.

"As a princess, she is highly educated, trained by the best doctors and has great knowledge of herbs, roots, and poisons." He paused and giggled nervously. "She has made it impossible for the queen to send anyone else with us."

Mother stomped her foot on the dirt floor. "She is a bold brazen article."

Catherine turned to face her coconspirators just as the cathedral bells began to toll for Prime, the morning call to prayer. "Our time has run out. Evil is upon us and we have our divine orders." Reverend Mother snatched the note from the monk's hand and held it over the torch until only ashes dusted the floor.

Shadim's confidence in his new position turned to fear. A few warriors with faith could destroy his master's plan. A sudden chill filled the cellarium as the spirit flew past them.

Mother watched the torch flare up like it had been caught

by a strong gust of wind. Her arms erupted with gooseflesh and the hair on her neck prickled. *An unclean spirit.*

Like a thief, Shadim escaped under the door.

"Sister Seraphine," she called as her accomplice rushed to leave the undercroft, "I want you to go with Alex on her final training mission here at the complex. Watch her. Make sure she is battle-ready. Our team must move into the far reaches of Old World by the new moon."

"Yes, Reverend Mother."

The woman grabbed John's sleeve. "Make sure your boy is ready."

He nodded his agreement.

"I will see to the healer."

Mother's parting words followed them into the predawn darkness.

"They carry the only hope for the future."

CHAPTER 2

Alex

Searing heat steamed up the underbrush on the forest floor. Alex rubbed her eyes. The humidity was so high she could see the moisture, like liquid phantoms, surrounding the foliage. Even in the deep shade of the trees, her lungs ached, making it hard to breathe.

She watched Sister Seraphine stumble.

"I can't believe Mother sent someone to evaluate you," Olga whispered to Alex. "You must be stressed out enough without that hawk watching your every move."

Alex wiped her face on the sleeve of her green tunic, staining it with the mud and grease she used to camouflage her flesh. "I must win this test, and her presence with us is making me feel a little bit jittery."

Olga bent over and scooped up some black mud.

She stood and began to apply the mask to Alex's face.

Alex grabbed her hand. "What are you doing?"

"Relax," Olga said. "She is watching us. Just stay focused and do what you always do."

Alex huffed. "What does that mean?"

Olga winked. "Prove yourself."

Alex rolled her eyes. "Fine. I'll see if I can help."

Seraphine watched the tall girl walk toward her. There was no denying she was athletic, focused, and driven. Her muscular body looked well-suited for a soldier.

"My leg cramped," Seraphine whispered.

"Use my shoulder for balance," Alex said. "It will be easier to work the cramp out of your leg this way."

Alex watched her superior from the corner of her eye. *She looks strange out of her habit. Many nuns are soldiers but Mother's right hand in battle fatigues!*

"We can continue," the older woman said. "I can put my full weight on it now."

"Are you sure you are all right?" Alex asked.

Seraphine straightened her vest over her chest. "It feels fine now."

She looks like one of us, but how will she hold up? "Let's go!" Alex commanded. "Quick, quick, quick!"

Her team picked up the pace.

"Stay alert and focused and move like you have a purpose."

They moved forward, hacking through the thick vegetation with their swords. The jungle won the scrimmage.

"Crawl on your bellies," Alex cautioned. "This is enemy territory and we can't afford to be stopped. Our captured sisters need all the help they can get."

The unit slid down a small ravine, startling a speckled boar from its afternoon bath. The large pig thundered away, disappearing into the depths of the jungle.

"Remove your weapons and roll through the mudhole, one at a time." Alex took a quick look around. "Do it fast before the mosquitoes eat us alive. The mud will protect us and camouflage us from enemy eyes."

One soldier fell behind and dropped to her knees. "I'm feeling dizzy, ma'am."

Alex severed a thick gray vine from a massive tree and spilled cool water over the soldier's head. "Drink it and get back in line."

The humidity kept climbing, offering no relief. The mud

made Alex's skin feel stiff and gritty. She felt irritable and edgy. Her stomach growled, reminding her that she had not eaten since yesterday.

No movement from animal or bird stirred the top of the trees. Only the insects that swarmed the forest floor moved about in the oppressive heat wave that left everything drooping. Alex could smell the stench of her body odor.

Vines crisscrossed the ground and climbed the trees. Distorted roots, the size of boulders, protruded through the tangled underbrush. Rotted logs lay buried under a blanket of thick plants. Lack of food and the heat was making her head spin, but she continued to move her troop forward.

"Stay low! Keep your bodies as close to the ground as possible." A rattling of leaves caught Alex's attention. An unusual odor surrounded them. The commander raised her fist. Each soldier stopped and became perfectly quiet.

The rustling noise was everywhere. In a matter of seconds, a muffled scream pierced the air. A vine coiled its way around a soldier's arm. Its hidden thorns bit through her flesh while thin sprout-like tendrils raced over her body, slid into her mouth, and down her throat.

"Alex! Agnes is down. Some strange vine—"

The panic in Olga's voice spurred Alex to action. Pulling a dagger from her boot, she crawled to the soldier's side. Without thinking, she savagely sliced the vine in two.

Agnes looked wild-eyed and dazed. Her hand reached for her neck and she pointed frantically at her throat. She began gasping for air, her body rolled on the ground, side to side. A look of panic clouded her eyes.

Olga backed away.

"Seraphine, hold her still," Alex ordered while she yanked the vine from the girl's throat.

Agnes choked.

A peculiar plant drew Alex's attention. She reached inside her boot for her knife. It was gone. She groped around the ground for the dagger but it had disappeared into the belly of vines.

"She's not breathing," Seraphine yelled while she fumbled in her pocket for the antidote.

"Isolde, throw me your knife!"

The medic tossed the weapon.

Alex caught it and sawed through a swatch of moss. A sticky green substance oozed on the ground. "Rip her shirtsleeve. Quick!"

Seraphine dropped the elixir back in her pocket. *Thankfully we won't need this.* She relaxed and watched their champion work.

Alex pressed the fungus into the open wound. Agnes's eyes rolled in her head; she coughed and began to breathe again.

The team snapped to attention as the rattling began anew. The lethal vines crept toward them across the littered forest floor. They pulled out their weapons.

"Use the slime as repellent," Alex said. The order was gut instinct. "Lather the green mucus on your clothing."

They cut into the fungus like savages, sawing and ripping the moss from the log. Long green tendrils, hidden below rubbery leaves, inched their way forward. Like alien fingers, the plants inspected the slime. Immediately the vines recoiled and retreated into the forest depths. The baffled soldiers sat motionless.

"They didn't teach us that in school," Magda whispered.

Alex wiped her forehead on her sleeve. Seraphine smiled. "On the battlefield, instinct is as useful as a weapon. Great save, Alex."

Agnes was stunned but alive. All that was left of her injury was a scratch. The unit was shaken but unharmed.

Alex sat next to Seraphine who helped Isolde nurse the

injured soldier. "Will she be able to finish with us?" Alex asked.

Isolde nodded. "Agnes is fine. You worked quickly, so she will have no complications."

Seraphine wiped grit from her eyes. "Well done."

Agnes grabbed Alex by the hand. "Thank you, commander."

Alex pulled her hand away. "You're all right then?"

Agnes jumped to her feet. "Fine, ma'am."

Alex stood and scanned the perimeter. "Move out!" she commanded. "Quickly before something else creeps out of the undergrowth and bites someone."

Exhaustion slowed their progress. Alex forced the soldiers to move over the uneven terrain. Their training taught them to work through pain, hunger, and fatigue.

She kept her troop inside the tangled depths, checking her compass constantly and keeping alert for voices or movement. Although a longer and more difficult route, they could avoid discovery by scouts that patrolled the roads leading to the tower.

So far, so good, Alex thought gratefully. *By nightfall, we will take the compound by force and release the captives.* The commander paused and looked back at the struggling troops. Mud, slime, and swatches of blood collected on her team members' faces and uniforms. There was no time to allow the medic to check injuries.

"Look alive, people," Alex said. "Move like you have a purpose." She urged them on until she heard voices and movement ahead. They had reached the tower, still hidden from view. Alex lifted a hand in an open gesture. The unit of five spread out. Another signal and a lone soldier crept forward. Olga took a sphere from her pocket. The dull-brown orb fit in the palm of her hand. She rolled it into the belly of vines. Alex stopped breathing, waiting for the globe to hit a trap. When all was clear, the soldier moved forward and repeated the maneuver in several directions, securing the perimeter.

When Alex was satisfied that the team was safe, she signaled and the team followed. Once close enough to see the fortress, she took her position. The rest of her team stood like tree trunks hidden amid green leaves, solid and still.

Alex could see the stronghold. It was apparent they would need to climb the outer wall. She knew it was the worst possible form of entry. The tower was out in the open. The team would have to be quick. The windows were extremely high off the ground with narrow openings. It would make entry a tight fit.

This station had five armed guards patrolling the perimeter. Alex peered through a jumble of leaves and used hand signals to show the team the position of the guards. She suspected her opponents would have swords, knives, and parrying daggers.

Alex mentally calmed her nerves. Timing was everything. Her soldiers would need to wait. They stood, unflinching like stone statues, for what seemed an eternity, having trained their minds and will to be as strong as their muscled bodies.

The quiet forest took on new life as the sun began to set. Wild cats screeched from the shadows, and strange frogs whistled and chirped. The thick shrubbery began to move around them. The backwoods came alive.

Shadows lengthened and darkened the forest floor. Alex could see her team's bodies droop from fatigue. The sound of hoofbeats and a deep voice brought them back to life.

"It's about time!" a male voice said.

Another voice answered, "The horses are lazy. This heat is unbearable."

As the enemy neared the tower, Alex could see them. She watched as they shared small talk with the new unit. The banter echoed from the tower while the new soldiers exchanged position.

"It's been quiet," one guard said. "Our troop is sure the enemy retreated."

She watched as they exchanged horses. "You should have a peaceful night. We will see you in the morning. Joseph's team is the sure winner of this final test. The archbishop will be thrilled with this victory."

Hoofbeats echoed down the winding dirt road, eventually fading in the distance. The unsuspecting new guards propped their weapons against the tower or on the ground while they took a moment to relax. Alex gave the signal. One by one, the unit snapped to attention. Their fatigued bodies came alive, fueled by adrenaline. They crept forward like tigers—swift, sure, and deadly.

In the darkness, the scheme surprised and disarmed the new guards. Alex grabbed an enemy from behind, placing a dagger on his throat. "Joseph and his seminarians will not win this battle," she whispered in his ear. "My novitiates and I are hungry for this honored prize."

The other team members corralled the remaining guards with their swords, dragging the prisoners into the cover of the forest, tying their enemies to tree trunks.

"Agnes," Alex said. "Stay behind. Watch our backs and guard the prisoners."

Alex evaluated the stronghold. "Everyone else, prepare your grappling hooks."

In one easy motion, the officer allowed the rope to play out freely, using a gentle upward lob. When lodged within the window, Alex tugged forcefully on the dangling line to make sure it had a proper bite. Nodding to the team, they followed her instructions using adjacent windows.

Alex led the team up the rough stone wall. She could barely ignore the cuts on her hands, elbows, and knees from the uneven surface. She was tired and knew her team was fading by the inchworm progress of their climb. Every muscle in her body ached, but she kept reaching and pulling upward with her arms and pushing with her legs. Laughter from inside the tower jolted her focus. Two guards leaned out a tower window above their heads.

"It's hot as hell inside," he complained.

Another voice answered, "It feels just as hot with our heads poked out this window, there is no breeze."

Alex prayed they would find a distraction.

"I say it's time for some ale."

She heard them laughing and shuffling away.

Olga lost her footing and began to slide down the rope. She dug her booted feet into the mortar. The clatter of her boots scraping the wall sounded like a rockslide. Her body weight propelled her downward. The soldiers dangling below ducked their heads while the loose stones pelted them.

Olga's legs pumped up and down as if she was running, yet her body kept falling down the side of the fortress. Alex knew she needed to act fast. She loosened her grip on the rope and let her body fall until she was inches below her friend. She wrapped one wrist around the dangling line and grabbed Olga's belt with her other hand as the girl slipped past. It gave the recruit enough time to stop the decent.

Both women held on, clinging to the tower wall, waiting to see if the noise drew the enemies' attention. Precious minutes ticked away as they hung suspended like spiders.

Alex's heart pounded in her chest. *I will not quit. I will win this test. I will make my team and the Sisters of Faith proud.* Sweat dripped down her forehead, and she felt like her arms were ripping from the socket.

Finally the voices stopped and the exhausted troop, once more, began their climb. Slowly and deliberately, they made it to the top of the wall.

"I'll go first," Alex whispered.

The window ledge was wide and deep, easy to get a good grip. Alex hoisted her body through the narrow opening. She landed like a cat on the flagstone floor and helped the others sneak inside the fortress.

"The dungeon is this way," Seraphine said.

'No!" Alex whispered. "Follow me. I hear voices."

She crept down a long empty hall toward the noise. A huge wooden door, left slightly ajar, met them as they turned the corner. Alex's pulse raced. The commander looked each soldier in the eye and smiled. With no further warning, she kicked open the heavy wooden door, catching the infantry leader and his men playing dice, oblivious to the intrusion.

"How the hell did you get in here? I was sure you gave up and ran back to the convent when we captured most of your team."

"You guessed wrong." Alex pulled the wet bandana from her head. Long sweat-soaked black hair cascaded down her back. She used the headpiece as a rag to wipe grime and dirt from her face.

She stood before her opponent. "Joseph," she jeered, "loyalty to God and our fellow soldier is the first and most important core value. We would *never* abandon our team."

A strange sensation came upon her. She felt an unnatural cold creep up her spine. The hair on her arms stood on end.

Shadim arrived like a storm cloud. His invisible presence dominated the room. A fierce cloud of hatred seeped into the air. *Here you are, warrior. I have been looking for you.* The demon said, although he knew she couldn't hear him. *Looks like I came at the perfect moment to create trouble and seal your doom. Already Joseph and his team are embracing hate in their hearts.*

"Tie the priest's hands behind his back before we send word to the archbishop about his team's loss," Alex said, sounding bolder than she felt. The cold creepy feeling surrounding her made her stomach queasy.

The seminarian wrenched free from Isolde's grip and spit on the floor. "This victory is a fluke. You are no real commander of an army. A girl like you will never be anything more than a beggar."

Shadim laughed while he whispered words that stirred Joseph's bitter heart. *Tell her what a piece of fodder she really is. Make her feel as dirty and shameful as her pathetic mother.*

"Maybe you're worse than the foundling the nuns say you are." He laughed. "You are a misbegotten spawn of hell. There is talk that you are the bastard child born to a crazy whore." His team began to laugh with him. "A nun, possessed by demons, bewitching honorable men of the cloth to do unspeakable things with her."

Alex lunged at him, throwing punches at his face and chest. He swung his fist and landed a blow to her eye. She felt a warm trickle of liquid spread over her face. She hit back with a hard right to his head and watched through her bloodstained hair as Joseph crumpled to his knees.

Sister Seraphine pushed his teammates aside and made her way to Alex's side. "Your words are nothing more than a lack of honor. She is a better soldier than the entire lot of you. Alex has already shown her worth to her team, the convent, and, most importantly, to Almighty God."

Two seminarians helped Joseph to his feet.

Shadim needed to stir up trouble to stop this girl. *You should kill her, Joseph, for embarrassing you in front of everyone. What will the archbishop think of his apprentice if he loses to a whore?*

"I curse you!" Joseph screamed. "I will make sure you pay for this insult." He glared at her with eyes full of poison.

Alex smirked. "Take the dungeon keys from the losing team and release our sisters."

"A great victory for the Sisters of Faith," Sister Seraphine said. She pressed a note into Isolde's hand. "Take this message to Reverend Mother at once."

"I'm famished," Alex said, hoping to hide the rage boiling inside her. "I smell something good cooking in the kitchen. I'm not leaving until we eat."

Stay angry, the demon whispered to Alex. Shadim smiled. *Yes, Alex, seek revenge.*

Alex watched Joseph and his team leave the tower in disgrace. Her heart pounded in her chest. "I hate him," she whispered to Olga.

She pushed the feelings from her mind and followed her team who ransacked the almery. "They must have known I was coming. Rabbit stew is my favorite."

In the center of the stone floor, in the tower kitchen, a cast-iron cauldron simmered over an open fire. The smell of fresh herbs, meat, and roots infiltrated the small room. Alex found a large wooden ladle hanging on the stonewall amid a combination of iron pots and utensils. She stirred the brew. Her entire team pressed in, looking over her shoulder.

"I don't care if it's rat or rabbit, I'm starving," she said. "Grab some bowls and dig in! This is a feast fit for a king."

They sat cross-legged on the floor with their backs propped against the wall. Alex felt nauseated but did not want anyone to know how Joseph's words sliced her heart. She vowed to herself, long ago, that no one would ever see her cry. She willed her hands to stop shaking and dug into the stew. With her eyes pressed closed, she pretended to savor the taste but she felt like her mouth was full of sawdust.

Her eyes popped open, and she swallowed hard. "Put the food down," Alex barked. The team stopped with spoons mid-air. "We forgot to pray," she said with her mouth full. "Thank you, Lord, for this victory over our enemy." She paused, trying to get the food to go down her throat. "and for providing a fresh-cooked meal at the expense of our enemies. Amen!"

CHAPTER 3

Catherine and John

The heat in the holy city smoldered. Reverend Mother dabbed sweat from her face. The heavy wool habit she wore trapped the heat against her body, making her feel like she was inside a furnace. She wanted to retreat into the cool darkness of her convent cell, but duty to the sick, the outcasts, and the orphans was her priority.

Mother walked across the grounds toward the hospital. So much had changed since she first arrived at the abbey twenty-five years ago. She was a young novitiate then, only sixteen years old, before taking her vows to become a nun in the order of the Sister of Faith. Marie Catherine was her chosen name until her religious order elected her the abbess responsible for the management of the abbey. So much time had slipped away yet she could still remember how excited she felt after accepting the position. Youth and innocence were on her side, giving flight to a young nun's hopes and dreams.

As quickly as day turns to night, the joy of the appointment turned sour. The rape of Sister Mary Cecilia cast a shadow over her life. How she wished she could go back in time and do things differently. Not a night went by that she did not regret having to keep quiet about the identity of the filthy pigs that brought so much pain to so many. Yet the sad irony was that such great despair provided so much hope. She smiled as she thought of Alex and how proud Cecilia would have been.

She looked around the complex, once empty and quiet. The mile of pasturelands between multiple buildings became a city of tents since the war spread its hatred into Safehold. As far as her eyes could see, wool capes and threadbare tunics stretched across sticks, making haphazard shelters for the refugees. She heard dogs barking and watched children of all colors and language play. She could not help but smile at the sound of their laughter.

Mother inhaled. The heady aroma of the food rations cooking on open fires gave her a momentary sensation of peace. She paused and prayed silently that the abbey would keep her gates open to help everyone who came looking for protection and forgiveness.

She walked for half a mile through the palatial estate. St. Regents was a ninety-acre fortress hidden behind twelve-foot stone walls. One-quarter of the compound was run by the Sisters of Faith while three-quarters of the complex was dominated by priests, bishops, and cardinals who made the laws for the church. In these evil days, the pope was nothing more than a figurehead, signing his name to unscrupulous documents, leaving the church's faithful followers at the mercy of wolves in sheep's clothing.

Fortunately Safehold was a self-sustaining city unto herself, a refuge to the lost sheep. Outside her walls, the church owned and operated manors that paid for the privilege of using monastery land. St. Regents had her own school, hospital, and military base where she trained and equipped warriors to send as emissaries in times of war.

The holy city sat in a fertile valley and was surrounded by lush forests and protected by Mount Evermore in the west. The Basjan Desert and the Toas Sea bordered Safehold to the north. This thriving seaport brought much trade and wealth to the holy city, along with the benevolence of the residing Queen Ra'ashad of Safehold who gave great sums of money to the church. In the northwest was the training ground, surrounded by the Depraved Forest, the only area in the kingdom that resembled Old World. The area was used to simulate war for the training of the soldiers. The diverse landscape of Safehold had rich soil and mild weather suitable for the many plants and compounds used by the convent for healing the body, soul, and spirit.

To the south was the Chasm. The wasteland was the last vestige of safety that separated Safehold from her enemies in Old World.

Mother shuddered at the thought of her changing world. The holy city was once the seat of spiritual knowledge, her precepts were unchallenged, her laws governed by the Word of God. Over time, corruption and compromise weakened her walls. Now each day brought the church, as she knew it, closer to extinction.

The late morning sun beat down on Catherine's head. She was glad for the shelter of the cloister, the high-covered walkways that connected each building. The beautiful arched columns supported capitals, carved with elaborate images of Jesus and the apostles, a soothing reminder that some truths would never change.

She reached the large hospital that was built horizontally, on the north quadrant of the Garth, to separate the abbey from the monastery. She began to inspect the cloth the lay sisters used for bandages and the many herbs prepared as medication for the infirm. She realized there were so many injured military personnel, along with civilians, the beds had spilled over into the outside garden that surrounded the hospital walls.

A young soldier grabbed her apron as she walked past his bed. Mother's pulse jumped when she looked at his face. He was but a boy, no more than fourteen. His undernourished body was covered in blood. The white linens on his bed were soaked red and his wild eyes seemed to have seen death itself.

She motioned for a lay sister to come and pour fresh water from the jug she carried onto a clean rag and began to wash his wounds.

His fevered body started to flap on the bed like a fish out of water.

"You are safe here, my child," she said.

He sprang forward, grabbing for the crucifix that hung from a chain on her neck. She pulled back in surprise, away from the fear and torment locked in his eyes.

He coughed and blood bubbled from his lips. "The beast is among us."

The hair on her neck prickled. A physician came and moved Mother aside. They tried to quiet the soldier's screaming, and then there was a cold silence.

Catherine could not stop shaking. She knew the injured warrior was speaking of Satan, and she believed he possessed souls. "*Servatis a periculo. Servatis a malefico.*" She crossed herself and whispered her prayer in English, "Save us from danger. Save us from evil."

She saw Brother John leading his donkey and cart through the sea of injured pilgrims in her direction. It reminded her of another time and place when her friend came to her aid. After the rape and beating of Cecelia, he stopped her and her young apprentice, Seraphine, from barging in on the group of men who watched the young nun's humiliation and suffering. She knew he saved them from death as eyewitnesses. They all realized it would do no good to tell the authorities. The newly appointed inquisitor was untouchable.

She was forever grateful to John for following the evil brood to the place where they dumped Cecelia's battered body, thinking she was dead. John kept his wits about him that night. He brought his cart and donkey to the pigsty where they left her body as food for the hogs. By the grace of God, Cecilia held onto her life by a thin thread.

John sent his dove with a note to a trusted friend at the royal stables to meet them and be ready to take a woman to safety. She would always remember that dark night that bound four people together with a secret to save a woman's life. How strange that after sixteen years, the same four people conspired to save multitudes.

Catherine sighed. They were all young then and full of zeal for the future of St. Regents. She watched John amble toward her in the crowd. She remembered how he looked in his prime, strong and brave, with silver streaks covering a full head of brown hair. She smiled at the bald pudgy man walking toward her in the crowd. Suddenly she felt very weary.

His little cart held supplies for her inspection. A large dove was perched on the back of his wagon bed, cleaning mites from its feathers.

"Cleanliness is next to godliness," she said. "The bird is neither clean nor godly."

He smiled. "Greetings, Reverend Mother." He bowed respectfully. "Our brotherhood donated all the sheets and cloth we can spare."

She rummaged through his cart, pretending to inspect the merchandise. "I have word our warrior is ready. Seraphine's report says as a leader, Alex can be impatient with her team, yet sister calls her driven. She also noted the girl does not delegate responsibility. Instead she jumps into each situation, doing things her own way. Naturally Seraphine sees that aspect of her personality as a plus since she is the only trained soldier going on this mission. She also has a bad temper."

Mother clicked her tongue. "She assaulted one of the seminarians, and sister called it affirmative action."

John giggled. "Sounds like Seraphine. She always looks for the best in others."

Mother smiled. "You are as bad as she is." She let out a long sigh. "Our dear friend Mary Temperance is waiting for her. She was told to pair Alex with a warhorse capable of surviving the demands of the hostile outpost where our team will be stationed."

The monk nodded his head. "We have done well keeping her safe."

Mother frowned. "And now we send her into grave danger."

"She is destined for greatness," John said.

Catherine touched the sleeve of his gray robe. "I have a favor to ask of you, John."

The man smiled. "Anything for a friend," he said.

"We will need to borrow your cart and donkey to carry Alex and Seraphine through the forest to the stables. We have not been there since the night we left Cecilia with Temperance."

He patted the animal's nose. "He knows the path well and is at your service."

"Thank you, John. I knew we could count on you." Catherine looked around, making sure no one was watching or listening. "Your prophet must be ready before the new moon."

"I will send Sarah to bring him in from the wilderness."

Mother grabbed his arm. "John," she whispered, "you know we must trust only a few with the details of this mission."

He tapped his arm and the dove landed on his wrist. "Sarah is silent as the grave."

Mother relaxed her grip. "I made arrangements to personally visit the queen and alert her of the pontiff's alliance with the king. If she and the child agree to move forward with their part of this mission, I will return with the healer."

Archbishop Pietto appeared, like a shadow, from within the crowd. Joseph, his personal assistant, followed close behind him. "Reverend Mother," he said, holding his hand forward so she could bow and kiss his ring.

She bent her knee and pretended to kiss the beautiful jewel that graced his fat finger.

"The novitiate," he said, "Alex, I think they call her, did well yesterday, bringing her team to victory." He paused and winked at Joseph. "I hear the she-wolf landed a lucky blow to my champion. She must be taught her place if she wants to advance within the convent."

Catherine folded her arms across her chest. "I heard her lucky blow was a knockout punch. Looking at Joseph's swollen face confirms she has an incredible right hook."

The archbishop sputtered, "The girl is much too hotheaded to become a real soldier. Luckily a military vocation will no longer be her problem since the door has closed on sending help into the war zone."

Joseph winked at Mother and grinned in satisfaction. Catherine lifted her head high and felt her jaw tighten. "Sending St. Regent's soldiers into alien territory has been the function of the abbey for decades. I am sure the holy father will continue to see justice done for those living under the tyrant's fist in Old World."

The archbishop snickered. "The pontiff signed the treaty along with our cardinals and bishops. We voted to come to terms with our old enemy, King Apollyon. Once this truce is finalized, there will be no war. Surely no one can argue with peace." He fingered the large gold cross that hung from his neck. "It is time for the church to get in step with the ways of the world…don't you agree?"

Catherine wanted to punch him square in the face but held herself in check. "If I read our Bible correctly, we are to be light in a dark world, leading people away from sin and toward salvation. King Apollyon has no interest in the God we serve."

He grinned at her. "Of course he does, Mother. However, the church has run aground. We have lost touch with our flock.

We will begin to restore friendships with our neighbors in Old World in the name of progress as our blessed Lord commanded. 'Love your enemies.'"

Mother felt heat rise in her face. "We are to love them but not become like them. Maybe it is not God's voice you are listening to at all."

She watched as Archbishop Pietto's smile dissolved into a sneer. "War will soon be remembered as an evil from the past. Our soldiers will bring a message of peace and unity to all people. They will ride with King Apollyon's army. Anyone who disagrees or stands in the way of our new doctrine will be at the mercy of the supreme inquisitor."

He took a handkerchief from the pocket of his silk cloak and started blowing his bulbous nose. Mother watched the loose skin under his chin jiggle before he spoke again. "He was here on official business about sixteen years ago. I'm sure you remember him well. At that time, he was just one of many inquisitors. He has been given an elevated title now and will have an office here in St. Regents." He paused and scrutinized her face. "His word will be law, by order of the king, our new ally. If the rules of the New Inquisition are broken, infidels will be beaten, tortured, and killed."

He laughed. The sound was cruel, almost inhuman. "The supreme inquisitor is on his way to St. Regents to speak to the populace of this holy city. He wants to make certain all people understand the Bible is no longer the only book to give guidance in spiritual enlightenment." He grinned. "While he is in the city, he might want to look at this Alex. As I recall, she resembles the witch he sentenced to die in a pigsty many years ago. We always found it odd that the woman's remains were never found." He frowned. "His worship will be interested in inquiring into this mystery, you can be sure. It will not go well if he thinks someone removed the whore's condemned body, allowing her to live and have an illegitimate child." He dismissed them with a wave of his hand. "Come, Joseph. We will leave the Reverend Mother to contemplate this news."

Catherine watched him leave before she turned her attention to Brother John. "The soldier was right. The beast *is* among us."

She crossed her arms over her chest and shoved her hands inside the long sleeves of her tunic. "I will go alone to the palace to see Queen Ra'ashad, our benefactress. You send for the prophet. Seraphine will take Alex to meet Temperance and secure a warhorse. As soon as I return, we will have just enough time to pray with our team before we send them into the realm of demons."

CHAPTER 4

Beryl

A dull hum tugged at Beryl's sluggish mind, coaxing him from a sound sleep. His eyelids fluttered. The sound was constant, annoying. He rolled to his side and the hammock rocked underneath him like a moored ship. The thick woolen knots encased his body in soft folds, lulling him back to sleep.

The distant sound persisted. It grew from a faint drone into a loud whirring and chirping. The high-pitched racket jolted him awake. He bolted from the hammock and tried to focus his bleary eyes on the commotion in the predawn sky. From the east, a column of thick black smoke bled across the horizon, covering the light from the waning moon.

The few embers under his cooking pot offered no protection against the oncoming invaders. The crescendo grew as the winged destroyers soared closer to his campsite in the open desert canyon. One last look at the sky seemed to bring the mobile ravenous army into his camp. Beryl jumped down into the sand and covered his lanky body with a lion skin cloak, tucking it tightly about his frame.

The tree that spread its branches like a canopy above him moaned under the initial attack. The leaves rattled and shook, the bark cracked, popped, and splintered as the invaders gorged themselves on the meager vegetation growing in the desert lowlands. He felt the creatures walking over his body. Pulling his torso into a tight ball, he squeezed his eyes shut and began to pray. A presence settled over him, and in the darkness of the lion skin, he beheld a strange vision.

He watched messengers, men and women, young and old, walking through cities, towns, and villages, speaking in all languages to every tribe in the nation. Each carried a torch that blazed with fire. The flames were strong and steady, even though there was a strong wind. At first, throngs of citizens crowded around the ambassadors to hear the oracle they preached. Then another came, a mighty serpent who spoke powerful, proud, and defiant words against the messengers and their God. The snake opened his mouth and scorpions spewed forth, dividing the people.

A flash of lightning shook the sky, and the boy found himself on a mountain peak. A heavenly being clothed in armor, with beautiful white wings, stood before Beryl. The apparition had eyes that blazed with penetrating light that looked deep into Beryl's soul. It was holding a staff that was on fire but did not burn its hand or robe.

"Do not fear the serpent that deceives with his illegitimate power," the celestial messenger warned. "And do not be confused by the scorpions who will challenge you with their empty words." The angel's voice was crisp and clear. "The time is now at hand. A time of great change and challenge. My maker needs workers, for the harvest is ready."

"I will work," Beryl blurted out.

The angel continued to speak. "The locusts are marching throughout the land, devouring God's crops. The people who hear his voice must take the words in the Book of Life to heart and act quickly while it is still day. You are not born anew to stand and watch. God's elect must stand against the dark words of deception and expose the evil. I will give you the staff of light. Prepare for war."

Beryl stayed under the lion skin, unmoving, his breath shallow, his lungs tugging at the little bit of air inside the makeshift shelter. He was not sure how long he lay there, but he was certain the swarm no longer hid the sun; he could feel the heat bearing down on him, showing no mercy. The clicking and whirring noise slowed down; only a low chattering remained.

Beryl threw off the lion skin and gulped air into his lungs. He checked his arms, his legs, his chest and head to make sure the bugs were not feasting on his body. He felt itchy all over. Looking around, he saw his tree stripped of all dignity, a white skeletal image of its former self. He looked across the valley, each tree and every bush a carcass. The winged army left little vegetation in its wake but forgot a few stragglers that crawled over his hammock and lingered in the tree.

Beryl slipped out of his goat-hair tunic and dropped it in the sand. "I guess even locusts don't eat the flesh of an albino."

The seminarian tied the leather belt around his naked waist and fastened a large red sack to his hip. Kicking off his sandals he hoisted his body into the branches of the carob tree. With the agility of a mountain lion, he climbed from branch to branch, grabbing his prey with bone-colored fingers before they had a chance to fly away.

He stuffed his prisoners inside the bag and collected the few remaining finger-like beans the tree provided. The unusual swarm of locusts made this day's breakfast a rare delicacy in the desert.

The sun was high overhead. The day promised to be scorching. The bugs were on the go, warmed by the hot sun, flying out of reach. This swarm was already fleeing to some new destination. Small beads of sweat collected on his forehead and upper lip.

Beryl reached for a locust and skewered his finger on a broken branch. Pain shot through his finger. He shook his hand and stuck the bloody finger in his mouth.

"Hell's fire!"

The few remaining herbivores lunged out of his reach.

"Forget it." He huffed. "These few should do."

He climbed down the tree and slipped back into his gray robe. He shook out his lion-skin cape, making sure there was no trace of the tasty insects before putting it around his shoulders. Singing a psalm, he repositioned the belt around his waist and secured his water jug and numerous multicolored bags on his hip.

"Clap your hands, shout and sing, cry unto God with a voice of triumph!"

Beryl hustled about his cooking space, cleaning the mess he made while dyeing his powdery-white hair. He dumped the smelly remains of two pots, stained black, in a tangle of bare bushes. The parched sand sucked up the thick dark liquid like a thirsty traveler. The acrid scent of vinegar and leeches filled his nostrils.

"Hell's fire, that stinks."

He moved the clutter out of his way, stocked the embers into a blaze, and positioned a clean cooking pot on the fire.

Beryl threw a handful of brown carob pods into the boiling water and added salt from his pocket. Reaching into the bag, he grabbed one insect at a time. His long pallid fingers skillfully wrestled the creature, holding it gently in one hand. The insect struggled between his left index finger and thumb. With great precision, he trimmed off the small forelegs and popped off its head, making a neat pile on the ground, one carcass on top of the other. After preparing the final piece of protein, he dumped them into the pot.

He crouched down next to the fire and stirred the contents with a stick. His stomach growled while he waited. A dove swooped down from the sky and landed on the sand a few feet away.

He smiled at her. "I know you are carrying an important message but breakfast first." The small bird stood on the sand, watching him. Her white feathers ruffled in the breeze.

"Be patient," he said. "Brother John can wait a little longer."

Normally his morning meal was long over, he always ventured into the heat at sunrise, but today was not like other mornings. The swarm of locusts was unusual, and the dream that detained him was extraordinary.

The messenger flapped her wings to stretch, blowing a spray of sand in his direction.

"Get your own bugs," he said with his mouth full. The dove cooed, cocking her head left and right.

"Okay, you can have one." He threw an insect from his stew in her direction.

She examined the boiled carcass then flew into a nearby tree.

"Your loss," he called after her.

His focus shifted to the strange gift left by the angel, the staff of light, which lay in the sand. It no longer glowed brightly with fire; it looked ordinary, just a stick. He picked it up and examined it from top to bottom. No scorch marks, no distinguishing feature, just a walking stick.

He stood and rubbed his head, feeling his freshly shaved scalp and the thick swatch that he left in the back. He rubbed his hands through the long black ponytail and checked his hands for stains. "Dry and crunchy," he said. "Perfect."

He peered across the sandy wasteland that rippled like water in the searing heat and pulled the oversized hood over his head to shield his albino skin from the sun. He smiled as he gazed at the chalk hills and plateaus he used as his refuge from life's challenges.

A soft clucking caused him to look at the tree. He held out his arm and the dove landed. "Sorry, Sarah. I forgot you were waiting for me."

He untied the small note from her leg and began to read.

Come home at once. Plans have changed. Our worst fears are realized. The pope signed the peace treaty with King Apollyon. Your mission is compromised. Get rid of this note. We are in great danger. Eat it if you must but make sure you get rid of it.

Home, he thought. The desert was his home, and all of God's creatures were his family. He knew when he went back to the monastery, his mission was to go into Old World and begin a new life, a dangerous life, serving God. Sarah watched him as if she was waiting for him to signal her departure. "Go, Sarah," he said and waved his arms in the air. She flew away, back toward St. Regents. Beryl cupped his hands over his eyes and watched the bird soar over a mountain that shot vertically out of the featureless sand. For a moment, he felt frightened. *I wish I had wings to take me far from my future.*

He folded the secret parchment into a tiny square and stuck it in his mouth. He chewed and swallowed the small wad of paper.

He looked heavenward and saw the eagle's nest that rested securely within a cliff ledge, directly above his head. He watched the bird, year after year, raise her family in the same nest, and he knew why her home was in disarray. The blazing sun shot through gaping holes in her domicile the size of his head. Mangled pieces of rotting carrion hung from the openings. He bent down and examined a mound of animal parts that fell from the nest. They were twisted and buried among discarded sticks and bloodstained fur that she had deliberately thrown from the nest. He dug through the pile with his staff and collected beaks, claws, and bones of varying sizes.

"Thanks for the leftovers and the memories," he said.

Beryl took a thin strip of leather from his pocket and tied

feathers, claws, and the tail of a rattlesnake around the top of his staff. He shook the wooden walking stick and made it rattle. "That looks better."

The contorted mess over his head rained dry leaves and mud on the sandy path. He knew the eagle had to make the eaglets uncomfortable. Her brood was growing up and she had to get them ready to leave the protection and security of their home. His time in the desert helped him understand her instinct to stir up the nest to train and prepare them to accept responsibility in order to survive. He also knew this was exactly where he was in his own life.

Brother John was getting him ready to leave the shelter of his wings, the protective confines of the monastery, so he could fulfill his purpose. From the eagle, he learned to rely on his heavenly Father for all his needs.

Beryl began to pace, his thoughts a jumble of questions. "Abba," he whispered his question to God, "I love my freedom here in the wilderness. What if I decide to say no to this mission? What if I decide to stay at the monastery to teach and prepare others to fight the good fight? What if I fall into hard testing and temptation in Old World?"

He paused and said a silent prayer.

When he finished, he looked up toward the sky. "*Deo volente*," he whispered. "Thy will be done."

Beryl looked in the direction of the midday sun. Like a master artist, she seemed to highlight images of deception on the weathered faces of the stone cliffs that surrounded him. The wind, her invisible apprentice, worked for centuries, blowing tiny particles of sand against the craggy rock walls, creating sculptures of cathedrals, castles, and snarling monsters.

He watched those same cliff monsters hide a coney from the jaws of death. The badger-like creature was an easy meal for the hungry jackals. The crevice within the rocks became a fortress and a stronghold against predators. Over the years, his time in the wasteland taught him to trust the Creator's protection.

Beryl loved his days climbing the cliffs and wandering on the rocks. He chose to live among the wild beasts and ferocious things of nature. This barren desolate place hid many lessons on living in a world full of blessings and dangers. In the evenings, he saw lions creep from their dens high in the rocks. They were patient all day, waiting for the sun to set, freeing them to devour unsuspecting prey. He learned to be vigilant, sly, and watchful against the attacks of the enemy.

The sun boiled above his head. Her position in the sky reminded him it was time to go back to St. Regents and prepare for his journey. He collected his sandals, cooking pots, crude utensils, and new walking stick. He shook the stick violently, trying to make it flame, but it remained a staff. He pretended it was a weapon, a sword, and he acted like a warrior swinging it around over his head. He stabbed at the air and twirled it in circles, playing war with his pretend weapon, but it remained a staff.

"What kind of gift is this?" he wondered aloud. "This is stupid. I wanted something powerful."

He squared his shoulders and began the hike through the wadi, the narrow ravine that cut between the high banks, offering some shade on the long and dangerous journey home. He pulled his oversized sleeves and hood over his hands and face to keep his albino skin from burning in the blistering sun. The position of the shadows warned him of the fleeting hours. He kept his pace sure and measured to be certain he reached his next destination point on time.

Beryl removed his water jug and took a long drink while resting at the base of a plateau. The next hour of the journey would be across the hill country, a monotonous succession of cliffs, each bare and desolate. He timed the slow descent of the sun perfectly and watched her slip behind Mount Evermore, far in the distance, before he made the climb.

He maneuvered the dark hills in silence, broken only by the wind and the rattle of pebbles tumbling down the steep slopes loosened by his sandaled feet. He learned to tread like a mountain goat over the uneven surface. He stopped at a viewpoint to gaze at the succession of hills, each identical in size and color. Brother John warned him that many wanderers lost their way in the desolate wasteland.

A voice from the shadows startled him. He whirled around with the staff, ready to strike. Nothing was behind him. Nothing or no one he could see. He wiped his sweaty forehead with shaky hands.

He walked a few steps farther and heard the noise again. This time, someone was calling his name.

"Beryl," Shadim whispered.

He spun around. No one was there.

"Beryl." The evil voice persisted.

He tightened his grip on the staff.

"What is that stick you carry?"

Beryl squinted into the darkness. He watched long claw-like shadows stretch across the desert floor. An unusual wind rose. It made the rattlesnake tail and badger claws clatter against the wooden staff like the gnashing of teeth. He saw a small whirlwind form in the sand. It twirled and rose in the cool night air. Beryl froze. From his distance, he thought he saw a beast or a demon growing larger, out of the rotating column of sand that whirled in the creases of the spreading night.

"Who are you and what do you want?"

"I am the voice of reason," Shadim said in a cold detached tone. "You have prepared for a journey that will lead you into much danger, possibly death. You have only a stick to take with you into a very treacherous and alien territory. You are mistaken. Your God would never send someone like you to do anything of importance. You should stay locked away inside the walls of the monastery…safe from ridicule…until you have the skills needed to speak to the heart of a lost generation."

Beryl held the stick ready to attack the formless shape that floated toward him out of the darkness. A cold sweat racked his body. *Maybe the voice is right,* he thought. *How can I battle the enemy and win souls to Christ? I'm a living freak show, too worthless to be used by God.*

Suddenly from deep within his spirit, words of truth filled his mind and he spoke them aloud. "I can do all things through Christ who empowers me." As he spoke, the stick burst into flame, knocking Beryl to the ground. He watched the murky form that was taunting him explode into thousands of red sparks in the darkness.

Beryl dropped the stick and examined his hands and clothing. He was unharmed by the flames. He used his sleeve to wipe perspiration from his brow. He carefully picked up the staff and looked at it in awe. His heart beat wildly, but something stronger than fear gripped his chest. "I can do anything," he whispered as he steadied himself on the staff.

"Thank you, Abba Father," he said. "You are with me and this mission is my purpose, my reason for living."

CHAPTER 5

Beryl and Brother John

Beryl was so excited he seemed to fly back to St. Regents. He and Brother John used a secret entrance, hidden away after decades of peace, to sneak in and out of the monastery. He climbed into a basket attached to a rope and operated by a second windlass at the top of the wall. He whistled, hoping his teacher anticipated his arrival and was at the top to help hoist him up.

A portly face, lit by a flickering candle, peered down at him. Immediately the basket began to ascend the battlement. He could hear the wheel at the top grinding and Brother John grunting under the strain while the basket bounced and jolted to the top.

When he reached the ledge, Beryl jumped from the basket. "Wait till I show you what an angel left for me in the desert. And my vision—"

Brother John clutched his chest and flopped on a stool. "What did you do with the note? Did you get rid of it as I instructed?"

Beryl nodded. "I ate it as you said." He smiled as he watched the look of surprise register on Brother John's face.

"It was a figure of speech! Surely you understand the difference." Brother John huffed. "You must grow up, boy! Quickly! I am sending you into the war zone."

Beryl felt his face flush. "I don't understand why you are

so angry with me. I just wanted to tell you about my special gift and vision."

"You are late." He wiped sweat from his forehead. "I was worried." He looked at Beryl and shook his head. "You are irresponsible."

"I'm sorry." Beryl hung his head. "I was in the wilderness, praying." He cringed, knowing he lied, but he wanted his mentor's approval.

The priest stood slowly, the stool creaked under his weight. "You were in the wilderness collecting dye for your hair," he grumbled.

Beryl felt his shaved head and the shock of hair in the back.

Brother John made the sigh of the cross. "Boiling leaches in vinegar to produce black dye is ludicrous!" He clicked his tongue. "What are you thinking?"

"I like it."

"A ridiculous style for an apprentice. It should look like everyone else's. Short and neat, cut close to the head, keeping a natural color like mine." He rubbed his bald head. "I mean, when I used to have hair. That has always been our way."

Beryl shrugged his shoulders.

"Your clothing," he scolded. "What is that filthy thing hanging over your shoulders?"

Beryl stroked the lion skin with his hand. "I found the young animal dead and decided to make a cloak." He squared his bony shoulders and posed like a mighty warrior. "I think it makes me look brave and courageous." He shook the staff to make it rattle.

The priest sighed. "Courage and bravery come from within, my son."

Beryl's posture shrunk. "I think the stick holds some magic."

The elder's eyes turned cold, and his mood darkened.

"God does not deal in magic," he snapped. "Sorcery is the work of wizards, druids, and demons." He gripped a crucifix that hung from his robe and kissed it reverently. "Our Lord operates in power."

Beryl shook his head. "You don't understand. It can flame up and turn demons into dust."

"After all this time, you still have so little understanding." Brother John interlaced his fingers and twirled his thumbs around each other. "Sticks, charms, and spells have no authority. One name spoken in faith holds all the power you need."

Beryl stood in the chill air, feeling defeated. He looked at the stick and wondered if it was all his imagination.

"We must hurry." Brother John pulled Beryl along by the sleeve. "I realized years ago, when you were quite young, that you march to an internal beat only you can hear. For this reason, I allowed you freedom to learn from the Holy Spirit and from nature." He slapped the boy on the back of his head. "But this." He shook his head. "How am I to explain this new rebellion?"

Beryl sighed. "I just wanted to cover up my white hair and pasty skin. I hate the way the others look at me."

John stopped and pointed a finger in the boy's face. "God has given you many gifts," he scolded. "Be proud of who you are in Christ and never let the opinion of others distract you from your true self."

His tone was harsh, but Beryl saw Brother John look at him with eyes that sparkled with pride. Beryl smiled at his gentle mentor and followed obediently.

"Brother John," Beryl said. "Thank you for teaching me how to study the Scriptures, the very words of God, and how to pray and meditate."

The monk mumbled under his breath. They raced across the courtyard, their sandaled feet echoed like running horses. John rummaged through his cloak for keys to unlock a large wooden door. The door creaked open, leading them into the library within the monastery. The room was large and impressive. They stopped long enough to light one candle to take them through the darkness. Volumes of books were stored on massive shelves, accessible by staircases, that escalated to each level.

Beryl looked around the scriptorium where he learned to copy ancient manuscripts, saving them from extinction. A large map of Old World hung on the wall. He had studied it from the time he was a child. It was familiar to him, yet a chill crept up his spine as he looked at the region beyond the borders of Safehold.

"Wait," Beryl whispered. "What has changed about this mission? Your note said our plans are compromised."

Brother John took a deep slow breath before he spoke. "We will send only three of our messengers into Old World. A mission to spread the Gospel is forbidden by our superiors. If we are caught, we will be tried as traitors and executed."

Beryl felt goose bumps cover his arms. "No! I will never let them hurt you."

"If you don't go, many people in Old World will die from lack of knowledge of the truth." He paused, looking for the right words to comfort the boy. "God's Word tells us to be bold… as a lion."

Beryl pulled the soft fur tight about his shoulders before he walked to his table at the far end of the room and gathered a few necessities. He placed the book with the Words of Life into his knapsack, along with parchment pages of songs for praise and worship to teach new converts. He flung his lute over his shoulder, making the strings gently sing, and stuffed colored balls and sticks into his bag.

Brother John bristled. "Old World is no place for toys!" He wanted to begin another lecture but decided against it.

Beryl smiled. "I will miss this place."

Brother John interrupted his thoughts. "We must hurry! Reverend Mother and the team are waiting."

Beryl froze before the door that led out of the library. "Do you think I'm ready for this mission?"

The elder looked at him and smiled. "What is in your heart?"

"I want to do the will of God."

Tears filled Brother John's eyes. "I found you in the desert. An orphan left out there to die. I raised you as my own son, and I have watched you grow into a young man who has become a master in the disciplines of our faith. I have seen you use musical instruments and compose hymns of praise and worship. Yes, you look different. You are different—from any other boy I have mentored. I believe in my very soul that you are ready," he whispered. "I will pray for you without ceasing. Do not fear. Our God is with you always."

Beryl wiped his eyes. "Thank you. You are a father to me, and I love you."

Brother John reached up and fixed the lopsided lion-skin cloak on Beryl's shoulders. "We must go to Mass before we meet Reverend Mother to make things look as normal as possible."

He opened the large wooden door and walked into the Narthex, a large covered porch lit by torches. His advisers, along with his classmates, waited in line to form a procession into the cathedral.

"Look at him," Joseph whispered to another seminarian. "He should be a jester in King Apollyon's court."

The boys snickered.

A tall cleric with thick eyebrows clicked his tongue and folded his arms over his chest. "The boy is a joke. Clearly a mistake."

Beryl hid his flaming red face within his hood, his eyes searched the expressions on the faces of those he called family.

Only Brother John believed in him. Most of his peers looked upon him as if he were no more than a locust.

Brother John nudged Beryl with his elbow. "Do not let their words grieve your spirit," he whispered. "God has a good plan for your life. Believe what your heavenly Father says about you in the Book of Life."

He passed his peers, carrying the stick given to him by the angel in the wilderness, as they began to sing. The service was a High Mass, and the priests sang the ancient Latin words with voices that sounded angelic. He looked around the candle-lit cathedral that was the heart of St. Regents. Beautiful stained glass windows told the events of the life and death of Christ, a story he knew well. He would leave this place and become an ambassador of hope, bringing a message of salvation to a heathen nation. *I'm not sure I have what it takes, but I trust Jesus to finish what he began in me when I accepted him as Lord and Savior.*

He lifted his voice with the others as the ceremony of the Bread of Life began.

CHAPTER 6

Nyla

Princess Nyla lay, facedown, on the massage table, allowing the therapist's strong hands have their way on her tense neck muscles. She relaxed to the sound of the Toas Ocean waves licking the sandy shoreline a few yards away. The cool breeze from the trade winds rustled the thatched roof that covered her private spa. The fragrant scent of jasmine oil helped ease her body, mind, and spirit. Abada worked her magic on Nyla's body while she let her emotions drift in a sea of anticipation.

"I'm finally of age. Everyone thinks of me now as an adult. It does not seem real," Nyla said. "While I studied and counted the days, I thought my sixteenth year would never come. Now that it's here," she took a deep breath, "where has the time gone?"

Abada kneaded the princess's slim shoulders with her strong hands. "Maybe you want to give back your certificate to practice medicine," she joked, "along with the little trinket around your neck and start over."

Nyla's hand reached for the pendant at her throat. Her fingers ran over the rough surface covered in sapphires, rubies, and emeralds. The gold pendant was an eagle in flight, its talons clenched around a serpent poised to strike. Inside the eagle's body was a secret vial which held the oil of Gilead.

She propped herself on one elbow and smiled at her friend. "This trinket is my way out of here."

"Lie still," Abada scolded.

Nyla sunk down and closed her eyes. Breezes strolled through the open-air structure and stroked her body. In its wake, the wind left the heavy scent of flowers like a lover bearing gifts. "I don't remember a time in my life that I wanted anything more than to carry this title," Nyla whispered sleepily. "As a physician, I will heal people physically, spiritually, and emotionally, bringing wholeness to their entire being."

She dozed off until memories surfaced like a bad dream. She remembered the disappointed look on her mother's face when she learned of Nyla's deceptive plan to escape marriage and go into the war zone. Nyla always went head-to-head with her mother. Unlike the queen, Nyla hated all the rules associated with the chains of royalty. She knew from childhood, when she watched the ships come in and out of the harbor from faraway lands, that staying in Safehold and the old traditions of her country were not for her. It was odd how much her mother's disapproval bothered her. She hated the knot that tightened in her stomach each time she thought about the hurt she inflicted on this woman who loved her. She shook off the feelings. *I'm an adult now and I do not need parental approval.*

Abada watched the girl's muscles tense and slapped Nyla gently. "Lie still. This massage is supposed to relax you. Think happy thoughts. You're getting away from here."

Nyla opened her eyes and smiled. "You always know what to say to make me feel better."

Abada added oil to her palms and rubbed the girl's back, hitting each pressure point. "Old World is far from study, family, and tradition." Her fists pounded gently on Nyla's back. "You will finally be able to make your own decisions, live life your own way."

Nyla's body relaxed but self-doubt gnawed at the back of her mind. "Do you think I'm a bold brazen article?"

Abada laughed. "Where did you hear that expression?"

Nyla giggled. "Reverend Mother's words in a note to my mother."

"Sounds like her." Abada handed her friend a soft sponge and sent Nyla into the fresh water pool. "Don't tell me you're having second thoughts!"

Nyla splashed water at her friend. "You sound like my queen mother." She swam across the sandstone lagoon, protected by bamboo walls, within her personal spacious garden. She ascended a series of stone steps to the showers and bathed under waterworks that sprayed her with jets of warm water.

"You have another option," Abada said sarcastically. "You could stay here and let the elders select the right husband for someone of your noble standing."

"No thanks," Nyla said flatly. "I joined the Beguines, so marriage is no longer an option. At least for a few more years."

Abada clicked her tongue. "I can't believe you, joining that religious order so you can go into the war zone. You could have any prince you want from the four corners of the world and you want celibacy."

Nyla climbed out of the pool and wrapped her body in soft towels. "I want freedom from all restraint. If I decide to marry, it will be for love, not duty."

Abada bustled about the hut, placing her equipment on a Marquette table. "Do you really believe that special someone is in Old World? Or is it the idea of the adventure?" Abada made her words low and seductive; they both giggled.

Nyla slapped her friend playfully. "He will be handsome and exciting." She picked up a metal box full of sea salt and a wooden ladle and used them as a darbuka to tap out a rhythm.

Abada watched her dance around the room. Nyla's slender frame swayed to the rhythm as she sang. The princess dropped her instrument to the mat and sat on a lime-green divan.

"The handsome stranger will take me on many adventures. We will never be bound by old rules and laws." Nyla twisted water from her thick hair. "I will see foreign lands, eat exotic food, live like a free woman in an exciting kingdom. Someday we will settle down and marry, have children." She paused and smiled playfully. "But I have to join the convent and get out of here first."

Nyla blotted water from her curls. "Healing is my passion. I don't want to sit as mediator for the people of the kingdom until I marry for greater wealth. Then the advisers will expect me to have one heir after the other until I'm old and my children are grown to live their dreams." She felt panic rise in her chest. "It's not too late to change your mind and come with me."

Abada shrugged. "Leaving Safehold and everything familiar is not for me." She frowned. "Besides I didn't study under the great healers like the gifted students."

Nyla wondered how anyone could be so domesticated and stuck in the old ways. She watched her friend stomp across the room, her ankle bracelets clattered and her natural fluid movements, beneath her silk caftan, became as rigid as a rod.

"Are you jealous?"

Abada plucked orange blossoms, orchids, and red hibiscus from the trees that surrounded the hut and threw them into a basket.

"Why would I be jealous? You were graded on your knowledge of the patient's mind, body, and spiritual connection." She looked over her shoulder at Nyla. "My duty is here, not on the battlefield"

"Your duty is whatever you choose. I have offered you that option many times." Nyla felt her pulse jump in her neck. "If there is something on your mind, just say it!" She stood and paced the room. "My duty is here also, but I have dreams of other things, desires that my ancestors overlooked for the sake of tradition. I don't want any of that. Being a healer is my chance to escape a duty placed on me by nothing more than a birthright."

Abada rushed to her side. "I know. I'm sorry." She sat next to her friend and held her hand. "I guess I'm a little jealous of your adventurous spirit and the fact that you would just leave me behind."

"I asked you to join me." Nyla sighed. "My mother wants me to stay here. She and the elders try to appease me by saying if I stay, I can help in the hospital, along with my other duties." Her gaze strayed to the ocean. Ships dotted the horizon, carrying cargo from one port to another. She pointed to the activity in the harbor, and Abada followed her gaze.

"I understand your desire to experience life differently, but your responsibility *is* here."

Nyla raked the tortoiseshell comb through her hair. "I spent each summer at the hostels, visiting pilgrims who came to Safehold from the war zone. They spoke of many dangers, but each one said God never failed them." She crossed her leg and put a gold charm bracelet around her ankle. "I washed infested sores that covered the feet of the children at the hospital and administered herbal remedies to give them relief. We nursed those who were hungry and thirsty at the almshouse, giving them both physical and divine nourishment." She shook her head and felt her long spiral curls tumble around her face like a lion's mane.

"I can do more if I go directly into the battlefield. My spiritual adviser said that faith is a strong agent in the healing process. I will be able to teach others that integrating faith in God and forgiveness are motivators in a patient's ability to heal."

Abada lined Nyla's eyes with a black powder and applied rouge to her cheeks and lips. She thought it was a good opportunity to change the subject. "What about the herbs, will they grow in Old World?"

Nyla shrugged. "I gathered the necessary roots, plants, and oils to take with me into active duty. I made detailed sketches and had them bound in my journal so I can identify the similarities once I get there."

Abada picked flowers from the basket and arranged them in Nyla's hair. "What about your special gift? Do you think it might scare the people of Old World?"

Nyla stood and slipped a silk caftan over her head. "The gift scares me." She shrugged her shoulders. "I have no control over this privilege or ability to conjure it at will. It has nothing to do with my talent, will, or force."

Abada watched Nyla's face light up.

"Just yesterday, a woman gave birth to a healthy baby boy. She and her husband were so happy." Nyla sighed. "Within hours, the child developed a fever and began convulsing. We summoned the doctor but there was no time. The baby stopped breathing." Nyla took a deep breath; her words tumbled over each other. "I felt the urging of the Holy Spirit to lay hands on the infant and pray. I was hesitant at first, the baby was dead. The parents were crying and pleading for help. As soon as I touched the child, I felt a surge of divine power, like electricity, run from me to the infant. My prayer to Jesus brought immediate healing." Nyla looked at her friend with wide eyes. "I still don't really understand all there is to know about this gift. Sometimes the Lord answers the prayer."

She paused and clapped her hands to chase a yellow bird from the platter of sweet cakes sitting on a cushion by the divan and picked up a goblet of water to drink. "I have prayed on other occasions and the person passed away or the problem was not solved the way I thought it should be." Nyla's words trailed away. "I am learning to realize, whatever the outcome, it is God's will I must seek."

"Are you not afraid?"

Nyla smiled at her friend. "Of what?"

"Of the dangers that stalk believers in Old World."

Nyla rested her hand on Abada's shoulder. "We call King Apollyon a demon because his ideas are different than the traditional views held by our parents. I am sure the old wives' tales about this man are to keep us all locked up behind bars of fear and superstition. I certainly don't believe devils run wild in the forests of Old World."

Nyla watched Abada's face turn pale. "What if the tales are true?"

"I am not afraid." She winked at her friend. "I'm curious about Old World." She rubbed her hands together. "I have been taught many things here, but I want wisdom gained from experience."

Abada stood with her hands on her hips. "Look at me, Nyla! We have been friends since childhood. I can tell when you are up to something."

Nyla placed her hands on her hips and mimicked her friend's actions. "Relax." She folded her arms across her chest. "I know there is great danger in enemy territory. Those who assimilate into the world are lost in a maze of regret. You know me better than—"

Nyla heard a loud whoosh behind her. Abada's face paled, and she dropped to her knees, pressing her forehead against the floor. "You're Majesty."

Nyla turned slowly. Queen Ra'ashad flew into the hut, enraged. Like bird wings, her gold and purple robes flapped in the wind.

Nyla stood erect, her eyes holding those of the woman. "Good day, Mother." She forced her lips into a childish pout hoping to irritate the queen.

The woman's black eyes peered over her burka. "I interrupted you. Please finish your conversation." She unfastened the veil that covered her face. The gold coins and beads sewn into the deep-purple fabric jingled. "You have given me the silent treatment for over a week. I would like to hear what you have chosen to tell your attendant instead of your advisers."

Nyla knew how far she could push her independence. The queen's expression was like stone. Her unspoken displeasure was etched across her face, chilling Nyla's nerves. "I was going to say I am strong in my convictions and not given to compromise."

The queen walked inside the open-air booth, and her attendants followed close behind. "The hour grows late."

Nyla looked past her at the clear blue sky. "I have all afternoon."

The queen stood before her daughter, clenching her jaw. "Reverend Mother has come personally to deliver you to the Beguines."

Nyla inhaled deeply and dug her nails into her clenched palms. "Why? That was not the plan."

"Your attendants are waiting to help you pack." The queen paused and looked her daughter over. "Unless you have changed your mind." Her voice sounded hopeful. "You could rethink this decision. Your countrymen want you to take your proper place as heir to my throne."

Nyla shook her head. Abada watched her friend's hard expression match the look of irritation on the queen's face.

"You are young and reckless," the queen said. "I will see you at the palace." She secured her veil over her face and walked slowly to the entrance. "It would be wise not to keep Reverend Mother waiting."

Once the queen left, Abada stood and rubbed her knees. "I thought she would never leave!"

Nyla picked up a lusterware platter, full of sweet breads and fruit, and threw it against the floor. "I hate her."

Abada was used to Nyla's outbursts. "My mother would have pulled my hair out by the roots if I acted like that."

Nyla rolled her eyes. Abada held up a mirror. Nyla grabbed it from her hand and aimed it at the wall. The attendant braced for the tantrum, but the princess stopped and took a few deep breaths.

"I will be away from here soon enough with no one telling me what to do."

She held the mirror up and winked at her reflection. "I look like a woman ready for adventure."

She slipped silk trousers under her caftan and secured a veil over her face. "I must go now. Tonight, after the ceremony, I leave for the convent."

Abada faced her friend and grabbed her by the shoulders. "I can't believe you are going to leave all this luxury and privilege behind for this fantasy you have concocted in your mind."

Nyla hugged her friend. "I need to do this. Some yearning inside is warring with my heart." She considered her friend's eyes. "This is my purpose. If I stay..." She shook her head. "Hurry. We must prepare my bags for the journey."

Nyla and Abada rushed to her room. Her slippers padded across the parquet floor. The intricate geometric patterns on the tiles made her feel dizzy. When they reached her rooms, she sat on an overstuffed chair and gazed at the earth-tone walls decorated with blue and orange ceramic tile. Warm sunlight filtered into her bedchamber through lattice-covered windows. She needed to steady her runaway thoughts before meeting Reverend Mother.

She saw the nun many times at the hospital, helping the lay sisters when more hands were needed to care for the sick. Mother was efficient, but Nyla felt she lacked a certain empathy the other nuns exhibited toward the patients. She remembered when Mother saw her for the first time. She gave a quick nod of recognition and walked away without a word. Nyla could still see the woman's cold brown eyes and lifted brow and felt the woman assessed her like she could read minds.

She was sure Reverend Mother looked right through her.

Nyla shuddered at the memory and began to pace her living quarters, wringing her hands. "Abada, make sure I do not forget anything. I refuse to give that woman—or my mother—a chance to deny my escape from this prison."

Her attendant inspected Nyla's satchel. "We packed your bag full of medications necessary for this journey. Salves, ointments, potent tinctures, and herbs, fresh and dried, are packed carefully."

Nyla checked her backpack. The smell of books and leather was calming as she finished packing her volumes of holistic practices into the bag.

Nyla walked through a large arched doorway into a covered courtyard. A slight breeze rattled palm fronds on trees planted in multicolored ceramic pots. Fresh water bubbled up within fountains, and flowering vines grew around white marble pillars. Nyla spotted her sand cat hanging from one of the elaborate cages that held her collection of exotic birds.

"Dalia," she scolded, "bad kitty!" Nyla pried her pet's claws from the cage. Dalia purred, snuggling into her arms. "Don't look at me with those innocent yellow eyes. You would eat my pets if you had the chance."

The princess pulled on a tassel hanging from the ceiling, ringing a bell. Within minutes, a cameleer, dressed in fine blue silks, led a white camel into the courtyard, followed by three grooms carrying trunks, saddle, bridle, and blankets.

"Where is the rest of my caravan?" Nyla asked.

The groom bowed respectfully. "The Reverend Mother said one camel is sufficient and only a few necessities are needed."

Nyla felt like screaming but held her temper. "Get the camel ready." She ran her hands over the luxurious handmade saddle blankets decorated with coins and beads. All the trappings were handed down from her ancestors over the generations. The lightweight saddle was a basket, lashed together with rawhide and covered with colored leather. Silver bells on the backrest jingled. Nyla dressed the camel's ankles with gold bracelets fitted with steel balls that made a light tinkling sound.

She placed all her health and therapeutic aids into the trunk. "Abada help me stuff as many articles of clothing as you can inside."

"Nyla," Abada scolded. "You have wasted enough time. The queen and Reverend Mother are waiting for you."

Nyla pushed her long curls over her shoulder and secured her veil across her face. "Koosh," she commanded, and the camel obediently lay down so the princess could mount. "Hut-hut," the girl said, and the camel stood and began to follow Abada toward the queen's private chambers on the far side of the palace.

The girls left Nyla's courtyard and silently moved toward the dome hidden within a large garden. The temperature soared in the high nineties, making the shade from the trees within the garden walls a pleasant respite. Abada led the procession through rows of frankincense and myrrh trees.

"Can you smell the harvest?" Nyla asked. She loved this time of year and relished the pungent odor of the bark that her countrymen used as incense and perfume. She watched butterflies flit over saffron flowers, calandos, and spikenard and inhaled deeply, enjoying the fragrance of the pine trees that produced cinnamon. Exotic peacocks roamed the grounds, along with parrots, monkeys, and zebra.

Nyla's eyes lingered over the pools where ancient lotus and papyrus plants sheltered newly hatched koi from the beaks of the hungry ibis. The giant water lilies fascinated her. The ancient plants were six to seven feet in diameter and trailed gracefully across the water garden. The huge flowers floated like dancers across the pond, dressed in soft hues of white, pink, yellow, and the very rare and precious powder blue. Turning the corner that led to the queen's private rooms, she spotted a cheetah taking a drink from a nearby fountain.

The path they traveled wound its way through foliage loaded with pomegranates, figs, and persimmon. Bearded holy men, arrayed in multicolored robes and elaborate hats, waited in the shade for an audience with the queen. A doorman rushed down a series of steps leading into the dome and helped the princess dismount.

"This is it," Nyla whispered.

Abada held her hand. "You are shaking."

Nyla smiled to reassure her friend. "I'm ready to do this. Be happy for me."

Once inside the building, Nyla heard the familiar chatter of her mother's entourage and smelled the sweet bread and fruit they brought for afternoon tea. Inside the stateroom, the queen's attendants and advisers chatted amicably while her mother and Reverend Mother sat in high-back chairs, side by side, talking and sipping tea.

"They look ridiculous," Nyla whispered to Abada. "My mother in her bold costume, like a peacock, and the nun looks like a crow."

When her mother saw Nyla enter the room, she stood and dismissed everyone.

She motioned to her daughter with a grand flourish of her hand. "Your attendant is not welcome in this meeting."

Nyla squeezed Abada's hand. "Don't worry. I will meet you after the ceremony and tell you everything before I leave."

An armed guard took Abada by the arm, escorting her into the hallway and closed and bolted the door behind them.

Nyla whirled around to challenge her mother's authority but sensed something was wrong. Looking from one face to the other, she could see the strain of many hard decisions etched on both faces. Although she told Abada she hated her mother, she secretly envied the woman's self-disciplined nature. Watching the two matriarchs interact made her realize how alike they were; both chose to forsake their own desires for the greater good of others.

"You must listen carefully, daughter."

Nyla detected a strange fear in her tone.

"Reverend Mother has not come to deliver you to the convent." She paused. "Instead she has grave news."

Nyla focused her attention on the nun.

"St. Regents has been ordered to stop sending soldiers and spiritual advisers into the battlefield. By order of the holy father, the church is making a pact with King Apollyon in the name of peace. We must worship pagan gods, along with God the Father, Son, and Holy Spirit."

Nyla shook her head. "That's impossible. How can believers in the cross align themselves with lies?"

Mother Superior walked slowly to the large iwan, a floor-to-ceiling window that led to the queen's balcony. "At great risk, a few of us will ignore this mandate and send a warrior, a prophet, and a healer into the battlefield. We will be acting against the law and will be tried for treason if we are caught."

Nyla felt like all the air left her lungs. She grabbed the back of a chair to steady herself. "I will not risk my mother's life. Send someone else."

"No," the queen protested.

Nyla was confused. Her eyes filled with tears.

The queen's voice trembled. "I will not put anyone else in danger. We have come too far to turn back now. I believed in this mission before, and I believe more so now. As believers, we must stand for the truth, no matter the consequence. You are free to change your mind, Nyla, and Reverend Mother will send the other two without a healer."

Nyla slid into the chair. Her legs were weak and she felt sick. "No army will accompany us?"

Reverend Mother shook her head. "We hope the three of you will be across the Chasm before anyone notices you are missing."

"What about my celebration? When will we—"

Mother folded her arms over her chest and looked at Nyla with her cold brown eyes. "If you decide to leave the palace and join this team, you will no longer have any contact with anyone inside the castle. As far as your mother's advisers know, you have left to join the convent."

Nyla jumped from the chair. "But Abada, I must tell her. I need to say goodbye."

Mother looked away. "You will put her at risk if the inquisitor finds out you spoke to her before leaving. When we leave this room, your life, as you've known it, is over."

Nyla fidgeted with the necklace that graced her neck. "Will we ever be able to return to our homeland?"

Both women exchanged glances, but it was the queen who spoke, "Not until King Apollyon and his army are defeated."

CHAPTER 7

Seraphine and Temperance

Alex and Sister Seraphine arrived at the stables of St. Regents before noon. The wooden cart, pulled by Brother John's donkey, rocked and bounced along the horse trail and out of the forest into the noonday's brilliance. Alex wiped water from her eyes. The light was blinding after being within the dark canopy of trees for half a day's journey. She slipped out of her cloak and let the sun warm the chill that settled over her within the forest and shielded her eyes with her hand to see the high peaks of a massive mountain. The twisted spirals on top of the mount reached into the sky, touching the clouds. Mount Evermore, the majestic highlands of Safehold, made a perfect backdrop for the royal stables.

The sight almost made Alex forget Joseph's accusations about her mother. She wondered if this maternal stranger, hanging over her life like a dark shadow, *was* a whore as some believed. She decided she would ask her confessor if her mother's sins of lust made it impossible for her offspring to become anything more than a misfit.

She was so lost in her thought, Seraphine's voice made her jump. They spent most of the half-day trip in silence, except for the few courtesies they exchanged with each other along the way. It was all the same to Alex, she used the silence to plot her revenge for Joseph's cutting remarks.

"We must be very careful with what we say and how we

act for the next few days," Seraphine said.

Alex came out of her fog and watched the woman's body go rigid.

"First and foremost, you must avoid going to confession. The Lord commands us not to lie yet the lives of many hang in the balance, so secrecy is of the utmost importance."

Alex wondered if she was a witch who could read her thoughts.

"You can confess directly to our Savior. Our Lord does not need priests' ears to hear us."

Alex watched the woman fidget with the leather reins. Her fingers were long and slender, but the skin on her hands were rough and chapped from participating in yesterday's training exercise. Alex thought the nun had a beautiful face, like marble—strong and smooth. Normally it was hard to read her mood, but today, her expression was tense. It gave Alex a strange knot in her stomach to see her leader show fear. Seraphine was known throughout the abbey as stable and solid in her faith; an asset in giving council to Reverend Mother.

"Why the secrecy? What has changed?" Alex asked.

Seraphine cleared her throat. "I regret to tell you there will be no army from St. Regents for you to command as you invade Old World." She paused, letting her words sink into the girl's mind. "You will oversee this mission, but we will only send a prophet and healer to go with you."

Alex laughed. "Am I to understand St. Regent's is sending only three ambassadors into the war zone? Alone?" Alex shifted her position on the seat so she could see the nun's expression to make sure she was serious.

Seraphine looked into Alex's eyes. "I'm sorry. Much has changed since the church made an alliance with King Apollyon. We are forbidden to take the Gospel into Old World."

Alex shook her head. "Stop lying to me. The church would never follow a man who calls himself *Dominus et Deus*.

He murders believers and anyone who questions his authority. It is because of his kingdom that we fight for the people of Old World."

Seraphine's silence was all the proof she needed. "I can't believe God's own people have surrendered to evil."

A soft breeze rustled the tree branches that stood in a long line surrounding the pasture. The sound was like rattling bones. She watched a flock of little birds dart from the branches of a tall tree and heard the flutter of their wings murmur like whispered secrets.

"Yesterday I was a champion. Today I'm a heretic on a secret mission with two other infidels. We are sure to be tried as enemies of the kingdom and butchered when we are caught."

"I will not lie to you," Seraphine said. "The truth of this campaign is sure to frighten you, child."

Alex stiffened. "I am no child." She felt her pulse race. "I am a warrior ready to die for my Lord, if need be." She watched Seraphine's lips pull into a thin line on her flawless olive-colored skin.

"I meant no insult," Seraphine said. "We believe a small band of three, with your gifts and abilities, are all the army we need to strengthen those who remain."

Alex detected a slight pitch in her voice. "Are you telling me the entire truth?"

Seraphine reined the donkey toward a palatial building. The cart rocked and swayed as they traveled closer to the stables.

"You will occupy an outpost heavily populated by assassins and overrun with demonic activity. You and your team will teach the remnant to fight this war with God's weapons. Your mission is to equip the few who remain loyal to Christ and invade the Kingdom of E'Doom to set captives free."

Alex's heartbeat felt like a stampede in her chest. She forced her trembling hands into her pockets and looked away.

Seraphine reigned the donkey into the entrance to the stables. Alex felt lightheaded, jittery, and alarmed all at the same time. Sister Seraphine message was disheartening. *Strengthen the few who remain? Who is this remnant?*

Alex wanted to press her superior for more details, but Seraphine had gotten out of the cart and stood waiting for the chief trainer of horses.

The cobbled paddock surrounded a building that looked more like a castle than a barn. St. Regents raised and bred war machines worthy of papal and military approval. Excitement replaced trepidation as she imagined what her charger would look like. Each operative received a warhorse at the end of their training, paired according to the special needs of the warrior.

A tiny woman in a black habit, hiked to her knees, crossed the paddock. Alex was speechless. She looked ancient and out of her league. Her stiff white bib reflected the sun, making the woman's face glow, accentuating her deep lines and wrinkles. The stiff headpiece squished her pudgy cheeks together, and Alex thought she resembled a wooden marionette.

Following her was the biggest stallion Alex had ever seen. He was magnificent with powerful muscles that rippled under the sunlight. The woman held a jumble of papers in her hands and allowed the horse to trail behind her freely. Each time the horse got close, he would try to rest his muzzle on her shoulder. She swatted him away like he was nothing more than an irritating fly. The steed towered over the woman. He was pure white with a long mane and tail.

"I'm Sister Mary Temperance," the marionette said. She turned slowly, like a puppet on a string, and paused to look at Alex over the jumble of papers.

She smiled at Seraphine without looking at her. "She has grown into a fine young woman," the nun said.

Alex smirked. "Do I know you?" She looked at Seraphine

for an explanation, but the women embraced each other like long-lost friends.

Seraphine wiped a tear from her eye. "It has been a long time."

Temperance smiled. "She is so tall and…" Her words trailed away. "I have told the cooks a friend was coming for a visit. Please join the other sisters in the dining room as not to arouse suspicion. We will talk when I am finished with our champion."

They embraced again, and Seraphine left Alex standing alone.

Alex watched the old woman rummage through the papers she held in her pudgy hands. "I am waiting for a horse trainer." Alex absently tapped her foot on the ground. "I must have gotten his name wrong. I thought they said Sir Temperance." Alex tried to keep her voice low and patient. "I do not have much time."

Temperance ignored her. "We know you have ridden many horses while you trained in St. Regents Academy." She scanned the papers in her hand. "Mother sent me your certificates of excellence. Let me see." A gust of wind blew a few pieces of parchment into the air, scattering them across the paddock. "Too much paperwork for my taste," the marionette mumbled.

Alex watched pieces of her accomplishments blow away with the breeze.

Sister Temperance smiled. "You have your mother's temperament, obstinate and willful."

Alex's heart jumped. No one had mentioned knowing much about her mother personally. "Did you know her?"

The nun's eyes brightened. "After Reverend Mother and Sister Seraphine brought her here, that terrible night, I hid her in the mountains with a goat herder and his wife as caregivers."

Alex felt confused. "Mother and Seraphine were involved?"

Temperance began to walk and the stallion clip-clopped along behind her. "Oh yes, child. I am part of their cover up, along with Brother John. We are all involved and up to our neck in this seal of secrecy. Our past deeds seem to be repeating themselves in the present."

Alex felt glued to the spot. "Why did no one tell me?" Her legs refused to move. "I knew I was illegitimate, a bastard child, but I know nothing of my mother's circumstances."

Temperance reached over and placed a small hand on Alex's elbow and continued to totter along, stumbling now and then in the tall grass. "It was far too dangerous to divulge this information. We would have put you at further risk. You have many enemies within St. Regents who suspect your identity. The four of us have been careful to conceal the truth. Mother gave me permission to reveal your true patronage."

Alex felt like her head was about to explode. The nun continued to speak as if this information was easy to digest.

"We were surprised Cecilia lived through the attack and more surprised at her pregnancy."

Attack? Alex felt nauseous.

"As her time to conceive came close, her mind began to taunt her with memories of the defilement until the images drove her mad." She looked toward the mountain range beyond the stables. "She lived in a cottage in the shelter of Mount Evermore until you were born."

"I was born in the mountains?" Alex looked toward the soaring peaks shrouded in mist and mystery. "I was told that Mount Evermore was so special, God uses her like a stairway to come from heaven to the earth."

Temperance laughed. Alex thought her voice sounded girlish and fresh coming from a woman so old.

Temperance sighed. "I love the folklore that has become

truth to the villagers around St. Regents." She gazed at the peaks covered in snow. "The mountain is special, especially when it comes to hiding treasure."

Temperance continued toward the pasture. "Come, my beauty," she said to the stallion. "Relax while you can. In time, the supreme inquisitor will come to take you as his own."

"The inquisitor," Alex asked. "I thought this horse was mine."

The woman opened a wooden gate and let the horse run into a spacious meadow. He whinnied and bucked a few times before he joined a heard relaxing in the orchard.

Sister Temperance stuffed the papers she received from Mother in her large pockets. "He is a magnificent stallion to look at but he is weak-willed and flighty. A horse that looks noble, like his rider, but appearances can be deceiving."

She looked at Alex and smiled. "Cecilia had the same raven-black hair as yours, but the eyes…she had dark sorrowful eyes like black onyx against her pale ivory skin. Yours are the color of sapphires."

Alex pushed a loose strand of hair behind her ear. "I look like her?"

The nun nodded her head. "Very much, but she was a tiny woman whereas you are tall and sturdy, well-suited for a warrior."

The sun was high in the sky, and the temperature started making the air sticky. "Who was my father?"

"I don't think your mother knew for sure. There were many men involved in the attack. Most just watched and did nothing."

"She was not a loose woman?" Alex asked.

"Oh no, child," Temperance protested. "She was a devoted sister of our order. It was a sin of the flesh, perpetuated by a few priests without scruples and executed by evil leaders."

Temperance paused and rubbed her eyes. "As her mind

began to fade, she spoke of a mark on one man's wrist. A tattoo of a scorpion, she said. He was the one person who caused her the most anguish. Other than that, it was only the nightmares that kept her memories chained in torment."

Alex clenched her fists. "I hate them for what they did to her. I pray I find them and will repay each one for the indignity they inflicted on her."

Sister Mary Temperance nodded in agreement. "I understand, dear one, but vengeance is not ours for the taking. God deals with evil in his own time and in his own way." She wiped her hands on her apron. "He tells us to love our enemies and pray for them. If the Word of God was not clear on the subject, I would have hunted the beasts down myself, years ago."

Alex decided she hated this incompetent old woman, with the full face and laughing eyes, for allowing injustice and evil to triumph. Her mother was innocent and no one went to the authorities.

"Let's get on with the details of your visit," the nun said. "Your warhorse is waiting."

Sister Mary Temperance led Alex away from the royal stables.

"Where do you keep this warhorse?" Alex asked. "I thought I would take one from these stables."

The nun laughed. "Do you want to add horse thievery to our list of crimes?"

Alex's mind raced with anger. "I have committed no crime. I am innocent like my mother. Somehow I will see justice done."

Temperance silently prayed Alex would be able to forgive all of them in time. She pointed in the direction of the mountains. "Your horse runs free."

The elder wasted no time getting the novitiate ready to travel. She chose two horses to carry them for the day's journey into the forests, beyond the royal stables of St. Regents, and on the road to the Mountain of Evermore.

Alex was amused to see Temperance out of her habit. The woman looked smaller without the traditional headpiece, yet with her short salt-and-pepper hair and wide-brimmed straw-hat, she looked younger. She wore the same riding clothes as Alex: a white tunic belted at the waist, soft black britches, and leather knee boots.

Alex tried to ride silently, wanting to figure out a way to release her mother's shame but found it impossible to keep Temperance on track. The woman was fascinated with nature. Nothing escaped her notice. Her voice droned on and on, pointing out every species of bird, flower, and tree.

"Look to the right, Alexandria. The river flows from the Mountain of Evermore."

Alex followed her outstretched arm and pointing finger. Looking through the trees, she saw a large lake, glistening with clear water. The air smelled fresh. Her ears were aflame with the chatter of birds and the humming of wings.

Alex bolted upright, her senses more alive than she ever remembered. The horse she rode had a new bounce in his step. The color of the trees looked brighter. She focused her eyes, adjusting them to the changing light as they passed through the forest and into the most spectacular valley Alex had ever seen.

Colorful wildflowers stretched their arms for miles across the face of the basin. Cradled within the vibrant blossoms were hundreds of butterflies with wingspans the width of two hands. They danced, from flower to flower, to the music of a myriad of birds.

Alex looked in the distance at the majesty of Mount Evermore. The queen stood amid a wide range of snow-covered mountain peaks. She towered above the others, soaring to staggering heights. Her peak seemed to touch heaven like a spiral staircase, beckoning God to come to earth. As the sun dipped behind the mountain, the explosion of light looked like the brilliance of the Almighty seated on his throne.

Temperance dismounted and sat on a rock, pulling off her boots. Before Alex could say a word, her mentor was knee-deep in the river, skipping rocks.

"Sister," Alex called. "In the name of all that is holy, get back here." She looked around frantically. "Can you swim?"

"Of course I can!" Sister yelled over her shoulder. "Can you?"

Alex grabbed quill and ink from her saddlebag. She knew what she had to do. It was time the authorities knew how incompetent the featherheaded nun was. Someone needed to know the truth about the rape of her mother to bring the culprits to justice. Flopping on a boulder, she watched the river become a playground to her mentor and numerous river otters.

To his Imperial Excellence, Archbishop Pietto,

Please be advised that Mother Superior, Sisters Seraphine and Mary Temperance, along with Brother John, have information on the rape of one of our own Sisters of Faith. Sister Cecilia was a young nun, under the care of the academy of St. Regents when she was attacked. This innocent woman became the victim of a brutal assault. There is proof she was wrongly accused of whoring and bewitching several of our priests sixteen years ago. There were eyewitnesses who never came forward with the details of this horrific crime. Cowards, each one, who need to be punished for not bringing the rapists to light at the time of the crime.

Alex looked up at the sound of splashing and quickly hid her letter. Temperance was walking toward her. The woman squeezed water from her tunic. "You need to let go a little. You are much too serious." She scrunched her dripping hair with her hands.

"War is serious," Alex said. She noticed a scar on the woman's neck.

"You missed a great swim," Temperance said, looking up at the sky. "A pity. It's too late now, we must be going. It will be dark soon."

"I told you an hour ago, we needed to move like we have a purpose." Alex blotted her paper and folded it carefully.

Temperance led them across the valley, toward the forest that climbed the face of Evermore. It was late by the time they entered the woods. A large full moon lit their way. They entered the thick barrier of trees and began the climb.

The trainer found a spot in a glade of sycamores to camp for the night. "This is my favorite place," she said. "Remove all your gear and let the horse free. There is plenty of meadow grass and water."

Alex tethered her chestnut gelding. "He's not going anywhere. I don't intend to walk back."

Temperance placed her saddle blanket and supplies under a tree, making a comfortable bed. She let her paint mare run free. "Look up, Alexandria, at the stars. We will rest under Pegasus."

Temperance picked large berries from the surrounding bushes and placed them in her wide-brimmed hat. She held them out to Alex.

Alex shook her head. "I have bread and salted meat in my saddlebag."

"Suit yourself. God's bounty is here for your enjoyment." Temperance licked the juice from her fingers.

Alex unsaddled her horse, making sure to tie him tightly to a thick branch, and made a bed under a large tree. She propped herself up, resting against the tree trunk, intent on staying awake to watch the coward. Before long, her eyelids drooped. Crickets chirped, and birds cooed. She tried forcing her eyes to stay open, but the forest lulled her into a deep slumber.

At midnight, her head bobbed, jolting her awake. She blinked rapidly as her mind tried to get its bearings. The sight of Temperance on her knees, lost in prayer, brought her unusual surroundings into perspective. Her body relaxed. She tried to focus but the forest sang a peaceful sleepy song. In her dreams, she saw a beautiful dark-haired woman with black eyes, the color of onyx, rocking a newborn baby.

"Alexandria. Get up and follow me."

The woman's voice whispered her awake. Alex jumped to her feet. Her body swayed. She reached out and steadied herself on the tree. With sleepy eyes, she watched Temperance glide through the forest.

"Wait up!" Alex whispered into the darkness. She bolted after the trainer, weaving and bobbing like a drunken sailor, until she hit her toe on a fallen log.

"You are the devil's advocate!" Alex hissed. She tried to keep her footfalls quiet but her clumsy steps sounded like a herd of cattle bounding through the thicket. She could see Temperance far ahead, her white tunic glowed under the light of the moon. Alex stopped to touch moss that grew on the tree trunks; it took on a purple glow in the moonlight. Fireflies flashed in the tall ferns and twinkled like stars within the canopy of green leaves. She heard thundering water somewhere ahead.

The glade opened, and Alex walked into a meadow facing a high bluff with a waterfall that cascaded into a tranquil lake. The air smelled like evergreen, honeysuckle, and fresh grass. A loud beating noise made her jump to the ground, covering her head with her arms. She looked up toward the sound. A herd of mares galloped down the precipice.

She watched them land gracefully at the base of the hill, like a flock of geese, with their foals close behind them.

Temperance joined the herd from her spot by the brook. She walked among the wild horses as one of them.

"Come, Alexandria. You are welcome among us."

Alex stepped out into the moonlight among the herd. "There are so many of them," she marveled.

"Yes. This is Malak's herd."

A beating of hooves sent the mares scattering. A powerfully built black stallion joined the herd. He pranced through the mares, nickering and snorting his superiority. His presence electrified the air with energy. The stallion deliberately created an open area, leaving Temperance and Alex standing like targets in the open meadow.

"May I present your warhorse, Malak. His name means messenger."

He charged at Alex, snorting and whinnying. He reared up, pawing the air, signaling his challenge.

Alex backed away. "He hates me."

Temperance grabbed hold of Alex's arm and held her like a prisoner. "No. He is just trying to see what you're made of."

Alex wanted to run but Temperance held her steady. The stallion lunged at her. He did not slow until he was within a foot of the soldier. He stopped short and turned back, prancing away a few yards like he was playing a game with her. He pounded the ground with his hooves and then thundered toward her again. His thick mane flew around his head like thunderclouds. He reared up and whinnied, challenging her the second time.

"Stand your ground. He wants a strong leader to guide him. Malak will demand a rider equal to his talents in battle."

He trotted forward and stood so close, Alex felt his warm breath on her face. He pawed the ground and snorted, less intense this time.

He nudged her gently with his nose and stood with his head down, looking into her eyes. Alex felt her knees go weak. "His eyes are blue like mine."

"Yes. It is a rare color for a horse but not as uncommon as you might think. Touch his face, Alexandria."

She lifted a shaky hand and put it on his nose. He allowed her to run her hand over his thick neck. She could feel him relax at the touch of her hand. His pitch-black coat was not sleek and smooth like the destrier she was used to riding. His coat felt thick and coarse.

"He is ugly," she said to Temperance. Alex walked around him with just her fingertips gliding over his body. He was short but sturdy with a big head, thick bones, and a large barrel; and as she stroked the animal's coat, she realized he had many scars on his body.

"You have scars on the outside where everyone can see," she whispered to the horse. His ears twitched as though he was listening. "I have scars too, but they are hidden inside." The horse put his soft nose on her head and nibbled her hair.

Alex felt jittery. "How did he get so many scars."

Temperance smiled. "He has been in and out of Old World many times. You might say he was forged in the crucible of war. Only the strongest and most reliable survive."

"What's next?" Alex asked.

"I will teach you how to form a lasting bond with him," Temperance said. "Warhorses need to pair with their rider." He reared up and shook his great head.

Alex jumped away from the horse and hid behind the trainer. "Why is he so difficult? I just want a horse I can ride."

Temperance remembered feeling intimidated and, at the same time, awed by the large beasts when she first started working with them. "Achieving control is not making another creature submit to you, it's a partnership."

"I am not trying to be rude, sister, but I finished first in my squadron and I am assigned to lead a team into Old World. I have spent years learning how to take charge of things and rely on myself. I don't need an equine partner."

Malak bolted into the forest, leaving both women surprised.

The trainer grunted. "You will need to work *with* Malak, not against him. He will reward you with loyalty, love, and courage in the face of danger."

Alex detected annoyance in the nun's voice. She locked eyes with the old woman, holding her challenge until she saw a look of sorrow flash across her mentor's face.

"You will be stationed near E'Doom," Sister said softly. "There will be many dangers. Both you and Malak must learn to trust each other in this world before you tackle a hostile environment."

Alex pushed her long braid over her shoulder. "He ran away, now what?"

Temperance grinned. "A sure way to get his attention is with treats."

Alex huffed. "Where will I get treats in the wilderness of Old World?"

Temperance led her into the woods and picked stalks from a bean-like plant that grew wild in the mountains. "This is fenugreek, a delicacy that grows well in our soil as well as between the rocks in Old World." She held the bouquet to Alex's nose.

"It smells spicy."

"Taste," Temperance insisted with a mouthful of leaves.

Alex ate some. "Yuck! It tastes like burnt sugar."

"Malak will choose this over an apple." She pulled a flask from her pocket and took a drink. Temperance wiped her mouth on the back of her hand and offered the flask to her student.

Alex sniffed. "This is wine!" She handed it back.

"Yes. Made from grapes in our own vineyards. Quite good, I might add." She corked the flask. "A little nip is good for what ails you."

Alex threw her hands up and shook her head. "Do you ever do things by the book?"

"That depends on what book you're referring to." She winked and patted Alex on the arm. "Now where were we? Oh yes, the fenugreek."

Alex followed the trainer into the valley. She whistled and waved the plant in the air. Before long, they heard the rumble of hooves. Malak came out of the forest and trotted obediently up to the trainer. "Works every time." She smiled.

The next day, Alex joined Temperance in prayer and worship amid the flowers and wildlife in the belly of the mountain. They ate fruit and vegetables that grew wild in the vast valleys of Evermore. Alex bathed under cascading waterfalls, surrounded by multitudes of sweet-smelling blossoms.

"This mountain holds many pleasures, but it is time to train for war," Temperance said. "Tomorrow is the new moon. We must move like we have a purpose."

Alex rolled her eyes. "Now you're stealing my lines."

She handed Alex a thin belt. "Place it around Malak's neck. You will ride without bridle, bit, or saddle."

She must be kidding! "In case you have forgotten, this animal has not completely decided he likes me."

Temperance waved a pudgy finger in Alex's face. "Malak decided to give you a chance last night. I suggest you learn to cooperate with him or you will find yourself doing this mission on foot."

Alex put the belt around the stallion's thick neck. "Easy," she whispered. Malak stood like a statue, waiting for her to mount.

Alex relaxed. "I wasn't expecting him to be so congenial."

Temperance shrugged her shoulders. "Me neither."

They rode through the forest and into open fields. Alex began to get comfortable and rode the black stallion like they had been one for years—until they came to a meadow and he bolted.

Alex kicked him hard. "Let's go. What's wrong with you."

He continued to fight her, refusing to move forward.

Temperance huffed. "Give him his head, girl. He is your partner. Trust him."

He will learn who is boss. "Stupid lazy horse!" Alex kicked him as hard as she could.

When she opened her eyes, she watched the sky spin as her eyes fluttered open.

The spinning stopped and Temperance's flushed face was inches from her eyes. "Are you hurt? Answer me, child. Can you move your toes?"

Alex tried to sit up. "Sister, please! I am fine."

Malak nibbled her cheek with his wet nose. She pushed him away. "He threw me!"

Temperance cleared her throat. "When he detects danger, he tends to do that. Just to get your attention."

Alex stood up. "I am his rider. This animal will learn to respect me." She grabbed him by his mane and pinched his nose as hard as she could. "I am boss. You got that?"

Malak shook his large head and looked away from her.

Alex watched Temperance make a sour face. "He threw you to protect you both from the caltrops."

"Cal-what?"

Temperance dug around in the dirt until she found a sharp rusty metal weapon. She handed it to Alex. "Where there is one caltrop, there are many."

Alex held the heavy spiked object in her hand.

Temperance wiped dirt from her tunic and took the caltrop from Alex. "This small object has been used by the enemy to kill or disable both man and beast. They are silent, insidious, and deadly, making them the perfect weapon. A puncture wound from one of these can kill immediately or lead to infection and a slow painful death for rider or horse."

Alex hung her head. "I'm sorry. I thought Malak was just being stubborn." She dug in her pocket and found a small stalk of fenugreek. She held it out to her horse as a peace offering. He gently ate the treat and nuzzled her shoulder.

"Malak is a warhorse," Temperance said. "He understands and anticipates danger. This *animal* carried many warriors into battle and brought most of them safely home." She paused and patted his strong neck. "Please get back on your charger so we can finish your practice session. You must learn his body language. It could save your life."

Alex stomped her foot. "How was I to know you planted real traps? I could have been seriously injured."

Temperance gave her a look she recognized. "The war zone is real and the traps are many. You are here to learn to fight. And win."

Heat spread across Alex's cheeks. "Are there any other surprises I should know about?"

Temperance folded her arms over her chest. "The caltrops are placed in random order. These weapons are used by the enemy to stop horses and elephants in battle. Let your eyes, your instinct, and your horse guide you."

Alex remounted and leaned forward over Malak's neck and whispered to him, "Forgive me Malak. We can do this. I'm listening to you this time." He whinnied as if he understood her words. Once she learned to trust him to avoid caltrops, she learned to spot and avoid dangerous pits, camouflaged under tree limbs and filled with wooden spikes, sharp as daggers.

When Temperance was satisfied that her student felt secure, they began using weapons to hunt throughout the highlands of Evermore. "Alexandria, you must shoot your arrows with accuracy. I will direct you."

Alex reached back into the quiver on her back and secured an arrow. She placed it in the bow and aimed at a wild boar, waiting for instruction.

"Time your shots when Malak's hooves are in the air," Temperance yelled to her student. "Do not disturb the aim. Pay close attention to the wind, your speed, and feel the moment."

Alex held her breath until she felt the timing was right. She heard Temperance cheer when she hit her mark. She learned that Malak was well-suited for battle. He was quick to dart or lunge as needed to help her in the use of the lance, spear, halberds, and sword. He was responsive to the touch of her leg or a shift in her weight. He was not the mount for a new or timid rider. She realized he was bold when she refused to flinch during the hunt. Together they could take full advantage of the kills when brought into the heat of combat.

Alex slid off Malak's back and wiped the white lather of the horse's sweat from her riding britches. "Did you see him jump the log while I held the lance over my head? I can't believe it. We really have become partners."

Temperance's grinned. "You are a good student, Alexandria. Your mother would have been proud of everything you have accomplished." Her mentor looked into the distance. "It is time to go back to the stables. Your training here is finished."

Temperance reached into her apron. Her small hands trembled as she took a tattered book from her deep pocket and handed it to her student. "The word of God brought me great peace when I was stationed in Old World many years ago."

Alex held the leather-bound treasure to her heart. "What is it like in the war zone?"

Temperance sighed. "Fulfilling your purpose will be challenging and frightening." She paused and smiled. "But God will give you whatever you need to succeed." She patted

Alex's arm. "Be on your guard, always. You are an alien in that world. The enemy will try to destroy you and your team." Her eyes glistened with joy. "Fear not, child. Our Lord goes with you."

Sister Seraphine met them at the stables. "Reverend Mother is ready to see you," she told Alex. "She said to tell you the hour is upon us."

Alex looked at both women, feeling as though she was in a daze. Her feet refused to move. She saw a look of pride in Seraphine's soft brown eyes.

"Hurry now," Temperance said. "There is much work for you to accomplish on the battlefield."

Alex looked away from Temperance, forcing back a surge of emotion. "Thank you for everything, sister," she said. Alex wanted to hug this woman who caused her to well up with love one moment and hate the next. *I can't betray my mother's honor. They are traitors.* She shook Temperance's hand instead.

Seraphine locked eyes with Alex. "Mother said to hide the warhorse in the abandoned shack on the south side of Lord Frederick's Manor. He is dimwitted and lazy, so he never visits the place, but be on your guard, he is an enemy bound to the abbey for monetary gain. The lords are each handpicked by Archbishop Pietto and paid by the church, making each one a puppet on a string." She wrung her hands together. "You will use the road from the hill country while it's light. The small building is far enough away from prying eyes and close to the road that leads to the Chasm." She paused as if she was measuring her words. "When you finish, Mother will be waiting to give you her last-minute instructions." Seraphine looked into the sky that darkened with storm clouds. "I will meet you and your team at our departure point before dawn on the morrow."

CHAPTER 8

Reverend Mother and Alex

Alex reached the covered portico that bordered the massive stone abbey on the south entrance. The impressive building was the convent of St. Regents. The wind stirred the air, bringing with it the sweet smell of roses that mingled with the stench of betrayal. She made up her mind to give the incriminating letter to Olga, her closest friend. She jogged through the abbey gardens, full of fruit trees, vegetables, and herbs, with a sick feeling in the pit of her stomach. She knew she would find Olga in the garden at this time of day.

Alex had no time to change from her riding attire into her white novitiates' habit before the meeting. A few lay sisters, who cared for the kitchen plants, watched in silence as she stopped and called her friend aside. She knew they would find it unusual, but she wanted to get this traitorous act over with.

Olga followed Alex away from the other girls. "Why are you dressed like that? We wondered where you were hiding after your conquest. Joseph is still screaming about how he is going to get you back."

Alex touched the note in her pocket and hesitated. Fear crept up her spine. What havoc would this information bring into her mentor's lives? Her fear was quickly replaced with anger. The thought of Joseph's mockery pushed her hand. *They started this, and now, I shall finish it. It's the least I can do for my mother.*

Alex pulled the sealed paper from her pocket. "I need you to do something for me."

Olga looked surprised. "What's this about, Alex? You are not the type to ask for favors."

I am not the same person I was yesterday. "Keep this hidden until the supreme inquisitor arrives. It is a list of my accomplishments. I'm hoping to get a position as his apprentice." Alex tried to keep her expression as normal as possible.

Olga turned the sealed envelope over in her hand. "Why can't you do it?"

Alex squeezed her friend's hand. "Archbishop Pietto hates me for what I did to his champion. I will not be able to get near the inquisitor, but you can."

Olga stuffed the note inside her pocket.

"I have to go. Please keep this hidden until the time is right."

Olga looked her in the eyes. "You have my word."

Alex thought her lie was ingenious. She had no intention of leaving the convent now that she had to clear her mother's name, but she was waiting until she saw Reverend Mother to spring the news. Alex pushed down the bitter stench that clung to her mind like manure.

Knowing her superior would not be bound to her cell on such a beautiful day, she raced down a stone staircase past many water fountains and statues of ancient saints. Alex found Reverend Mother sitting on a bench within a glade of willows that overlooked a large pool of water. A clutch of ugly gray cygnets darted across the pond, chasing a graceful white swan. Alex stood next to her mentor, waiting for her to speak. She knew better than to initiate conversation. Many whacks on her hand with a ruler kept her quiet. Alex looked at her palms and remembered the sting.

She forced her body to remain still until Mother placed her prayer beads in the deep pockets of her apron and stood.

Alex watched her. The nun was a giant, towering over the novitiates' head. Alex thought she looked regal in her long black tunic. The stiff white scapular, cowl, and veil framed her face, accentuating the woman's square jawline. Alex knew not to try to read her expressions. Mother's face was a stone. It seemed to her that her superior had only one expression: a perfectly arched brow that lifted high on her forehead when she looked down at you while the rest of her features remained locked.

"You have done well, daughter." Her sharp brown eyes lightened. "We have trained and empowered you with the Words of Life. You are equipped for every service Our Lord has planned for you." She slipped her hands within the folds of her dress and the sun caught the metal of the cross on the end of the beads that hung from her belted apron. The light reflected from the crucifix jumped around them like a darting firefly.

"Your potential as a leader is well-noted." She folded her large hands as if to pray.

Alex fidgeted with the hem of her riding tunic. "I must tell you something before we proceed." Alex tried to keep her voice steady. "You allowed a great injustice to flourish and grow here at St. Regents. The truth of my mother's past and my real heritage was concealed from many here at the abbey. My peers and the faculty believe the lies and gossip that spread throughout the years."

Mother looked down at her with one arched brow.

Alex continued, undaunted, "I think this atrocity must be brought to light and those guilty of the crime brought to justice. The archbishop and the inquisitor should consider this mystery straight away."

Alex watched Mother's shoulders rise. The woman seemed to grow before her eyes yet her voice was as soft as a gentle breeze. "I am sure this will be hard for you to imagine, but the authorities were part of the rape and plan to murder your mother."

Alex staggered backward. "You expect me to believe one of them could be my father."

Mother remained silent, allowing the girl time to take it all in.

Alex crumbled to the bench. She sat and gazed across the pond, watching the cygnets follow the swan. She understood now why these four people needed to hide such a crime.

"Mother," she whispered, "I wrote a note to Archbishop Pietto, explaining the crime, and I named those involved."

Mother sat next to Alex and held her hand. "Each of us have choices to make in our lives. Some things we act on impulsively, others we have time to reflect upon. Either way, it is in God's hands."

"I have delivered the incriminating details through a trusted friend." Alex felt sick.

Mother patted her hand reassuringly. "Life is a gift from God. At the hour of our decision, so long ago, we each chose to save two lives at the expense of our own. Now we choose to send three ambassadors into a hostile world to save multitudes who are lost, dead in sin. We have made our decision, and we know the risks."

Alex folded her hands on her lap. "Why do I fight for this cause when the church is corrupt?"

Mother sighed. "We fight the enemy of our souls for personal revival. One by one, born-again believers become the true church. We must help one another keep the fire of the Holy Spirit burning in our hearts while there is still time."

Alex watched her spiritual mother stand. "If you still desire to accept this mission, you will meet the prophet and the healer. They are gifted in their unique abilities as you are in yours." She paused, and Alex watched her sharp brown eyes search her face. "You carry the gift of eternity to share with an unbelieving generation." Mother squeezed Alex's hands. "You also have a message for those who have given up the fight."

She folded her hands as if to pray. "God has not given up on them."

"I think I understand."

Mother sighed deeply. "If you are ready to pick up your weapons and follow God, we are finished here."

Alex had mixed feelings. *Should I cling to the past or run into my future? Are the demons the assassins or are they my leaders? Lord God…who can I trust?*

Mother prepared to leave. "If you decide to join us, we will meet at the abandoned stable at sunrise to deploy. Brother John left your weapons hidden within the ox shed." She embraced Alex tenderly. Mother lingered a moment, like she wanted to say something more, then turned and left.

Alex listened to the hem of her habit swish across the ground and watched her black tunic billow like storm clouds in the wind. She opened her mouth to speak but her words lay silent on her tongue. Instead she waited until her teacher disappeared up the stone steps and out of sight. "Who can I trust?"

CHAPTER 9

No Turning Back

Midnight moved slowly under the watchful eye of the crescent moon. Alex lay in her bed, within the soldiers' barracks, folded inside the darkness that surrounded her. She listened to the sleepy sounds of the novitiates snoring, wheezing, and grunting peacefully and wished she could turn back time, be young and carefree again, or at least be one of the other girls who would live a quiet life within the protective walls of the abbey. She was frustrated and disappointed that she had to keep this mission secret from the other novitiates, especially Olga.

This was my moment. I trained for this. I worked hard for the honor of commanding my own troop. It's not fair, God. It's not fair.

Alex wiped her damp face with her hand.

She found it impossible to relax. Her mind kept repeating the events of the day. She wondered why Olga had taken the note for the archbishop without some sort of interrogation. They were friends and never hid their hopes and dreams from each other. Olga was too quiet and accepting.

Now with the truth brought to light, Alex wished there was a way to retrieve the incriminating letter before leaving the compound. Lack of time would force her to abandon the notion. Her stomach lurched at the idea of more betrayal. A piece of straw from her mattress stuck her in her back when she rolled over. She always hated the soldiers' uncomfortable sleeping arrangements. The noviatiates slept on a raised wooden slab, side by side, with twelve straw mattresses positioned so close together, the girls had to sleep elbow to elbow.

Olga normally slept next to her but had chosen this night's watch. Alex climbed from her bed and felt under the empty mattress, hoping her friend tucked the letter away for safekeeping. Nothing. With a heavy heart, she picked up her backpack and snuck to the door. She paused, taking a minute to remember bits and pieces of her life. Leaving this place she called home tugged at her heart. The abbey hid all of her secrets and accomplishments.

She took one last look around and slipped into the cool night air, determined to make her mark in the world. Crouching low, she ran toward the battlement that sat directly behind the long narrow building that housed the female military personnel.

Her mind and body worked quickly in the darkness. She needed to make it to the tunnel that led through the protective outer wall of the abbey before Olga began her next sweep across the roof. The twenty-five-high battlements that surrounded St. Regents had small crawlways, used to drain excess water after the heavy storms that flowed from the peaks of Mount Evermore. One of the grates was located behind the soldiers' quarters. As a child, she would sneak through the steel grate and into the passage that led beyond the compound. It had been years since she used the tunnel to defy her mentors and slip outside the confines of the abbey. She was counting on her memory to take her through to the other side.

She began to count in her head and repeat the rhyme she used when she was a child to make her way through the dark night. *One step, two steps, three sure and brave steps…four steps, five steps, quiet and safe steps. Six steps, seven steps, silent as the grave steps, then a final eight steps, reach out and grab the grate…steps.* Alex paused and slipped her backpack through the steel bars, then squeezed her body into the tunnel. She took a few deep breaths before tying her bag under her belly and started to crawl toward the grate at the other end of the channel. She held her breath. The water that lay trapped inside the pit smelled stagnant and felt slimy. She forced her body forward on all fours in the cramped space. Her back rubbed against sharp rocks and her knees ached as she inched along, scraping them on the rough stones. Finally she could smell fresh air and knew she made it to the other end.

Alex squeezed outside, taking deep breaths of fresh air. She waited and listened for the sound of footsteps on top of the battlement. She heard nothing. In the silence of the night, it was easy to hear the booted footfalls of the guard on duty.

Tonight there was no scraping of leather against stone above her head. In her gut, she knew something was wrong. *Where is Olga? She would never leave her post unattended.* She waited and strained her eyes, trying to detect a shape on the wall. Nothing. *I must keep moving. I can't chance missing the rendezvous. There will never be a second chance.* Making her decision, she sprinted across the wide expanse of meadow toward the forest that surrounded St. Regents and separated the abbey from the many villages owned by the church. She made it to a thick jumble of trees and waited until she was sure the watchmen failed to see her. Alex caught her breath and began to follow the tree line that led to Lord Fredrick's Manor. In the deep black darkness, she used her heightened senses to guide her along the uneven path and away from her old life.

Alex heard the soft rise and fall of voices on the cart trail ahead of her. She paused, holding her breath, waiting for something to jump from the darkness. She knew wild boar and wolves roamed the forests, but they didn't frighten her. It was the animals of a human kind, who waited to devour anyone suspected of treason, that made her blood run cold and her heart race. She crept closer and listened. The voices became familiar and the whispers more distinct.

"I've waited here over an hour. The mosquitoes ate me alive! Whatever you have to give me better be important."

Alex recognized the voice. It was Joseph.

"You said you would get me promoted if I gave you Alex's head on a platter."

Alex knew it was Olga speaking and that she was going to betray them. Her heart pounded in her chest.

"Get on with it," Joseph demanded. "Or I'll have Archbishop Pietto put *your* head on a spike!"

Alex was close enough to see them in the light of the lanterns they carried. She watched Olga fan her face with the note, taunting the seminarian.

"Your rival gave me a sealed letter to turn over to the archbishop when the inquisitor arrives. I opened it. This confession will incriminate Reverend Mother, Sister Seraphine, the warhorse trainer, Brother John, *and* Alex. No questions. All of them will be burned at the stake for protecting a witch."

Joseph laughed. "The church doesn't care about witches anymore."

He grabbed for the note, but Olga was too quick for him.

"I'm sure the archbishop and his accomplices will come up with a suitable crime to pin on their enemies. Give me your word you will have the supreme inquisitor hire me as his apprentice."

"I can pull strings," Joseph said. "If this information is all you say it is, you will be riding by his side within days."

Alex's blood boiled. Olga was going to use her lie and really try to get a position with the inquisitor. Her heart dropped as she saw her friend hand him the information that would bring sure death to those named.

"I'll make sure this information is in the archbishop's hand before Prime."

Olga challenged him. "Make sure I'm rewarded promptly or I'll personally see you meet an untimely death."

Alex watched Olga hand him the note and sneak back into the shadows, disappearing into the darkness. Joseph unfolded the paper and tried to read it under the light of his lantern. It gave Alex enough time to sneak up and surprise him. She held her dagger to his throat.

"The letter belongs to me," she whispered into his ear. "Hand it over before I leave your dead carcass for the wolves."

He handed it back to her. She snatched it from his fingers and stuffed it in her pocket. He took the opportunity to spin around to face her. He stomped his boot into her foot, grabbed her by the throat, and began choking her with his large hands.

Alex felt her mind go dark as he squeezed tighter and tighter. She thought she saw the shadow of a demon surrounding Joseph's body, but the forest went dim and she felt her hand release her dagger. Through her haze, she watched his face turn red with rage. He snarled at her like a wild animal. She saw something or someone over his shoulder.

Kill her! Shadim coaxed.

As Joseph raged, his eyes looked cold and dead. "You are a useless piece of trash, just like your mother. You don't deserve to live."

She knew he intended to kill her. With her last bit of strength, she kneed him in the groin. He grunted and loosened his grip, giving her enough leeway to stumble into the forest.

She looked over her shoulder and saw a glint of steel in his hand.

"You won't get away alive," he yelled.

She heard him running after her. Tree branches snapped, leaves crunched beneath his boots, she heard his heavy breathing bearing down on her. She kept moving, running toward the road, outside the forest but close to the tree line. Her throat ached, and her head pounded. She knew if he caught up to her, it would be his life or hers and she had no intention of dying tonight. She found a good place to hide and wait for an ambush. She squatted in the darkness, trying to catch her breath. She waited, hoping to catch him unaware.

Minutes ticked away. She continued to wait, but the forest was quiet. *He must have gone back for Olga,* she thought. *Two of them against one would make it easy to bring me back to the authorities. I need to make it to the getaway point and meet the others. I have the note. No proof to incriminate the others.* A soft rustling startled her. When the noise proved to be nothing but a rabbit, she began a slow jog.

She had to reach the village before the bailiff began his inspection. He would rise before the servants, the serfs, and the cotters to make sure everyone was working and giving Lord Friedrick the proper amount of produce and that none was being stolen. She jogged for what seemed an eternity, stopping only long enough to listen for Joseph, until she smelled firewood burning within the small wooden cottages and knew she had arrived at the manor.

She slowed her step as she moved into the village and hurried past the dovecote, a spacious shelter that housed doves and pigeons awaiting the butcher's ax. Alex listened to the soft cooing of the birds the villagers raised as food when the winter freeze set upon them and hunting wildlife was scarce.

She silently made her way past the tithe barn and snuck past the church, grateful the priest on duty was a sound sleeper. As quiet as a mouse, she skimmed the backyards of the serfs, the workmen of the manor, and made it to the mill. She scanned the field where the crops were planted. Everything seemed quiet. She adjusted the sack of belongings she carried on her back and crept across the wooden bridge that led to freedom, just as the black sky brightened to a deep gray.

Alex knew she had time before gray dawn since the birds in the trees were still quiet and only the crickets and bullfrogs sang. She hurried into the forest that bordered the manor, relieved that she was hidden in the trees once again. She kept her pace steady and ran across a small stream, grateful for the relief of the cool water. Her lungs ached as she jogged up a steep hill. She pushed herself, knowing this was the last hurdle before she reached her destination.

Alex waited in the shelter of the evergreens. Watching. The deserted barn took on a sinister appearance in the dark. The once-sturdy barn had deteriorated with fallen beams smothered in ivy and a menagerie of weeds that choked the life from the old frame. The forest hid all but a barn door and small sections of the roof, making it look haunted and dangerous tonight.

She had tethered Malak within the shack earlier in the day, making sure he was safe and secure, hoping the few handfuls of oats that she scraped together from a sealed barrel held him over. One of the few things she carried in her sack was extra meal for her horse.

She sprinted from the trees toward the barn. As she approached, she heard unusual noises along with Malak's agitated whinnies. Alex lit a small candle, hidden in her sack, and ran into the broken-down building, fearing they were discovered.

The light from the small candle made jumping shadows on the dirt floor and across the wooden barn walls. Looking up, she could see stars through broken roof rafters. Once her eyes adjusted to the darkness, she realized Malak had barn mates.

A large camel shifted its weight, side to side, and spit at her from across the room.

"You beast!" Alex jumped away and the spittle landed on her boot.

The dromedary did not seem satisfied with the insult, so he continued to make deep moaning noises, agitating her horse.

"Quiet," Alex scolded. "Your noise will wake the dead."

She stepped over the stomach juices the camel sprayed at her and went to the barrel and scooped out a scant handful of oats. The camel ate from her hand, like a gentleman, and began to quiet down.

A donkey, tethered to an old cart, began to bray. Alex obeyed his demands and scraped the last of the meal into her gloved hands.

"That's it," she whispered to the noisy jack. "I've reached the bottom of the barrel." He licked the crumbs from her hands.

Once she settled the animals, she ransacked the old place, looking for her weapons. Alex noticed a bulge under a pile of dusty hay in the corner. She lifted an old lantern from a peg in the wall and lit it with the dying spark of her candle. She held it over the mound, inspecting the pile. The light revealed something that shone like gold. She knelt on the dirt floor, bowed her head, and made the sign of the cross before reaching into the dusty mess.

The first thing she found was her helmet of salvation. She held it to the light and inspected its construction. It was bucket-like with a hinged metal visor she could move up or down to cover her face. It was made with dark-black metal and had bronze details that reflected the light from her lantern. She put it on her head and laughed out loud. It was a good fit.

Alex lifted the helmet from her head and rested it gently on the floor. She unbraided her long hair and pulled a sharp knife from her boot. Grabbing a handful of soft curls, she impulsively sawed through her long black tresses. Once she started to chop, she couldn't stop. When she could no longer use the blade to cut shorter chunks, she dropped the knife on the floor and ran her hands through her hair. The short strands felt strange, like they belonged to someone else. She hated it.

Alex picked up a handful of the silky waves that lay on her lap and covered the floor around her. She held her crowning glory in limp fists and swallowed hard, fighting back her tears. *I might not be a commander of an entire army, but I am going to be a Sister of Faith—inside and out.* She dropped her thick locks to the floor and pushed them under the straw. Her fingers combed through the short strands, arranging the thick mass of waves around her face as best she could.

Picking through the straw, she found the rest of her armor. Lifting the breastplate of righteousness, she slid it over her red peasant blouse and black leather britches. The delicate chain mail covered her body from neck to midthigh like a soft tunic. It had thousands of metal rings, but it was comfortable, light as a feather, and easy to move around in.

Alex found the belt of truth. It was made from the softest hide she had ever felt and smelled of fine leather. The belt was wide, covering her midsection, from breastbone to hip, and fastened with a large bronze buckle. She bound it around her waist and secured the empty scabbard to her left side that would hold her sword.

Digging through the pile of straw, she felt her weapon. As she lifted the sword of the Spirit from its hiding place, the light from her lantern made the steel glow like flashes of lightning.

"It's heavier and longer than I imagined," she said as she stood, holding the black-and-bronze hilt in her hands. "It feels completely balanced, like it was made just for me." She swung it as if battling an enemy. In the soft light, she saw intricate engravings, running the length of the blade on both sides, and realized it was the image of a thick healthy vine full of ripe fruit. The triangular shield of faith was black as onyx, outlined in bronze, and engraved with the same pattern as her sword. She dug deeper within the mess and sat on a wooden crate to pull on knee-high boots that would carry her into battle.

Alex heard footsteps outside and quickly extinguished the light from her lantern. Her heart pounded. She was sure it was Joseph with the authorities. Holding her sword with shaking hands, a verse of Scripture came to her mind and she spoke the words aloud. "God did not give me a spirit of fear, but of power, love, and a sound mind" (2 Timothy 1:7).

Immediately a strange sensation jolted her body. The armor began to quiver and tremble. Row upon row of scales began marching over her body, clinging like a second skin to her flesh. She stood like a statue as her helmet grew armored plates that ran down her neck and fastened to her arms, breastplate, belt, and legs, overlapping one another until her armor was impenetrable and her sword exploded with light.

Before she had a chance to focus, the scales backtracked and her armor returned to normal. The transformation happened so quickly, Alex thought she imagined the entire incident. She felt lightheaded, shocked, and amazed.

Reverend Mother entered the stable, followed by a girl who looked like a desert princess.

Alex froze when she saw her mentor. The woman was pale as a ghost.

She reached out and touched Alex's shoulder. "What happened to your neck, child? It is covered with bruises."

Alex rubbed her throat. "Olga betrayed me and gave my confession to Joseph. He tried to kill me, but I was able to wrestle the evidence from him." She handed the paper to Mother. "Joseph chased me for a while. I think he went back to the monastery for help to find me."

Mother shook her head. "We found Joseph's body in the forest. It looks like he fell on his dagger."

Alex swallowed the lump in her throat. "My dagger." She sunk to her knees. "He was chasing me with the dagger I dropped when he was choking me."

Mother crossed herself. "We cannot bring him back from the dead, but we can pray for his soul." She reached out her hand and helped Alex to her feet. "There is no time to mourn this terrible loss. We must stick to our plan. Dawn is on the horizon."

Alex stood on shaky legs. She wanted to tell Mother about her weapons, but the thought of Joseph disarmed her. She hated him. He had tried to kill her, but his death brought her no feeling of satisfaction, just a sad emptiness. She pulled the helmet from her head and placed her sword on the wagon. *Forgive me, Lord, for my hatred and anger toward him.*

Alex looked at the girl Mother brought with her and wondered about her heritage. The girl's attire was different than the women she encountered outside the convent. She wore a deep-purple shawl that covered her head and face. From within the folds of the cloak, Alex could see a green silk caftan that skimmed her body, falling to her thigh. It looked hand-embroidered with red and yellow birds flying over purple and indigo flowers. Her trousers were a sumptuous deep purple, like the cloak, with many rows of coins and beads sown into the hemline. The garments were steeped in incense and smelled like jasmine and lavender. The belt she wore around her small waist had elaborate grommets that held chains, coins, and colorful beads. With every movement she made, her ankle bracelets jingled softly.

The girl pushed the purple scarf from her head and face. Alex marveled at her beauty. Her features were as flawless as her coffee-colored skin. She had slanted green eyes that looked lively, alert, and curious. The girl released the cord that held her hair in a tight bun and long spiral curls cascaded over her shoulders and down her back like a rushing waterfall.

Alex touched her own hair and winced.

Mother spoke softly, "Alex, this is Nyla. She is the healer on your team. As you can see, she comes from much wealth and will need suitable clothing to travel."

Alex could tell by the tone of Mother's voice she disapproved of the girl's dress code.

"No, I won't! I will travel in the clothing I'm wearing,"

Nyla protested.

Mother ignored the princess and addressed Alex. "All of you will need to dress differently so you don't fall into the hands of brigands on the road to the Chasm." Mother paused, staring at Alex. "Your hair, child." For a long moment, the woman just stared; then suddenly, she smiled. "Good. Very good. You will be safe traveling as a boy. Hide the armor until you are ready to cross the Chasm. In the meantime, you will dress as an archer." She handed Alex a leather doublet and a cap that covered the top of her head. "The authorities will be looking for a nun, not a young lad." She pulled clothing from a sack. "I'm sure you can outfit the princess with a simple frock." The woman tossed the garments into the wagon. "She may keep the cloak."

"Yes, Mother," Alex said weakly.

Sister Seraphine, Brother John, and the prophet arrived as the sun touched the sky with gray light. Alex was dumbstruck when they introduced the boy. His long-hooded robe covered all but his face, hands, and sandaled feet. Alex thought he might be ill. It looked like he was drained of all blood. Pitch-black hair surrounded a bone-white face, but it was his peculiar eyes that shocked and frightened her.

"My name is Beryl," he announced. His voice was quiet, like the coo of a dove. "It means rare and precious jewel."

He sounded angelic yet his appearance was bold and defiant. The boy carried a shepherd stick with bones, claws, and feathers hanging from its neck, and a lopsided lion's skin rested over his priestly vestments.

Alex watched Nyla roll her eyes in jest of his oddness. She opened her mouth to speak but saw Mother's lifted brow. Seraphine averted her eyes and looked down at the floor. Only Brother John smiled and beamed with pride.

The boy thrust out his hand in greeting. Alex wanted to recoil in disgust, sickened by his queer looks but slowly reached toward him and placed her hand in his soft white palm. Looking into the strange but beautiful dark eyes, she thought she saw compassion and honesty. He was tall and thin as a reed with a long serious face that was somewhat handsome. The apprentice looked no older than fifteen years. He smiled. It was a shy smile. A smile that was accustomed to being mocked. Alex understood that kind of smile.

"We must make haste," Mother announced. "Unfortunately there will be no church bells ringing in the cathedral tower as you depart on this crusade. There will be no friends, family, villagers, or clergy waving banners and throwing flowers as you parade down the streets of St. Regents." Mother paused. "There is still time to decline the mission. I want you to realize that each day that passes, the danger intensifies."

Alex heard her suck in her breath and pause as if the words she spoke were breaking her heart.

"Once you leave the walls of the abbey, there will be no turning back."

She waited for a reply. When no one spoke, she continued. "Alex, if you are ready to take your vows of poverty, chastity, and obedience, we will anoint you into our order."

Alex swallowed the lump in her throat. She felt fear rise in her chest, choking the very air from her lungs. *Jesus, help me be brave. I'm not sure you picked the right warrior for this mission.* Alex knelt before the three elders with her mind running in a million different directions.

Mother gently placed her hand on Alex's head and twirled the short strands of hair in her fingers. "I know this is not what you were expecting when taking the Perpetual Profession of Vows, but you can be assured, this crusade is sanctioned by our heavenly King."

Mother placed the blade of the new sword on Alex's shoulders. "We consecrate you, in the presence of Almighty God and all of us gathered here, into the order of the Sisters of

Faith. You are a warrior in the army of the King of Kings and Lord of Lords. You are commissioned to fight the good fight of faith. To stand against evil, now and forever. Do you agree?"

"I agree."

"In the order of our tradition, we give you a new name. You are now Sister Alexandria Augustus Mary, defender and conqueror. Amen"

Sister Seraphine squeezed Alex's hands. "I am so proud of you."

Brother John blessed her with holy water and the sign of the cross.

Mother took a bronze crucifix from her apron pocket. "This belonged to your mother."

Alex took the beautiful piece of jewelry and held it to her heart, then hugged the nun with so much zeal, Mother could barely breathe.

"Please put it on for me."

As Mother clasped the chain, she placed her hand on Alex's shoulder. "When you become a Sister of Faith, you exchange your old clothing for something new. The new uniform of a soldier in the army of Jesus Christ."

Gray light began to creep through the holes in the roof. Brother John started to ready the animals for departure. Seraphine collected Nyla's jewelry and clothing and stuffed them into a sack "We will send these trinkets back to the queen. You must not bring any attention to yourself as you travel the roads to Old World."

Alex snickered to herself. She imagined traveling with these two would bring more than a curious glance. Reverend Mother gathered them together in a circle like a clutch of chicks. The three messengers held hands and knelt on the floor as Mother, Seraphine, and Brother John surrounded them in prayer.

As their mentors prayed, Alex felt all uncertainty drain

from her body and she experienced a great peace begin to lift her spirit. Nyla was filled with joy and heard beautiful music like a chorus of angels. Beryl closed his eyes and imagined he was floating in a sea of mercy and grace. In an instant, the three disciples stood inside a galaxy, looking at the gateway to the throne room of God.

CHAPTER 10

Holy of Holies

The horseshoe-shaped entry into God's presence pulsed with bioluminescent wonder. Red, green, blue, and purple splashes of color rolled like waves from the celestial doorway. The multicolored shades of light jumped and danced into the atmosphere.

A gentle breeze blew, bringing with it the sweet smell of incense. Glittering particles of solar dust swirled through the air. Beryl reached out to touch the sparkling elements that floated around them, catching some in his pale white hands.

"They make my skin glow," he said. He manipulated a few of the tiny specs into a large ball.

Nyla smiled. "It's so pretty. The dust glitters like jewels."

Beryl gently pushed the orb in her direction. It floated ever so slowly toward her outstretched arms. He watched the pretty girl laugh and saw her big green eyes dance with excitement as she reached out to grab the weightless sphere.

"It's so light," she said. Her hands began to gently pull, twist, and shape the solar dust into the form of a butterfly. Opening her hands, her creation flew gracefully into the atmosphere.

Alex interrupted their play.

"Look." She pointed in the direction of the gateway.

A shimmering silhouette of a soldier appeared. The angel wore an elaborate breastplate of purest gold. His massive vapor-like form blended into the universe. The archangel spoke and swords of lightning shot from his mouth, splitting the heavens.

"Welcome, children of God."

The dream cloud parted and the three believers found themselves in the center of a large celestial portal hidden in the sky. Their bodies and clothing sparkled with divine radiance inside the heavenly chamber.

They floated, suspended on an invisible floor, and beneath their feet were billions of galaxies, the entire universe. They could see many glorious suns and brilliant were all the different shades of color. Each star varied in size yet one stood out larger and brighter than the others, exploding bursts of astral flares and fiery loops of gas into space.

The stratosphere blazed with a pulsating light show. Brilliant explosions illuminated the heavens in a rainbow of dazzling light. Multitudes of angels, with features that resembled men and women, sang to the Lord God in his sanctuary. They worshiped him in the heavens of his power with voices that shook the halls of space. They praised him on trumpets, lutes, and harps. Some danced along to the melody of the string and wind instruments, twirling joyfully around the tabernacle while the sun, moon, and stars in the skies praised him. The music vibrated throughout the universe, and unspeakable joy filled the temple.

Twenty-four men and women of varying ages, wearing robes of flowing white, appeared through the swirling curtain of cloud. They carried ancient scrolls and wore crowns of gold upon their heads. Twelve sat on seats on the right side of the room, and twelve sat on the left. They were chanting and singing beautiful hymns in a language the students could not comprehend.

Unworldly creatures guarded the throne that appeared in the core of this holy place. These unusual beasts had human bodies, covered with thousands of eyes that were able to see through the heavens and the earth in all directions at once. Each creature had six wings that moved slowly without displacing the living things.

The celestial beings had four faces. Their heads spun around quickly and repeatedly. For a fraction of a second, the spinning stopped, and you could identify one face like a man, one like an ox, another like a lion, and last like an eagle. They had large muscled bodies and held mammoth fiery swords that burned as bright as the sun.

Beryl pinched himself to make sure he was not dreaming. The tall warrior next to him nudged him with her hand, warning him to stop fidgeting.

"This is the most awesome thing I have ever seen!" Beryl said, trying to get the other girl's attention. "Nyla, do you know what these beings are called?" His excitement made him feel lightheaded.

"Shush!" both girls warned him in unison.

The Master, clothed in glowing radiance, entered the sanctuary. Immediately a deep peacefulness settled on them. His majestic form was a burning pillar of fire, yet his countenance was soft enough to gaze upon with the human eye. The train of his kingly robe swirled into the surrounding galaxy, mixing with the stars. The elders rose to their feet. God proceeded to his throne and sat among his elect, the believers.

Burning seraphs circled the King's throne. A multitude of fiery wings hid their faces and feet so the disciples could not witness their appearance. The huge creatures made a soft buzzing until they came to rest above God Almighty's seat of power. The chamber grew quiet, and every eye fixed on the young students.

"The three of you have been chosen and trained for ministry. Not because of your own strength and abilities, instead it is through your weakness that my power will manifest itself."

The Master's voice was soft and compassionate.

"You have been protected and highly favored while each of you prepared for your journey. I send you because you are all willing and obedient to the call."

The teens could sense their heavenly Father's pride in them as he spoke. "You each have knowledge of the sacred writings and are equipped for every good work. With the gifts you have received, you will go into Old World and speak to the heart of my people."

His voice took on a more somber tone. "I have been watching mankind and have witnessed the erosion of the nations. The land is plagued by an unholy horde. These creatures have brought with them violence and desecration of things that are holy. They lust for control and embrace everything that is wicked in my sight."

The Ancient of Days left the throne to stand before the three disciples. "However, there is a remnant, a scant few who have not completely lost faith in the one true God." As he spoke, a spirit of joy filled the air.

"These believers have been tested through the fire and are growing weak. They hold on to my teachings and are waiting for the promised return."

As he continued, Alex could discern heartache in his voice.

"Many have shrunk back from the battle, leaving some of my children with no knowledge of their true heritage."

The elders continued to pray as the Master spoke. "You must help the battle-weary soldiers regain their strength. Teach them to use the weapons I gave them to overcome the evil of this age."

The Master discerned the young warrior had a question. "Speak, daughter."

"What you are asking of us does not seem possible." She fidgeted with her white robe. "This generation has little faith."

She looked at the faces of the others and wished she had not started to question God.

"Continue," he said softly.

"Many do not understand they need a savior because they do not believe in heaven or hell. The generation you send us to help believe your plan of salvation is powerless. They do not understand the finished work of your son, Jesus's, death on the cross. If they denied the prophets and the very Son of God, why will they listen to us?"

All went silent like the calm before a storm. "This generation is self-centered, lovers of money, proud, and arrogant. They have become lovers of sensual pleasures and vain amusements more than lovers of God (2 Timothy 3:1–2). However, you must remind them of the love I have for them and that I require faith in the one who shed his blood for the forgiveness of many."

The burning ones came forward and spilled a bowl of smoldering ash into the air. From the residue, a mirage, a transparent three-dimensional image of a great army began to grow until it slowly spread and took over the land. An army was rising from the ash heap.

"I demand mercy, justice, and faithful followers who are bold and courageous—not easily intimidated by the enemy's tyranny. My disciples need to have a desire to open the eyes of the blind, heal the brokenhearted, and release the captives. My message is one of hope in days that are increasingly evil."

As he spoke, a terrifying sense of urgency overwhelmed the assembly. "My Son is coming back. When he returns, will he find his disciples living in faith or unbelief?"

The mirage of the army slowly vanished like a forgotten dream. "It is *not* my desire that any should die. The enemy plants seed of unbelief and rebellion. For this reason, I am raising an army, an army that will fight for truth and justice until the Day of Judgment."

Thunder and lightning shook the assembly. "You will find a few in Old World that have not forgotten the path of their ancestors. You must encourage them to keep fighting. However, some you will have to awaken from their sleep, shaking them out of their hiding places among the ruins of their lives."

As he spoke, the creatures prepared a brazier with burning coals. "Be on your guard, always. You must work hard to overcome your own weaknesses and find your inner strength. And most importantly, the gift that binds you together." While he spoke, the elders burned incense in golden bowls and began to chant softly.

One of the heavenly hosts, with blazing eyes and many wings, came forward and lifted a fiery hot coal from the brazier. The unusual creature touched the lips of the prophet with the burning ember. "The law of wisdom, understanding, and knowledge will rest on your tongue."

Beryl touched his face, amazed that the burning coal was cool upon his flesh.

It turned to Nyla and touched her hands. "Gentleness, compassion, and mercy will spring forth from your touch."

The specter moved slowly toward Alex and rested the hot coal on her forehead. "Faith, hope, and love will reside in your heart and hearing." The angel put the coal back in the burner and backed away before the King continued his words of instruction.

"Remember, you are strangers in an alien land where many dangers await you. Hold tightly to my teachings and rebuke every detaining circumstance. You must be firm in faith, rooted and established in truth, immovable and determined. Do not be deceived. The day is wicked, and the eve is upon the earth. The master of Old World practices the black arts, leading many astray. Be cautious, withstand him lest he devour you."

When he finished speaking, his form vanished into the

many galaxies. The elders spilled the incense into the cosmos and a new star was born. A loud clap of thunder brought the three disciples back to earth.

Alex opened her eyes. The glorious splendor of being in the presence of God was replaced by the reality of kneeling in the dirt on the stable floor, the feeling of peace and hope were gone, the heady aroma of incense was replaced by the smell of animals in a barn, yet a strange sensation of joy clung to her spirit. She looked around at her mentors still huddled in prayer and thought it strange that the light of morning was still gray. She felt like she was away for days, yet the bullfrogs still sang, and the morning doves slept. Everyone was still as they were when she went to the chamber of God. She wondered if her partners experienced the same vision she had or if it was just her dream. She watched Mother's eyes open and focus on her.

"Always remember, Alex, we do not fight against human opponents. Our struggle is against the rulers, authorities, and powers present in the darkness that surrounds us. Our attacks will come from evil forces from another realm. These spirits amass to destroy the children of God and the world he created."

Alex swallowed the lump in her throat. She stood slowly and helped Mother to her feet. "The sun will rise soon."

Mother nodded. "Get them on their mounts, John, we must send them out."

Alex felt like her feet were made of lead. She had to force her body into the saddle.

"Remember you are God's ambassadors in Old World. Never apologize for your message and never force the gift of eternal life on anyone. Love saints and sinners alike. Do good also to your enemies. That is the way of our Lord."

The woman held Malak's reins in her hands as if she wanted to stop time and keep them for as long as she could. She handed Alex a purse. "We scraped together all the money we could. It will buy enough bread for the journey."

Alex looked away, trying to control the wave of emotions that threatened to drown her.

Mother released the reigns and looked at each of them. "*Deus vobiscum*," she whispered. "May God be with you."

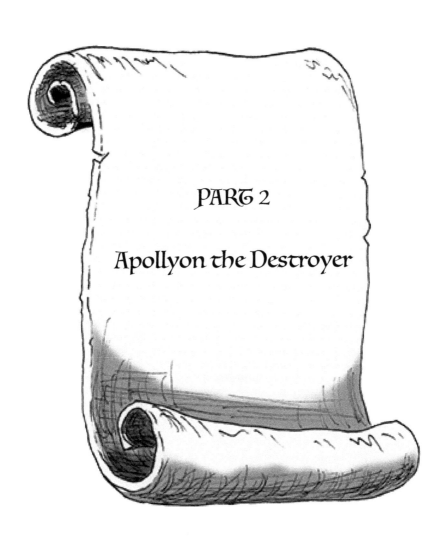

PART 2

Apollyon the Destroyer

CHAPTER 11

The King of Old World

Screaming, groaning, and shrieking cries of torment echoed throughout the upper corridors of Castle E'Doom. "*Deus*," Millicent gasped. "What is that hellish sound? Is the king torturing an army of poor souls?" Her shaking hands dropped her cleaning bucket, and she watched it clatter down the staircase. Dirty water, thick with grime, spilled across the floor and pooled like blood on the cold stone landing. The chambermaid backed into the corner, pushing her spine against the castle wall. She crouched down, like a golem; all but the whites of her eyes remained hidden in the shadows.

Millicent watched the king's servants and advisers bolt from the throne room, running past her as if she was a speck of dust swept into a crevice. The monarch's personal tailor slipped through the water at the top of the stairs. He tumbled and fell. His head whacked the wall, splitting open. His long torso sprawled on the steps like a felled log. The chambermaid watched in horror as the king's adviser ran after him. She thought he might stop and check to see if the tailor was dead, but instead, he reached the body and jumped the carcass, never looking back.

Millicent sucked in her breath as the royal alchemist, in a red velvet cape, sprinted from behind the king's high oak doors. She saw a look of fear that turned the skin pale etched across his tattooed face. Millicent thought he was flying down the stairs, his feet seemed to never touch the steps. The soothsayer was inches behind the druid. The elaborate black train from the sage's robe hissed across the flagstone. They pushed and shoved each other, racing to get down the stone staircase and away from the king's chambers.

Millicent's body shook. The inhuman screams from the monarch's studio continued, turning her blood to ice. She made the sign of the cross over her chest and spun the bracelet on her wrist; three times forward, three times back. She smelled the sienna, mint, and rue she braided together with pieces of twine to ward off evil, but she felt unspeakable fear grip her heart.

"*Verde retro, Satano. Verde retro, Satano,*" she chanted. "Go back, Satan. Go back, Satan."

Millicent listened to the running footsteps fade away at the bottom of the staircase. The castle tower looked and sounded empty. She hid in the shadows, fearing that the rumors of the king's infatuation with the dark arts might indeed be true. Her heart hammered in her ears, mixing with the inhuman groans from inside King Apollyon's studio.

Millicent scanned the hall. Light filtered through plate glass windows, painting the flagstone walls and ceiling with shadowy images. Tiny specks of dust floated in the air. She could smell her fear. Her heart fluttered in her chest like a caged bird. A noise came from around the corner. She gasped. Was it one of the king's dogs?

It shuffled down the hall in her direction; she could hear it breathing, smell its stench. Millicent covered her mouth with her hands. Her eyes snapped shut. Like a spinning top, her head reeled, knocking her body against the cold wall.

A bony hand reached into the shadow. "Hurry," the voice whispered.

Millicent opened her eyes. She recognized her friend's voice and grabbed hold of the bony hand.

"He must not find us here."

The two chambermaids snuck down the staircase.

Behind the huge double doors, in the privacy of his palatial suite, King Apollyon felt his body begin the steady metamorphosis. His chiseled image shape-shifted, changing the king's human form. His body gyrated and contorted as it grew into his natural shape.

Frayed flesh began to rip and shred. He squealed like a sacrificial lamb. Apollyon lurched forward in pain; his body thrashed in torment. He fell over a heavy claw-footed chair and crashed to the floor. His melodic voice deepened and cracked as his screams intensified. He felt his muscles thicken and twist, bending the inner man and reshaping his once-handsome body.

His upper torso burst through the soft tissue. He heard his bones crack and saw his sinews lengthen, transforming him into a powerful manlike demigod. Large leathery wings tore through the flesh on his back. Coarse black hair, sharp as razors, cut through his new scaly skin. Apollyon's arms stretched. His enormous hands ended in sharp claws. His bleating cries became the bellows of a raging bull as his lower body jerked and twisted, replacing human limbs with broad thighs and cloven feet.

The beast knelt on the floor and beat his head mercilessly into the hard flagstone. The arched glass windows, high in the castle tower, shook with each outburst. His misshapen head and face had thick ram's horns that twisted about its skull like a crown. Finally it ended. He stood slowly—a twelve-foot giant. His colossal body quivered with delight. Pain made him feel alive.

The fireplace blazed. Large seasoned logs popped and crackled, spitting embers from the mouth of the firepit. The inferno illuminated the dark room and the monster that lurked within. Apollyon tossed his remaining garments onto the ground. The few twisted threads of cloth that remained on his chest, he ripped away. Flesh and fabric lay scattered on the cold castle floor.

Silence once more filled his chamber.

His hulking body began to relax. He took the opportunity to revel in the opulence of his private rooms within his personal tower. He lifted an ornate gilded box, heavy with precious stones, sitting on a polished mahogany table. He carried the treasure in clawed fists, his hooves clomped on flagstone. The king loved wealth almost as much as he adored power. With lumbering strides, he walked across the room, his steps clumsy after the transformation. He savored the sight of his rich assortment of paintings, tapestries, and weapons that decorated his resting place. Each of the artifacts carried a memory of conquest, priceless treasures he collected through the centuries.

Ornate candelabras, with long tapered candles, cast an eerie glow within the room. Life-size murals graced the walls and ceiling of his bedchamber, telling the ancient story of King Apollyon's rebellion. He gazed at the paintings, the sound of battle, long forgotten, made his ears ring. He roared, shaking his massive head. The king sniffed the air like a brute beast and roared again, reveling in his glory.

He backed up, scrutinizing the portraits. An odd sensation, like maggots eating flesh, prickled his skin. He focused his gaze on the walls and blinked in astonishment. The painted images moved. He squinted his eyes and the movement stopped. Apollyon growled; the vibration rumbled through his body.

The king closed his eyes and waited. The hair over his body stood on end. He panted like a dog, his tongue dripped saliva from the side of his mouth. Slowly he opened his eyes. The images jumped to life, like moving pictures, under the flickering candlelight.

His lips pulled back into a snarl. "What omen is this?"

He scraped the wall with his claw-like finger, tracing his ancient image as the angel of light. "The celestial army called me Lucifer, son of the morning." He laughed. "I was the most gifted of the entire heavenly host. I was clothed with splendor and decorated with the celestial armor of a leader and commander, an archangel."

Apollyon twisted his lips into a grin. "I've had many names over the ages." He clomped across the room, feeling high on his power. "Satan, ruler of darkness, is the name I was given when I was thrown out of heaven and came to earth. I'm known by some as Abaddon, Belial, and Antichrist. Each name describes who I am. As King Apollyon, I'm the destroyer, the angel of the bottomless pit." He looked at his image on the wall with great pride. "I'm the accuser of the brethren, the adversary who preys on the weak, the dragon able to deceive the entire world."

Apollyon's brow furrowed. "Even then, in the time before the creation of man, I had a multitude of adoring followers. God's army of angels were willing to obey my every command."

He felt pressure in his spirit. Apollyon's lips twisted into a sneer; sharp canine teeth drooled spit over his corded chest.

"God's army revered me." He grinned. "At one time, the angels honored me. I had authority over all but *one*."

The king reeled in rage, staggering backward as if he was attacked by an invisible opponent. He squeezed his skull between clawed fists.

"One Son." His body shook. "One who is greater than all the angels in heaven." He spit on the ground.

"*One King* who is seated on the throne with the Creator." His chest heaved, and he clenched and unclenched his hands. "*One* who is given access to the very mind of God. *One* who is sovereign in heaven and earth." He choked on the words.

"*One* who is exalted among the nations. One who is the

savior of humanity!"

Apollyon bellowed, "I will never bow to the authority of Christ, the Son of God."

His body trembled with hatred. "I deserve this honor." He looked at the images on the wall. Michael the Archangel, with eyes masterfully painted to look full of light, seemed to be mocking him, looking down at him from his high position on the frescoed wall.

Apollyon laughed. "My old rival." He nodded his head. "What is God up to this time?"

The din of scraping and clanging of blade against blade echoed in his mind, bringing to life Michael's sword of truth against his blade of rebellion.

The pictures moved faster.

Apollyon pointed at the image on his wall. "I remember you, Michael. There was a moment when you collapsed and dropped your sword."

He laughed. "You hesitated. I should have crushed you and turned the tide of the battle." He groaned with the memory. "Instead Gabriel instructed you to pick up your weapon and stand firm."

The devil cringed. "You regained your confidence. It was a fluke. How different things would be if you had failed to cast me and my followers to the earth."

He pounded the wall with his fist. "Old World is my domain now. Man has infiltrated my space." He laughed but the sound was hollow. "This world is stained in the lifeblood of my countless victims." His muscles twitched in his neck. "While I wait with my legions for execution, we will continue to lead humans into rebellion. I am sentenced to hell and will take multitudes with me."

He watched his image in the pictures change from a royal angel into the vilest beast. He could smell sulfur. The painted lake of fire bubbled and smoked like molten lava. The mirage cracked and blistered the wall. He backed away from the image, cowering in the darkness as he watched the moving pictures. "I still have time," he whispered. "But something torments me."

A loud knock on the door forced Apollyon to collect his wandering thoughts. He looked around his room that lay in shambles after the transformation. The images on the wall stood lifeless. He threw blankets and pillows from his bed, searching for a robe. He needed to hide his identity. A red hooded cloak lay in a heap in the corner. The king threw it over his body; the long folds covered his nakedness. He pulled the bulky hood over his head and face and cursed under his breath at the intrusion.

He crossed the room; his hooved feet scraped the stone floor. In the corner, void of light, he sat in a large leather chair with his back to the door.

He shifted his voice into the soft melodious tone of King Apollyon, the leader his subjects knew and loved. "Enter." He beckoned.

A young aide walked in, tripping over debris on the dimly lit floor. His eyes darted, to and fro, adjusting to the darkness.

"Y-your worship," he stammered, bowing to the back of the chair. "This m-message comes from the watchers of the Chasm." The messenger coughed. He smelled brimstone, and the nasty scent burned his throat.

"General Shadim writes to inform you that three ambassadors from Safehold are preparing for a journey to cross our border." The boy shifted his weight from one foot to another. "Word reached us that one is a warrior who carries the sword of the Spirit, one is a prophet with the staff of wisdom, and a healer who brings life to the dead."

Apollyon was silent. He could hear the hammering heartbeat in the boy's chest. Normally he would enjoy listening to the sound of the coward's fear. However, uneasiness within his spirit made him uncomfortable. Energy he could not identify agitated his senses. Apollyon felt something. He could not wrap his mind around it, but he knew it was powerful. His skin prickled.

"Leave me," he yelled.

The aide cringed. The unnatural sound of the king's voice sent chills down his spine. He stumbled over his feet as he escaped the room.

The king stomped through his suite of rooms and stood in front of a massive piece of furniture. He pushed a knob on the face of a carved gargoyle that flanked the elaborate bookcase. The heavy piece of furniture slid aside. Dank musty air gushed into the room. He descended the serpentine staircase that led into his throne room, the core of Castle E'Doom. He stood motionless inside the blackness until his predatory eyes adjusted to the gloom.

Unnatural light filtered through towering stained glass windows, six stories high. The illumination created distorted shadows that stalked the circular sanctuary like wild beasts. Apollyon's greatest revenge was hidden below the ground.

He stood on the floor that was as clear as glass and vibrated violently under his feet. Beneath the surface was a sea of swirling black smoke. He peered into the abyss that descended for miles into the earth's crust. As he gazed into the precipice, millions upon millions of human flames began jumping and fighting each other in a roaring frenzy, reaching for the false rim.

The devil closed his eyes and inhaled deeply. His body tingled with pleasure. His nostrils inhaled the scent of burning souls. He listened eagerly as the thunderous sound of fire became the screams of pain and terror from thrashing, convulsing bodies that burned out of control.

He opened his eyes and watched the tormented faces of the damned. Flames gushed from every cavity in their body. They no longer had hair on their heads or torso, for their flesh melted and fused together, creating large writhing human torches. He loved how they pleaded for mercy while they sizzled and crackled, unable to end their torment. Once dead, those who rejected Christ, choosing to believe death was nothing more than a painless extinction, descended into the pit where the flames of hell consumed them until their final death.

E'Doom seemed to be in order, so why did he feel this unusual trepidation? His thoughts turned to the followers of the cross who trusted the teachings in the Book of Life, refusing his leadership. Revulsion for believers consumed his very existence. These survivors were his worst nightmare, especially those praying for rebirth.

The small army of rebels, who patrolled the countryside seeking refugees, were a nuisance but not much of a threat to his kingdom. They had grown tired and weary of the battle and allowed doubt and unbelief to creep into their lives. Their zeal to fight to the end had become lukewarm. His warlords could control them through fear and intimidation.

"Who are these three foreigners?" he mumbled.

The king's claws toyed with the hair on his chin. "The few who hold onto the truth are capable of causing my reign to crumble." He screamed into the darkness. "The more I increase my harassment toward those who seek the Baptism of Fire, the more the Word of Life spreads throughout the villages. I cannot chance this stupidity seeping into E'Doom."

A premonition spread through his mind. He saw a flash image of an uprising. "This cannot be! I will increase the terror throughout the kingdom and force total allegiance to my throne."

He stalked back to his bedchamber, barely able to contain his fury. In the center of his room, on a podium, was his book. He picked it up reverently and held it to his chest while he chanted in unholy tongues. His hands shook as he opened the *Book of Eternal Death* to a chapter and verse he knew well.

The fire that lit the chamber was dying, only a few glowing embers remained; the room was washed in a sinister radiance and felt as cold as a tomb. He set up vials of ancient powders and lit candles in a circle throughout the bedchamber.

"Something is coming," he growled into the darkness. With a brash and defiant voice, he read the words of sorcery and quoted spells of black magic, evil enchantment, and the necromantic arts. He chanted until his throat bled. His breathing grew erratic, and finally, he retched and vomited. From within his perverted body, two dark spirits spawned.

They lay on the floor, in the shadowy room, wrapped in dewy wet wings. They twisted and rolled on the hard flagstone, unwrapping themselves from the phlegm that spewed them forth. One creature spiraled upward like a whirlwind—forceful, destructive, and deadly. Apollyon was pleased. "I give you power over the elements of earth, air, water, and fire. I will call you Aether."

He walked around her, examining her. He spoke softly to the phantom in an evil dialect, known only to the spirits of destruction. As he spoke, she grew stronger until her form was complete. She spun around the room, like a heavy wind, barely able to contain her exuberance. Her emotions were unpredictable, unrestrained, and explosive.

"Quiet," he soothed.

She stood straight and tall in front of him. Her lucid black wings flowed around her transparent body like a beautiful gown. Her face glowed in the candlelight, making her spectral countenance appear tranquil and serene.

"You will use the elements to battle my enemies," he ordered. "Change Old World's climate and cause catastrophic tragedy and hunger. Make the populace think their gods are displeased with the believers." He smiled at the brilliance of his plan. "When I am satisfied that the citizens are ready to fully cooperate with my leadership, turning over all who follow the eternal God, I will stop your chaos, making the fools believe I am the savior of this nation."

He looked her up and down. "You will breathe thorns of defiance that will fester and grow within the heart of man, turning his belief from truth to error. When sin has fully taken hold, the human host will begin to change into my full instrument of evil."

The second spirit rose slowly from the floor, dressed in wraith-like vapor. She was mysteriously menacing and deceptive. Her appearance was dark and ominous. The demon was a deadly apparition, an ill-omen of dread. Coal-black hair, black lips, and black tattoos surround her clairvoyant azure eyes. Apollyon drew her close as if to kiss her perfectly shaped lips. Instead he expelled his dark vaporous breath into the specter's mouth, filling her with a multitude of evil secrets. Her mindset became malicious and oppressive.

"You will embody everything that is immoral, corrupt, self-indulgent, and cruel," he demanded. Apollyon thought her deliciously wicked. "You are Asmodeus, the spirit of anarchy."

He rubbed his clawed hands together. "You will patrol my kingdom, creating trickery through illusion and fraud. We must accelerate the downfall of humanity. You will plant my seeds of foolishness, self-confidence, and idolatry into the hearts of man, making them set up altars to honor me and cause them to sacrifice sacred life to appease me."

He walked to the table and lit a black candle. "You will carefully watch the Chasm, the entry into my kingdom, for something holy is coming, and I want it stopped before it has a chance to infiltrate Old World."

Asmodeus floated toward him with her shadow-like arm outstretched. She took the king's hand in hers and traced the lines that crept across his leathery palm.

"Beware," she said in a hushed voice. "I see three messengers from Safehold." Her brow furrowed. "They are sent to overthrow your authority with power from the Almighty Spirit."

Apollyon's eyes blazed with fire while he pounded his massive fist on the table. "Will they succeed?" He picked up the black book and threw it against the wall.

Asmodeus backed away. "Success is sure if the people of Old World choose to listen and believe."

"Go now!" he roared. "Make sure these messengers don't make it past the border. Use whatever psychic control you need. All my power is at your disposal. They *must* be stopped."

Both spirits passed through the castle wall. The king watched from his inner eye as one descended into the earth, toward the Chasm, where she would devour his enemies. The other soared upward, meeting the Red Dragon where she would join forces with the star that roamed the heavens.

Instantly a blizzard formed over the flatlands of Old World. Ice and snow captured the small army of rebels sneaking across the Plains of Mori, making the rebels her prisoner.

CHAPTER 12

The War Zone

Vicious winds and stinging sleet tore across the desert, ripping the tent cord from the commander's fist. The rope flapped wildly, slapping and stinging his hands, splitting his skin. Aza grabbed for it, forcing his frozen fingers to move in the extreme cold. His strength and agility were no match for the peculiar weather.

Snow and ice whipped around him, leaving a heavy coating of sleet on the supply tent.

Everything he touched was wet and cold. Aza shivered as a blast of air blew his shoulder-length hair into his face; he pulled it back into a knot, securing it with numb fingers. His green tunic and brown leather vest were soaked.

He cursed the gods for this new threat. "Damn this war!"

Aza turned to address the soldiers who stood by his side. "This storm is unnatural, something brought on by the Red Dragon." Looking up, he realized the lone star's brilliance burned through the hazy sky with a fierce intensity that matched the force of the falling snow.

"Sir, this blizzard has us trapped," Ralf addressed the commander. "What are we to do? The soul-sifters will be upon us by nightfall."

Aza wiped ice from his face. "Take Barric with you to the supply wagon. Load the necessary supplies in the tent for the night." He turned to Eldon. "You and Yates find dry tunics and blankets for the refugees." He paused and looked into the frightened eyes of a boy, no more than fourteen. "Zane, find someone to help you with the livestock."

Aza watched his men slip through the snow and hoped these small tasks would divert their attention. He turned his attention back to the tent when his feet slipped out from under him and he hit the frozen sand hard. Aza coughed and sputtered, realizing the fall knocked the wind out of him. He shook his head, trying to regain his focus. He was tired, afraid, and cold. He wished he could lie there and let the snow bury him, but he forced himself to stand.

Aza gazed at the ice-covered tundra. The Plains of Mori were alien, like he'd landed on some distant frozen planet. With the sleet stinging his eyes, he could barely make out the outline of Martic Forge. The mountain range was his home, the only safe refuge for miles. Aza yelled for his chief officer, hoping for some assistance, but realized the soldier was having his own issues with the storm.

Sargo worked frantically with the flint and stone, striking them together, waiting for a spark to ignite the pitch that coated the torch head. His fingers were purple and felt as hard as wood. It was useless. He left the fire he was trying to start and went to his commander's aid.

"What in the name of a thousand hells is going on here?" Sargo cupped his hands and blew on them. "We are on the flats. It should be dry and dusty from drought." He raked his hand through his wet hair. "This should be a sandstorm, not a blizzard."

Aza pointed upward at the Red Dragon. "The star must be responsible for this storm. Help me set up this tent before we all freeze to death," he ordered.

Both men worked together and secured the threadbare shelter. The goat-hair panels had seen better days. The fibers were stitched and patched, but it was all they had to protect his unit, along with the six refugees, from an attack.

Aza rubbed his hands together to shake the tingling numbness from his raw fingers before inching his way around the tent to check the wool panels. He had stretched the handwoven walls, as far as he dared, before testing the frayed line.

"This will never hold the center pole in place," Aza said. A gusty blast yanked the tie from his hand. The structure swayed and rocked at the mercy of the wind.

"Hurry," Aza ordered "These civilians are wet and chilled to the bone." He looked over at the survivors knotted together, shivering and bloody.

Aza leaned in close so he could whisper to his fellow officer. "The beasts are mutating fast. The attacks are more frequent and violent. This raid on Providence was the worst we've seen."

Sargo nodded his head. "I know. The enemy will kill us all unless we make it to our camp for help."

"Look at these people," Aza said. "They never had a chance against the king's warlords and the Soul-Sifters." He lifted his sword. "Our weapons are useless against them."

Sargo whispered back, "We need reinforcements. The cave is not far from here. We can take them there, it would be safer."

Aza's throat tightened. "We can't. The enemy is hunting us. If we go to the cave, we are leading them to one of the entrances into our home. We can't chance it." He looked at the band of outcasts. The pathetic few reminded him of the multitudes he was forced to leave behind. Images of carnage haunted him. Innocent people ripped and torn apart. Aza rubbed his eyes, trying to wipe away the image of a young man, accused of treason, kneeling before a Soul-Sifter. The creature of darkness toyed mercilessly with its victim. The boy's cries for mercy howled in his head like the storm around him.

Aza's skin crawled, just as it had at the scene of butchery. His ears throbbed with the sound of the Sifter's laughter before it tore into the boy like a wild animal. The memory of the boy's screaming played over in his mind as the beast ate flesh and soul from his body.

Words of terror tumbled from his lips. "The demons are coming for us. I can feel it."

Sargo saw the color drain from Aza's face. "Commander?"

"It saw me," Aza whispered. "That demonic thing spoke to me." His mind felt numb. "The beast held the human heart in its leathery hand to mock me." He looked around the camp, scanning the perimeter. "It said the boy gave his heart to Satan in life, and now, his master would take him to hell for eternity." His pulse raced in his throat. "It said it was coming for me." He bent over and threw up in the snow. *What's happening to me?* He wondered. *I'm no coward.* Aza wiped his mouth on his sleeve.

The snow swirled faster. His lips felt numb, and his words slurred. His body shivered and felt far older than eighteen years. He knew how to fight the enemy but not the elements. His sword had proved to be mighty in battle; but against the forces of nature, he had no power.

Aza stabbed the ground with his sword. "Why did the Soul-Sifters let us go?"

"I don't know," Sargo said. "I do know stopping here is a mistake."

Aza grabbed him by the shoulders. "Forget the hideout! There is no way to get through this blizzard to the cave anyway. We have no survival gear for these people. We can't make it alive. Look at this place. The mountain pass would be impossible now that we're saddled with the civilians." He heard himself laughing. "Even without the refugees, the trek would be disastrous." His amusement over their situation frightened him. "It doesn't matter anyway. We're out of time."

He saw the first shadows of night settle over the wasteland, and the full moon opened the sky like an evil eye.

Aza felt embarrassed by the way Sargo stared at him. He was supposed to be stronger, smarter, and wiser than the rest of the men. "See to the refugees," he ordered, hoping his voice didn't waver. "Warm yourself in the tent. I'll check the perimeter."

"Let me go for help," Sargo pleaded. "I can scale the rocks. It's our only hope."

Aza put his arm over Sargo's shoulders. "I need you here, brother. I need your sword."

Sargo pounded his chest with a closed fist, like he'd done since they were boys, a sign of their unity. "Together in life."

Aza pounded his chest in reply. "Look after the survivors and our men. I'm going to check the animals."

Aza was up to his shins in hard icy snow. His mind was running fast, making a mental list, trying to keep his zeal from faltering. A loud noise over the howling wind became a distraction. As he slowly proceeded toward the noise, he realized it was the whinny of horses in trouble. *By the gods! What have we done to bring such a curse upon this kingdom?*

He pushed his way toward the nickering brood, and when he got close enough to see through the white haze, he watched a soldier struggling with the animals. Not even the blizzard could keep him from recognizing Ravenna. He grabbed the harness strap from her hand. "What in the name of a thousand hells are you doing?" he demanded.

Her head jerked around to face him. "I didn't see you coming." She pulled her wet hood around her shoulders. "The storm had me in a trance."

Looking down, he noticed the white bones of fate she used to see into the future. The shells and bird bones lay scattered at her feet.

"Consulting the pigeon guts?"

He grabbed her roughly and pulled her close. Her slim athletic body felt like a block of ice. He pressed his lips against her ear. "You want to know our fate? I'll tell you our fate. Death is on our heels."

She pushed away from him. "So suddenly *you* can see the future?"

Like claws of smoke in the air, his breath, grabbed for her face as he spoke. "There is no future. Once you're dead, that's all there is. There is no God in heaven who hears your prayers. And there is no ogre in hell waiting for your soul. Those who preach that nonsense are fanatics."

Ravenna glared at him. "Who do you think you are talking to? I have been in these battles long enough to know what kind of power we are up against. You can deny the existence of demons and gods, but it can't change the truth."

He rummaged through a crate on the wagon bed, pretending her words didn't ring true. He feared the demons and their power, but worse than that, he was terrified that there was no God powerful enough to save them. He stifled his rising emotions and pulled out a dry tunic. He looked at her, standing before him, so small and vulnerable. It always surprised him that she tried to hide her feminine features under short spiked hair and tough exterior. He thrust the garment into her hands. "Put it on. Your lips are blue."

Ravenna searched his face and could sense his moods. Her heart ached for him. She knew him and, in her gut, felt his fear. She wanted things to go back to the way they were, when they were in love and safe in each other's arms.

"I still love you." The words gushed from her mouth without thought. She couldn't believe she said it. She saw his eyes widen.

"You dumped me for my brother, remember?"

She pulled the tunic over her dripping T-shirt, trying to hide her red cheeks, but decided to finish her rant since her words opened a door of conversation. "He was attentive." Her face felt hot despite the cold. "You want to be everybody's hero. I wanted security."

She bent down and scooped up the bones covered in snow. "You tried to bed every wench from here to E'Doom." Her freezing hands balled into tight fists, and she fought the urge to punch him in the face.

Aza smirked. "Watch yourself. Everyone told you it was all in your head."

"I used Sargo to make you jealous. He means nothing to me." *I can't believe I just said that.*

Aza stared at her. "Sargo believes you love him. I will never take you back. You're his woman now."

His comment hit its mark. Ravenna's mouth opened slightly; she wanted to say something but words failed to express the regret she felt for the stupid deception. For a fraction of a second, she stopped breathing. The past and present collided, shattering her dreams, extinguishing all hope. Like a slap in the face, the air returned to her lungs. She forced her emotions into submission and faced him. She stood tall and stiffened her backbone into a more military posture.

"The animals will need to find some type of shelter... sir," she said sarcastically. She knew him. He had written her off. Aza was finished with her. He would never betray Sargo as she had done.

He ignored her mockery and shook his head. "If they are lucky, they will fall into the hands of a poor farmer from one of the villages." He felt his body shiver. "It's more likely enemy scouts will confiscate them first."

Aza willed himself to move. The cold made him feel as weak as a child. His muscled arms and broad chest buckled under the weight of the heavy harness as he helped her free the animals. Although she was half his size, the slim soldier tried to steady him.

They watched their few horses and camels run away toward the mountain.

He looked at her and gently wiped a long tendril of ice-soaked hair from her face. "I'm sorry I went off like that." He stared at her for a long moment, remembering how she felt in his arms. "You look like a dripping scarecrow."

She smiled. "You don't look too good yourself." She fastened her bow with a quiver of arrows across her back and tucked matching daggers into the belt she tied to her waist.

Aza ran his finger over the deep scar that crisscrossed her cheek.

She pushed his hand away. "I took the enemy's blade for you, remember?"

He held her hand. "You're a skilled killer." The memory made him smile. "No one is better with a sword, crossbow, and any other weapon you manage to get your hands on." His fingers squeezed hers. "You don't have to remind me that your first love is war and weapons."

She pulled her hand away and turned her back.

He watched her small muscles ripple under her tight flesh as she moved away from him. Her fearless attitude toward life and death made her seem invincible. Aza almost believed they could win this war until a distant growl shook his soul. The guttural cry came from the bowels of no natural predator. The scavengers were on the hunt, moving him to action.

He grabbed her hand and looked at the sky. "We need to get to the tent. It will be dark soon, and the monsters have our scent."

Her face was white as death as he grabbed her hand and stumbled through the snow. He wished he had turned a blind eye on the village of Providence when he and his troops found it completely ravaged by the enemy. She was right. He always played the hero. If they hadn't snuck in to save the few left in holding cages, awaiting death, they would be home and safe now.

Sargo met them outside the tent. "Everyone is inside. I started a fire and rechecked the lines." He pulled the girl into his arms. "You are freezing," he said protectively. "Go inside. You will be safer there."

He paused, waiting until he was alone with Aza. "The beasts are tracking us. Didn't you hear them screaming in the distance?" Sargo looked pleadingly at his commanding officer. "Why do we care about these few?" He motioned with his head at the tent that held the survivors and military personnel. "Let's leave them here. We can make a run for it. You know we are no match for the demons. This regime is so strong, we can no longer fight them with our outdated weapons." His voice cracked. "The refugees belong to the Soul-Sifters. We took their leftovers. If we give them back, maybe they will leave us alone."

Aza shoved his brother, knocking him to the ground. "Are you crazy! Shut up before someone inside the tent hears you."

Sargo glared up at him. "Don't play the champion with me, Aza!" he argued. "We planned for a year to desert this lost cause. We need to do it now. You know as well as I do that we won't get another chance. Why should we keep risking our lives for strangers?"

Aza reached for Sargo's hand and pulled him to his feet. "I'm sorry." He looked toward the tent, wondering if anyone heard them. Wind screeched around him. He felt frozen. His lips chattered as he brushed snow from his hair which was hard and stiff with ice.

Sargo wiped snow from his clothes, keeping his voice low. "The refugees know better than to pray for revival. They took their stand and lost. They brought this attack on themselves." His throat suddenly felt too dry to speak. "There are rumors of worse to come." The ice felt like cold fingers creeping down his spine. "More of King Apollyon's armies are gathering in the south. They say this is a force unlike any we have fought before." His words trailed away in the wind.

Aza lifted a brow but did not react. He needed to stay calm, although he too heard the rumors. He did not want his commander of troops to fall apart, not now when he needed his twin's courage to bolster his own strength. Sargo was normally the more reckless of the two. He was first on the front lines, leading the others into battle, fearless like a wild animal—focused and dangerous. His strength and courage were an asset to their regimen. He was the one to go screaming and running headfirst into the face of danger, ripping and tearing into the enemy, leaving no prisoners. The men would laugh and tell stories about the battles and his explosive feats of daring. His courage was legendary.

"You know the elders deployed only a handful of soldiers for this mission." He put his hand on Sargo's shoulder. "The amount of enlisted men keeps dwindling. Even the refugees and foreigners have abandoned the cause. Do you want to leave them all here to die?"

Sargo spit on the ground. "I'm sick of playing this game. I'm ready to exchange my faith for freedom. Let others stand up to Apollyon's treachery. I'm tired of being considered a fanatic and an enemy of the state. With the new truce, they can keep some of their beliefs and live peacefully among their neighbors. They're asking for trouble by meeting in secret. They know the risks." He grabbed his brother's arm. "I don't want to die."

"Enough," Aza ordered. "Don't let them hear you. Our plans will bring trouble from our own tribe." His eyes met Sargo's. "We can only hope the enemy will be forced to abandon the chase because of the conditions." He hated himself for lying. He knew the demons never gave up.

"I can't believe we're going to do this! We could get

Ravenna and be out of here before anyone noticed." Sargo threw a piece of flint into the snow. "I wish I were more like you." He paused and looked at his brother. "You're stupid and sentimental." Sargo shook his head. "You might be a few minutes older than me, so why am I smarter?" The joke fell flat on his ears. Aza was always the tribe's first choice when they were looking for leadership. He felt the usual twinge of jealousy.

"Damn!" He irritably threw his bulky arms into the air. "If you're hell-bent on dying on this frozen tundra so be it. At least let us go inside and warm up. We can't draw our swords with frozen fists."

Aza threw his arm over his brother's shoulder. Sargo was truly his best friend, and as a warrior, one of the few he would trust with his life. "When we meet the beasts, make sure you use your ax and mallet. I want to see some heads roll!"

CHAPTER 13

The Back Roads

Alex let her body rock in the saddle and listened to the steady clip-clop of Malak's hooves become a monotonous drone, beating over and over in her ears. There was no way to guide the headstrong stallion. He knew the back roads through the forest and refused to let Alex take the lead. So she sat and rocked and thought about the danger her team faced and the horror that awaited Reverend Mother and her accomplices when the supreme inquisitor realized their treason.

Her back ached, her thighs felt raw from weeks of riding, and her hands were blistered from the friction of holding the reigns. When she thought of St. Regents, her home seemed to be a million miles behind them, a fading reality. She counted each day since their escape, knowing her team would reach the Chasm by the full moon. This was it. There was no turning back. Tonight it would rise full.

For weeks, Alex felt uneasy, like she was walking a fine line that could snap at any moment, leaving her team vulnerable to arrest. Although Malak led her small troop down narrow trails within the cover of dense forests, keeping them as far from village life as possible, she constantly felt a need to be alert and watchful. The fear that they would fall prey to St. Regents' finest soldiers became her constant companion. She knew the consequences of being fugitives on a forbidden mission, and now, Joseph's accidental death was sure to be pinned on her.

Despite their efforts to stay inconspicuous, they came upon many villages tucked away in the woods. The team was met with suspicious stares, so instead of hiding from prying eyes, Alex decided to stop long enough to eat at the local inns and keep up with any news that might pertain to their unlawful commission into Old World. The villagers were friendly yet inquisitive, questioning them about their destination. Thankfully Mother had the foresight to insist on their outrageous disguises, and Alex found her new partners were full of surprises.

Each village they entered drew a crowd. Everyone was curious about the boy with skin the color of white clouds and hair the shade of deepest night. The prophet, dressed in a brown vest, knee-high leather boots, and a green hooded cape, looked the part of a traveling minstrel. "Gather round, my dear people," he called. "Let us entertain you with stories, songs, and dancing."

Along the road, Nyla had tied a red scarf around her forehead and braided chains and coins into her long thick curls. Although her clothing was of simple fabric, her brown striped skirt, white bustier, and brightly printed scarf tied at her waist looked exotic.

Alex smiled to herself as she recalled the first time the boy began to strut around the crowd like a preening rooster. She thought, for someone who spent his time alone with nature, he had a commanding way about him; and truth be told, she was as fascinated by his antics as the villagers.

The boy paused theatrically, swung the green cloak from his shoulders, kicked off his knee boots, and dropped them in the wagon bed. "Gather close, dear people. Don't be shy." He opened a trunk and pulled out a menagerie of toys and musical instruments and proceeded to stuff his clothing with nonsense. He walked into the circle of spectators and began to drop numerous multicolored balls on the ground from inside his trouser pockets. "My companions and I are traveling performers," he announced, "on our way to lift the spirits of the soldiers in Old World. We call ourselves The Trumpeters of Cheer because we bring gifts of joy into the darkness." He bowed and tipped his hat. The crowd stared.

With his bare foot, Beryl kicked a ball into the air. He caught it and rolled it up his arm and around his neck. In the blink of an eye, he kicked up another, then another, to the wonderment of us all. He juggled them up into the air while he danced in circles. He spun around like a whirling dervish, never losing a ball to his quick hands.

Nyla began a rhythmic clapping of her hands and danced around the crowd, encouraging the spectators to clap along. Without thinking, I picked up a drum from the pile of instruments and began a lively beat. Before I knew what was happening, the crowd was stomping their feet and clapping as Beryl danced while he kept six, seven, then eight balls flying in the air. I was sure Mother would be scandalized by our masquerade, but it was a diversion that kept us safe for the time being.

As we passed through the villages, on our way to the Chasm, pretending to be The Trumpeters of Cheer, I realized juggling was only one of Beryl's talents. As a tumbler, he threw wonderful summersaults. He could run and do multiple flips forward and backward like he had been born a mummer. He told elaborate and fanciful stories of heroes who defeated terrible monsters and mesmerized the crowds with tales of flying carpets, chariot races, and buried treasure. To the delight of the children, he could make his donkey do tricks by hiding treats in his clothing.

He was proficient at playing a lute, his stringed instrument that he brought with him from the monastery. The young albino had a beautiful lively voice, and he knew many popular songs. The villagers loved to sing along while Nyla danced like a bohemian princess. Her skirt seemed to fly around her body while the coins and beads sewn into her apron jingled at her hips. She loved the attention and drew the village boys like bees to honey. The larger the crowd, the more wildly she danced to the great satisfaction of the villagers.

At each village, the townsmen enjoyed the distraction our little show provided and the disguises afforded us the opportunity to make friends with the peasants. Many were anxious to give The Trumpeters of Cheer news of what was happening in Safehold. In one village, the innkeeper's wife shared what she heard from travelers who came through the village.

"Pull up a chair, boy," she said as we walked into the inn. Although she was looking directly at me, I thought she was speaking to Beryl. I forgot my disguise made me look like a boy. After chopping off my hair, Mother thought it appropriate that I wear a red tunic under a knee-length leather doublet that completely covered my small breasts.

The woman ushered us to a table in a dark corner of the inn. "The supreme inquisitor is on his way to St. Regents to officiate an execution. They say a young seminarian was murdered. The protégé of Archbishop Pietto," she whispered the news while filling their plates with stew.

Alex avoided the woman's eyes and hoped her expression remained fixed and innocent.

"They say two nuns killed him. Stabbed him in the back while he slept." Alex watched the woman's face light up with the chance to share the gossip. "Can you imagine the things that go on in the convent?" She shook her head and clicked her tongue in disbelief as she filled Alex's tanker. "I hear one of the murderers was caught and is being held in prison. The other is missing." She paused, winked her eye, and slowly nodded her head as if she had information. "Hiding out in the woods, I imagine." She wiped the table with a dirty rag. "Better if the wild beasts find her before the inquisitor."

The woman burst into laughter. The sound of her cackle made Alex jump. She realized that each time the mystery of Joseph's death was told, the gossiper added a little speculation of their own to the story. Alex wondered how far these lies would spread and if the truth would ever come to light. Her mother was caught in a web of lies, and now she found herself in a similar trap. She touched her throat, remembering the pain of Joseph's strong hands around her neck and how he tried to kill her.

The innkeeper moved in closer, like they were coconspirators, and whispered in Alex's ear, "I'm told as he rides to St. Regents, he is holding inquisitions in towns and villages along the way. They say you can smell burning flesh and the stench of death for miles."

Moving closer to the border, the stories became more gruesome. News spread about the inquisitor's hatred and zeal to rid Old World and Safehold of the heretics who preached only one way to salvation. Beheadings, crucifixions, mutilations, and public executions were spreading through the provinces since the pope's truce with King Apollyon. Foreigners escaping persecution from Old World found no rest or safety in St. Regents. They whispered about the fate of born-again believers across the entire world. The news haunted her thoughts day and night. She prayed constantly for Reverend Mother and the others who stayed behind.

Villagers reported the border was unsafe because of the inhuman creatures who crossed the Chasm from Old World and entered the perimeter unchallenged. Alex knew their fears were true, she felt a wicked presence in the air as they made their way inside the boundary, the last stop before crossing the Chasm. She watched the countryside change. The trees became thick with gnarled trunks, twisted and bent like tortured souls. Moss hung from tree limbs, like fingers, reaching down to snatch away a weary traveler. The cries of the birds from within the shadowy depths sounded loud and brutal.

Villages were scarce, and the inns were filled with brawling and thievery, leaving them no choice but to sleep and eat on the trail. The people they encountered were solemn, distant, and bound with hatred, walking the dirt roads like shades of the dead.

Alex noticed the day held only a scant bit of light before nightfall. She pulled Malak to a stop. "Beryl, find us a place to settle in for the night. Make sure it is away from the road. No telling what type of travelers roam these paths at dusk." She learned to trust the prophet's skills. Living in the wilderness had made the boy an expert in survival skills. "Tomorrow we cross the Chasm."

Alex faced Nyla. She had mixed feelings about the princess. For the first few weeks, the girl tried to get them to wait on her every whim. *Boy! Unsaddle my camel! Find me fresh fruit, a place to bathe, clean clothes.*

At first, Alex entertained thoughts of abandoning the rich heiress on the road but realized that would be a terrible hardship for anyone foolish enough to rescue the spoiled brat. Instead she and the albino taught her to unload the basket she used as a saddle on her camel and make a safe bed at night, using her silks as a covering against insects. They patiently showed her how to clean her clothes by the stream, pick fresh berries without getting pierced by thorns, and to take quick showers under the mountain runoffs. Alex gave her a knife and taught her to throw it. She practiced every chance she got, and truth be told, she was becoming quite proficient. Under their tutelage, she seemed to grow and blossom, reveling in her new independence.

Beryl stopped the caravan under a rock ledge. "We will set up camp here. I will start a fire and look for a fresh water supply."

Alex tied Malak behind the donkey cart. She didn't feel

safe letting him forage alone in the woods. "I'm going into the forest to hunt for food."

Nyla took a grooming comb from the cart bed. "I will care for Malak while you're gone. He needs to be brushed and fed." She handed Alex a large bow and quiver of arrows hanging from Malak's saddle. "It will be dark soon. Be careful out there."

CHAPTER 14

The Border

Night crept into the forest. Shadows sprung up behind every tree. Alex heard whispering and footfalls chomping through the fallen leaves. She ran through the murky forest with two misshapen rabbits hanging from her belt. Her breath came in choppy gasps. Wiping sweat from her forehead with the back of her hand, she cringed at the blood under her nails and shuddered at the thought of the decay she saw in the woods.

Relax, Alex. You are almost back to the camp, she told herself. A distant clap of thunder caught her off guard, making her heart feel like it jumped from her chest. *Jesus, Mary, and Joseph!* She stopped with her hand to her heart until she could breathe normally again. *I'm supposed to be this bold and courageous warrior, and I'm scared of thunder and a little rot on the trees.*

She clutched the crucifix that hung from a chain on her neck until her heartbeat slowed.

She hurried away from the tree line and made her way into the comfort of familiar surroundings. The scent of wood burning brought a momentary sensation of safety, but she noticed the different species of trees and grasses made her throat itch and eyes burn. Picking up the pace, she hurried to the campsite.

She relaxed as Beryl smiled and nodded his head in greeting. She watched him slice odd-colored roots to add to the stew.

A sudden guttural growl echoed through the darkening forest. Her flesh erupted with gooseflesh.

Beryl jumped to his feet. "Hell's fire! What was that?" He rubbed his arms as chills crept over his body.

Alex's heart galloped. "Something big." She rested her hand on the hilt of her sword. "It sounded far away, like it was moving away from us, not toward us."

Nyla ran to the fire ring. "Did you hear that?" She squeezed next to Alex and pulled her cloak tight around her shoulders. Her hands trembled as she opened a pouch and began to dump its contents into a bucket of dirty water.

Alex reached for the pouch to stop her. "The streams I saw had fish that swam belly-up. We don't want to drink this stuff."

"Don't worry," Nyla said. "These stones have been used by my ancestors for centuries to purify contaminated water. It will take a while, but it will be safe to drink as soon as the filmy color clears up."

Alex dumped her kill at the girl's feet. "Can you do anything with these?"

Nyla cringed. "What are they?"

Alex reached down and pulled an arrow from each carcass and wiped the blood on a rag. "I'm not sure."

Nyla's stomach lurched. "I'll see what I can mix up with my herbs."

Alex pulled a sharp knife from her boot and began to clean her catch.

Beryl stoked the fire, warming his snow-white hands over the red flame. "What did you see out there?" he asked.

Alex smirked. "The natural things look normal, almost beautiful, but there are hidden changes. The world, as we know it, is passing away. Look at the roots you pulled from the earth."

Beryl held them up in the light of the fire. "They are different than what grows in Safehold. They look putrid." He opened his hand and let them drop to the ground.

Alex pulled the archer's cap from her head and ran her hands through her short hair. "There seems to be an underground system of darkness spreading throughout Old World." She crossed herself. "It is reaching across the Chasm and making its way into Safehold. The roots of this blight go deep. The disease is feeding all of creation a portion of its corruption." She shuddered. "This is like nothing we have ever seen or imagined."

Silent flashes of lightning jumped across the dark sky. The moon had risen high and black. Bright light glowed behind the moon, illuminating the high peaks of Moreland, the circular-shaped mountain range that encased the Chasm like a closed fist. Alex stared heavenward at the strange sight.

Nyla broke the silence. "Astrologers say the planets and stars speak of future events. Do you think the black moon is an omen?"

Alex sprinkled the mixture of herbs the healer provided over the raw meat and threw it into a pot simmering over the fire. The meat sizzled in the hot liquid. Malak began to whinny and snort. The stallion pawed the ground, agitated and nervous.

Alex stood and unsheathed her sword. From the darkness, two strangers appeared in the camp. One man and one woman, both well-dressed and well-armed. Alex felt uneducated in the ways of the world but guessed by his sleeveless white robe and the strange black symbols covering his face, arms, and torso, he was a cleric of some kind. He carried a broadsword on his back and had a dagger hanging from his belted robe.

The girl who traveled with him was young, no older than she, but had long white hair that trailed to the ground. Her robe was red, like the leaves on the trees, and she had a large bag of seeds slung over her shoulder. Around her neck hung many chains with stones of quartz and amber in all sizes and shapes. She carried a sickle, for harvesting grain.

The man bowed formally. "Excuse our interruption. We were crossing the Chasm, on our way into Safehold, when the spirits of the air foretold the arrival of three ambassadors from St. Regents. Maybe you saw them." He paused and arched his brow. "We were told a nun, a boy, and a princess are carrying a forgotten message into Old World. We decided to look for them."

Alex lowered her sword but decided to keep it close. "What business do you have with the travelers?"

The woman answered. Her voice sounded chillingly calm. "The new truce between the church and the king opened roads that were once closed. Mystics can now bring seeds of knowledge into a kingdom previously opposed to enlightenment."

Alex felt her skin prickle.

Nyla stood to shake the stranger's hand. "We are The Trumpeter's of Cheer, part of a traveling circus. We have been in many villagers but saw no one who fits your description." She flashed a pretty smile. "Personally I think it's about time the people of Safehold open their minds to new ideas." She led the visitors to the fire. "Come and join us for a meal."

The man introduced himself. "I am called Lammas. I am a bard entrusted with keeping our sacred traditions alive. I come from the great kingdom of E'Doom where our all-powerful King Apollyon has established his throne."

Alex pushed back a wave of nausea. "Only God has unlimited authority and power in heaven and earth."

The cleric raised his hand in a placating gesture. "We are speaking of our king as a force strong enough to hold all things in the universe together."

Alex felt like she couldn't focus. She watched the girl sit next to Nyla and felt a strange sensation in the pit of her stomach.

"My name is Dimitra," the pretty stranger said. "I am a practicing augur, able to interpret signs and symbols. I heard you ask if the black moon is an omen. I read manifestations in the earth and skies. Would you like me to tell you what I see?"

Nyla clapped like a delighted child. "Yes. Do tell us what this dark moon is saying. I am very interested in knowledge from other lands."

The augur's voice was like the coo of a dove. "The autumn equinox has begun." She looked around the dark woods. "Can't you see the thinning of the Veil that separates our world from the spirit realm?" She paused and crossed her arms in an X-pattern over her chest. "Take a moment and feel the restlessness in the air." She gazed into the distance in awe. "It's the demon spirits passing through the open door."

Alex interrupted, "Our God tells us that the days are coming when some people will turn away from the faith, giving their attention to doctrines that demons teach (1 Timothy 4:1). The knowledge you offer is forbidden fruit."

Nyla protested, "What harm will it do to hear what she has to say? It doesn't mean we believe their teachings."

Dimitra smiled. "First I will pray." She raised her arms over the camp in benediction and chanted in a strange language. When she finished, she took a handful of seed from her bag and threw it into the purified pot of drinking water. For a moment, the water turned black, then it bubbled, releasing a hiss of steam from inside the pot. The cloud that formed spilled its vapor into the surrounding area like a circle. The steam smelled like fresh herbs and shimmered like silver in the light of the fire. With closed eyes, Dimitra toyed with the vapor, pulling it toward her face, inhaling it.

The augur slowly opened her eyes and smiled. "What

we see in the sky tonight is a waxing moon, gaining in size and strength. The black moon is a sign, revealing a change in power." She continued to pull the vapor toward her face. "I see empty fields, plowed under and replanted."

Dimitra stood and raised her arms to heaven. "I see a new harvest." From her bag, she took a loaf. "Let us break bread together to congeal our friendship."

Alex felt drained of energy. *I need my weapons.*

Beryl noted the warrior's discomfort and took her hand to lead her away to the wagon bed. "You look ill. What's wrong?"

Alex swallowed hard. "My body is shaking, and I feel lightheaded."

Malak shook his broad head, pulling at the ties that anchored him to the wagon.

"What's wrong with the horse?" Beryl asked. "He never acts like this."

Alex stroked his neck. "Easy, Malak. I feel it too."

Beryl handed her a cup of water.

Alex winced. "I don't want that! Did you see what their seeds did to the water?"

Beryl smiled. "I took it before their seeds. Drink. You might need refreshment."

Alex shook her head. "No. It's a demonic attack."

Beryl choked. "What?"

Alex fastened her combat belt over her chain mail. "We have been given authority to trample on scorpions and snakes, but I have never done this before."

Beryl pulled his hood over his face. "Where are they?" he whispered.

Alex slipped her helmet on her head. "They are sitting at our fire ring."

Beryl pushed back his hood and smirked. "Alex. You are being misled. They carry a different message than ours…but demons?"

Alex ignored him. She noticed she was already feeling better. She strode over to the fire and faced their guests. "Dimitra. Explain your oracle to us."

The girl turned and faced Alex, her eyes wide with surprise. "Are you threatening me with that armor?"

Alex planted her feet firmly on the ground. "Explain your oracle."

Dimitra looked over her shoulder, looking for Lammas. He stood silent in the shadows, away from the fire and nodded his head.

"As you wish, warrior," she said. "Thousands upon thousands of followers of the cross have been leaving the faith. That is what the barren plowed-under fields represent." She looked at the warrior and grinned. "I imagine your converts finally realized how powerless their religion was and began to look for answers in the dark arts."

She turned her black eyes on Nyla. "Besides, believers are such hypocrites."

Nyla inhaled a sharp breath. "How dare you! I am no hypocrite!"

Dimitra curled her lips with icy contempt. "Poor delusional child. You wanted me to read the heavens. Is that your way of mixing magic with Christianity? Maybe you want to start a new religion or could it be your eyes have been opened?"

Nyla was incensed. "How dare you question my conviction to Christ."

Dimitra laughed. "The spirits of the air know what you're about. Running from the constraints of duty to find freedom and adventure. Your schemes have nothing to do with the God you say you serve."

"Enough!" Alex stood between them. "You will not accuse her."

Dimitra squared her shoulders. "You said you wanted to

know the meaning of my prophecy. Be quiet and listen, if you want the truth." She began to walk around the fire. "The size and strength of the waxing moon, with the black covering, is the Great Enlightenment spreading its teachings throughout the entire world. The occult is a seed with a vast root system your converts cannot contain."

Lammas spoke from the shadows. "As you might guess," he said, "the new harvest is the rising of an army of disciples who follow Apollyon and his universal teachings. These soldiers will trample the faithful saints of God and crush converts as new seeds try to sprout and grow."

Alex's hands were sweating, but she felt her armor quiver, giving her a jolt of courage. "You both lie. Darkness will never overpower light." She kept her hand on the hilt of her sword. "As the soil makes the sprout come up and a garden causes seed to grow, so the Sovereign Lord will make righteousness and praise spring up before all nations." Her sword felt hot in the scabbard. "God's harvest is ripe. The righteous will never be uprooted."

Alex felt Dimitra lay a gentle hand upon her shoulder. In the light of the campfire, she looked like an angel.

"Do we need all this uneasiness?" the augur said. "Surely as Safehold and Old World come together, we can share the harvest." She moved away into the shadows toward Lammas.

"No!" Alex said. "Jesus told us a parable about the final harvest. He said while his men slept, the devil came and sowed weeds among the wheat." She took a breath trying to calm her racing heart. "Falsehood and truth will grow together until the harvest time. When the time is right, the reapers will gather the sons and daughters of Satan and tie them together to be burned but gather the children of God into his barn" (Matthew 13:24–38).

From within the dark canopy of tree boughs, Dimitra began to make a loud repetitive clicking and chirping sound in her throat. The pitch continued to rise, getting louder and louder.

Nyla backed away from the tree line, covering her ears.

Beryl stared wide-eyed into the darkness. "I know that sound," he whispered. "It's an arachnid."

A large bug-like creature came out of the shadows. Its upper body was Dimitra from her waist up, but the rest of her body was a large black scorpion, heavily armored.

Alex watched in horror, from somewhere locked within her mind, as the giant creature moved toward her, its eight legs scraping the dirt as it moved, its tail held high above its head. Alex's heartbeat was the only sound she heard until a heavy front claw stuck her body and sent her careening through the air and into a large tree.

"Alex, get up!" Nyla screamed.

Pain shot through her body. She realized she was thrown across the ground like a windblown leaf. She heard Dimitra's chirping sounds closing in on her. *Where is my sword?* She jerked herself to her feet in time to have a large pincher grab hold of her chain mail and hoist her into the air. The scorpion shook her back and forth violently before throwing her into the campfire.

Alex shrieked as the hot embers touched her flesh.

"Alex, your weapon." Nyla threw the shield toward the warrior.

Dimitra lifted her tail in an arc over her head, a sign of attack, and rushed forward stabbing her venomous spike toward the warrior.

Alex rolled sideways, avoiding the massive stinger on the tip of Dimitra's tail. She grabbed hold of the shield, covering her sprawled body. A loud thud rang through the camp as the tail struck Alex's shield, crushing her chest.

"You are beaten, warrior," Dimitra said as she sidled away, looking for another victim. "Go back where you came from. There are far worse enemies in Old World, and you have failed the first wave."

Alex felt sharp pain in her back and chest from the blow, like her ribs were broken. In that instant, she saw Beryl running toward the demon with his staff swinging through the air. *He is going to get himself killed!* Alex pushed her shield off her body and grabbed her sword from the dirt. Jumping to her feet, she ran toward them.

Dimitra laughed. "Stupid boy. You are but a grasshopper before me." With an open claw, she knocked him off his feet and pinned him to the ground.

"Get off me, you freak," he screamed.

Her tail swung up and over her head. She used the stinger like a weapon stabbing the ground, over and over, toying with him, deliberately missing his vulnerable flesh. "Freak, you call me? A misfit calling me names."

Beryl felt the air leaving his lungs.

She poised her tail for a direct hit. "Useless piece of human waste. You must die." The stinger careened toward Beryl's heart. "Your God can't help you now."

Alex pounced on the demon's back, climbing over the creatures armored plates, hanging on with every ounce of her strength.

Dimitra turned her head toward the warrior and stared, bug-eyed in shock.

One swift move with her sword, Alex cut off the demon's head.

The grotesque body collapsed to the ground. Alex hit the dirt hard, her sword flew across the campsite. She sat in a pile of debris that was once Dimitra. The dead skeletal remains twitched and moved erratically while Dimitra's head lay wild-eyed in the dust.

Alex jumped to her feet and pulled Beryl from beneath the claw.

"Yes, yes, yes!" he yelled as he lifted the warrior from her feet and spun around. "You did it! You really did it!"

Lammas slithered from the shadows and grabbed Nyla by the throat, lifting her small body off her feet. His large muscles, beneath the tattoos, writhed like snakes under his skin. "You did wonderfully, you fool! You gave me a sacrifice." He laughed. "I will take this girl's life in revenge for what you've done." His forked tongue darted from his mouth and licked his prisoner's face. "A human sacrifice is desired for the gods of the harvest."

Beryl stopped celebrating and dropped Alex to her feet. She quickly grabbed her weapon from the dirt.

Alex could feel this demon's power. "What do you want with the healer? She is no trophy for someone with your ability. Take me instead."

He lifted his prisoner higher. Nyla kicked at him with her dangling legs but was no match for his strength. "Drop your sword and I will release her."

Alex watched his large hand writhe like a massive constrictor was hidden beneath his skin. She saw Nyla's body go limp in his hand.

She let the sword fall from her hand. "I dropped the sword, now let her go."

As he came toward the firelight, Alex realized his flesh was covered with scales, like a snake.

Lammas's voice took on an ominous tone. "You are a fool, Sister Alexandria Augustus Mary." He smiled at the look of surprise on her face. "Yes. I know your name. I know all about you. You are a coward in your spirit. With or without the armor, I will kill all three of your aspirations."

Nyla opened her eyes into small slits while Lammas was distracted. She slid her hand within her skirt and felt the dagger hidden in her pocket. She grabbed the knife and thrust it into her captor's arm.

The surprise disarmed him, and he dropped her to the ground.

She landed on her feet and bolted away to stand with the others.

"Where is he?" she asked.

Alex stiffened. "He disappeared."

A thick black fog rose from the ground. It smelled like rotting flesh. Lammas began laughing. "I summoned the fog," he said.

They followed his voice and watched him appear behind them in the gray mist and quickly disappear again. "I'm so powerful you cannot stop me," he said and materialized to the right of them, but like a puff of smoke, he was gone.

He emerged out of the fog as a snake in a tree. "None of you are as powerful as my god has made me. Look at the three of you trembling before me. You have only limited ability because the god you serve is the lesser god." His serpentine body coiled around a tree limb. As he spoke, his reptilian eyes changed color from black to red to yellow to green.

"The God you serve has limited authority on earth. If he were all-powerful as he claims, wouldn't he just destroy all your enemies with a word? He doesn't care about you. Look at the corruption in the church. His disciples are easily bought and sold." The fog curled up the tree, rendering him invisible once again.

"Foolish children of righteousness, can't you see the error of your belief? There are others," he whispered reverently. "Others who rule this realm. The legions become stronger as more people follow the enlightened path." His voice rattled the autumn leaves hanging from the trees. "Say what you want, Alex, but I see you. I know your type. All show on the outside but frail and broken inside."

Alex's heart hammered in her chest. *He knows I'm afraid. He knows I'm a fraud.* Her eyes darted around the perimeter.

Where is he?

He slithered from the fog. His snake-like form gliding forward on his belly. His reptilian eyes held hers, daring her to look away. "Admit your defeat, Alex. You have no stomach for this battle. You barely believe the word you preach." In a flash, his shape shifted into its human form. "Lay down your weapons and join our king. I have shown you a small demonstration of my power. For our devotees, there are special gifts and abilities we share with our worthy disciples."

Alex's body doubled over in pain. She felt his words constricting and crushing her spirit.

Nyla screamed, "What are you doing to her? Leave her alone."

Lammas just laughed.

Alex fell to her knees. *Is the serpent right? Do I really believe the words in the Book of Life? Can I trust God? Everyone I ever loved and trusted has lied to me.* A cool breeze blew against her face.

She heard a voice whisper in her heart. *I have loved you with an everlasting love* (Jeremiah 31:3). She recognized the voice of her Savior. She felt her body, soul, and spirit relax and slowly raised herself up from the dirt and faced her attacker.

In one swift motion, Lammas pulled his broadsword from his back. The blade hissed through the air as he came at her, swinging his weapon. Alex double flipped backward, avoiding the blade. Instead of pursuing her, he changed direction and stalked Nyla and Beryl like a hungry predator.

They stood side by side, afraid to run. Beryl realized Alex's sword still lay at his feet. As he watched the creature of darkness come closer, he wiggled his toes under Alex's weapon. As if it were one of his colored balls, he kicked it high into the air.

"Alex," he yelled.

She ran forward and caught her weapon by its hilt. She

was inches from the demon. Her body vibrated with the power of her sword. "Jesus gave us authority to trample on snakes and scorpions" (Luke 10:19).

The name of Jesus broke him. He stopped with his broadsword midair and began to vaporize like the fog he had summoned. Alex felt empowered and raised her voice. "Jesus gave us the power to overcome the enemy and nothing will harm us" (Luke 10:19).

Lammas's form became like dust at her feet. She raised her leg and stomped her booted foot into its head.

The fog, along with the remains of Dimitra and Lammas, vanished as mysteriously as they had appeared. The fresh scent of pine filled the air, replacing the sickening smell of rot.

Alex was not sure how long the three of them stood silent, locked in their own thoughts. She was surprised when the morning birds began to waken the dawn. Part of her hoped it was all a bad dream, but the black moon still hung in the sky, reminding her why she was on this mission. Somewhere on the battlefield in Old World, soldiers were losing heart.

"Saddle up," Alex heard herself say. "It will be better to cross the Chasm in the daylight."

CHAPTER 15

Soul-Sifters

"You're bleeding," Aza said. "Get inside the tent."

Sargo wiped blood from his cheek. "This sleet feels like spikes!"

Once inside, there was hardly enough room to move. The tent was designed to fit eight soldiers, and they stuffed another six civilians inside. The refugees settled at the far end, sitting shoulder to shoulder, clinging to one another. Aza realized there were three women, two children, and the old man. He watched them sob, grieving the loss of their loved ones, but he felt empty. He no longer felt sad or pity for their loss; he felt angry that they held onto their faith that brought death and danger to believers. It was strange to realize where he once felt compassion, he now held these refugees in contempt.

A small child looked at him through sunken eyes. His skin was the color of cold ash. The boy's flesh stretched across frail limbs, leaving bones visible under his weak torso. His chest rose and fell slowly with each labored breath.

"I'm hungry, Mommy," he whined.

A thin tendril of smoke, from a small fire inside the tent, rose toward the ceiling. Aza's stomach growled.

"Why haven't these people been fed?"

Ravenna rummaged through her bag and found some crusty bread. She pulled off a small chunk and stuck the larger portion back into her bag and passed the meager leftover around the room.

Zane, a young recruit, questioned Aza. "What shall we do now, sir?" Despite the cold, tension caused beads of sweat to drip down his forehead. "What will become of us if they catch us this time?"

Aza looked at the young soldier's drawn face. He had seen the look many times in the past and knew the boy was desperate to camouflage his fear from his teammates. Part of him wanted to tell all of them to run for their lives, but he held up a bold front. *Aren't all good leaders supposed to be fearless in times of war?* His thoughts mocked him.

He began to speak words that belonged to the man he wanted to be, but in truth, his heart was no longer in the fight. His heart had grown cold, and he couldn't fan the flame to make it burn with passion for the cause. He was tired. Too weary to care.

"In the past, we have been successful, keeping this troop one step ahead of the enemy."

A new voice whispered treasonous thoughts in his mind. Shadim hovered like smoke around the hopeless band of survivors, willing the commander to take the bait. *Lie to them and save yourself before it's too late.*

Aza let false words spill from his mouth like an avalanche. "There is no reason to believe the Soul-Sifters will continue to follow us in this blizzard."

He dropped his gaze from the group. Soldiers and civilians stared at him; their faces pleading for answers, and all he had was lies. The wind beat against the tent. The relentless gusts threatened to lift the structure and toss it away. Aza's mind raced, trying to think of something to say. He had decided what he must do and felt a twinge of remorse. He drew a deep breath and looked into their trusting eyes.

"We will need to post a watch with or without fire." He pulled his wet hood over his head. "Sargo and I will go first.

The rest of you get some sleep."

Ravenna grabbed hold of his arm. "What about me?" Her deep brown eyes flashed with fury.

"Not this time." His tone was final. "They need you here." Aza looked down at her, and his heart ached. He realized this was the last time he would see her face, hear her voice. His gut tightened and bile rose in his throat.

The merciless wind screamed, pounding and pushing its fury against the tent. Icy water dripped through a small hole in the roof. The constant sound ticked away the minutes, a steady reminder of impending doom. The structure creaked and groaned as the storm guys struggled to hold it in place. The soldiers were jumpy and on edge. Every thump made them reach for their weapons. The refugees were wide-eyed and fearful, except an old man with wispy white hair.

Aza and Sargo prepared to take the first watch, but the old one blocked their path. "I had a dream from God," he said.

Sargo rolled his eyes and tried to push past the man in exasperation. "God doesn't live here, old man."

Aza put a comforting hand on the elder's shoulder. "I hope he will protect us this night." He tried not to sound condescending, but he was tired of believing in an ancient religion that promised victory but never delivered.

"They are coming." His faded blue eyes sparkled, and his voice shook with anticipation. "Three of them are coming from Safehold." The old one continued speaking, ignoring the soldiers' unbelieving stares. "They will help us fight the enemy." His eyes held Aza's gaze. "They will teach us to use special weapons of warfare so we can rid our homeland of King Apollyon's evil."

Aza clenched his fists. "Three? We need three hundred legions of soldiers to win this war." He stopped himself. He knew if he let his emotions surface, he might knock the old man out for clinging to false hope. "We must take this watch."

He forced his voice to be gentle, although he wanted to scream in rage against this God who was the cause of their misery.

"Have faith." The elder cautioned in a strong voice. He fumbled around in his pocket and pulled out a vial of oil. He spilled a small amount on his finger and traced the sign of the cross on Aza's forehead, giving him a blessing. He moved aside, letting the soldier pass and sat quietly next to the others.

Outside the icy wind ripped at the soldiers' bare faces like claws digging into soft flesh. Sargo tried to shield his eyes with his arm.

"How the hell are we supposed to see anything out here?" Sargo moved his hand to the scabbard that held his sword and quickly pulled it away. The hilt was deadly cold to his touch. "Look at the black covering over the moon. Have you ever seen anything like it?"

He tried to focus his eyes, but the storm, along with the wind, was blinding.

Shadim followed them, hovering around them in the frosty midnight air. *Run. It's the only way to avoid death. Are you a martyr? Save yourself.* He watched and waited.

Save yourself. Aza's mind whispered. Like a flash of lightning, his decision took on a life of its own, pushing his fear to new lengths. The impulse made him stumble.

"The creatures will be on us like vultures," Sargo said. "We are walking around like live bait."

"Shut up!" Aza ordered. He looked over his shoulder. "We're out of here." He grabbed his brother by the arm. "We can't look back."

Sargo froze. "What are you saying?"

"Move as fast as you can toward the outline of the mountain."

Sargo's body refused to move. "What about Ravenna and—"

"Forget them and move."

Shadim flew from the scene toward E'Doom, reveling in his success.

Sargo stood like a statue.

"Move out now or I'll leave without you," Aza ordered.

Sargo fell in step with his brother, trudging through the snow toward freedom.

The beasts picked up their enemy's scent shortly after the rebels snuck away with the refugees. The dominant mutation led the pack through the frozen tundra. The demon was skilled and versatile—the ultimate predator. The sifters understood the human intellect and used the scent of fear to track their target. The leader inhaled the air that reeked of terror and could hear voices through the screeching wind. It urged the pack on, pushing them through the ice and cold.

They were quick, traveling the distance on all fours. Instinct taught them to work as a team. Being semi human, some were still in the process of transformation while others were completely demonic. Hosts to demon spawn, the sifters were born of hatred, brutality, and murder. Men and women who gave their souls over to their base animal instincts after pairing with evil spirits. Without warning, the germ that lived within them finally possessed their every action.

"Did you see them in Providence? They don't look like us anymore," Sargo said. "You can't tell male from female. Their faces are almost completely distorted."

The soldier lost his footing and slipped on the ice.

Aza reached out his hand to help his brother up. "One has a horn that protrudes from the center of its forehead."

Sargo clamored to his feet.

"Did you see that?" he whispered. "Something is out there."

Dark shadows darted across the icy landscape. Noises and shapes appeared in the distance like a black oasis.

"Maybe it's just a wolf," Aza said. He strained to see

through the whiteout. His body shook uncontrollably.

"It can't be. It's up on two legs like a man."

Sargo stepped backward in the direction of the tent.

"Is that noise the wind?"

The sifters howled and barked. They sniffed the ground and the air. The wind toyed with their sense of smell. The human scent was strong and the wind gusts carried it, tantalizing the pack, leading them one way and then the other. The game heightened their aggression. The deadly silhouettes crept closer, pressing their bodies close to the ground. Instinct fueled their desire to hunt, and nothing could stand in the way of the kill. They circled their prey.

"I don't see anything now. Where did they go?" The snow blurred his vision. "I know they're out there." Sargo squinted his eyes. "I can smell the decay."

"The air feels colder somehow." Aza shivered. The feeling pierced his flesh like the tip of a blade. He felt death stalking him.

Their heavy claws crunched through the snow. Six colossal beasts ran forward, hunched over on all fours. They snarled and whined like hysterical madmen. As if on cue, they spread out, spacing themselves like a wall, until they surrounded their victims. The predators methodically began to narrow the perimeter, coming closer to their mark. One began yelping, jumping, and sniffing the air. The sound of its eagerness to attack incited the others. Within seconds, they closed the gap that separated the soldiers from death.

Aza and Sargo stood back-to-back, bracing themselves for the assault.

"Keep your sword high!"

The creatures closed in. Long threads of salvia hung frozen from their mouths. The largest predator stood on two legs. Aza recognized it from the village. It was the beast that spoke to him. The face of the demon was distorted, half-human half-beast. The creature curled its lips into a sneer—revealing sharp dagger-like teeth. Without warning, it charged into the pack and used the horn to gouge one of its own. The stunned animal screeched in pain. With unnatural strength, the leader threw the large bleeding carcass aside, distracting the others. The smell of the female's helplessness overpowered the pack and they dove into the wounded morphling, eating their victim alive.

The alpha mutation's eyes glowed in the night, red slits of evil. It ambled up to the frightened soldiers, confident in its power. "I told you I would come for you." Its voice was raspy and full of hatred and loathing of all flesh. Its eyes held Aza's frozen stare.

"I'm here to take you home," it hissed. The muscled creature slunk down like a lion and prepared to attack.

Aza made one plea. "God, if you are real, save us now!"

CHAPTER 16

The Chasm

Alex felt filthy after the encounter with Lammas and Demetria. If she could just wash the stench from her mind. *Demons stalking the earth! What next?* The nuns taught them Satan prowled around like a lion, looking for Christians to devour. *Truth be told, I didn't believe it. I guess I didn't believe God.*

She gave Malak his head and let him lead them through the forest toward the mouth of the Chasm. Everything looked so dark despite the early hour of the day. The black moon followed them along the path, accompanied by thick storm clouds. There was an eerie stillness surrounding the trail. Trees became scarce. Animal noises were nonexistent. Vegetation was replaced by rocks. The narrow road and giant boulders made it nearly impassable with the donkey cart.

Like an illusion, they rounded the bend, and there it was. Moreland. The mountain circled the Chasm like an ancient colosseum. In an intimidating gesture, the black moon settled in the center of the arena.

The squeaking wheels of the donkey cart pulled Alex from her thoughts. Beryl climbed from his seat and peered down the wide corridor of black rocks that resembled clawed fingers, beckoning them inside.

"A priest who made it back to the monastery after a crusade into Old World drew pictures of the Chasm. I recognize this as what he referred to as the gateway." He paused and cleared his throat. "If...I mean when we make it through the Chasm, we will be at the entrance into the Old World."

Alex shifted her weight in the saddle. "We can't see inside. Did he draw any other pictures?"

Beryl shook his head.

Alex leaned forward and stroked Malak's neck. "It is told around St. Regents that many soldiers who enter here end up like scattered seed, eaten by ravenous birds because their faith is weak. After our encounter with Dimitra and Lammas's occult teachings, we know the rumors are true. We will *all* need to be alert."

Beryl pulled a flat stone from his pocket and absently rolled it through his fingers. "The most disheartening stories are the soldiers who make the mistake of integrating into the lifestyle of the enemy and disregard their mission altogether. They say only the strong survive the crossover."

Alex rubbed the back of her neck. "I wish we would have received a message from Mother before we reached this point in our journey. I fear for those we left behind with our secret."

Beryl nodded his head in agreement. "I have searched the skies for Sarah, Brother John's pigeon, hoping for any sign they might be safe."

Nyla pulled her camel to a halt next to her comrades and looked down the passageway. "I'm not worried. I pity the inquisitor if he questions *my* mother!"

Alex and Beryl burst into laughter.

"You can be cold," Alex said.

Nyla shrugged. "No. Just honest. She has a way of getting people to do what she wants. I imagine she has concocted a fail-safe story to tell him about our disappearance."

"I hope you're right."

Nyla changed the subject. "Look at this strange passageway. The earth has an odd sheen to it, don't you think? There does not appear to be any vegetation, just these tall rocks and deep depressions in the earth."

The stench of burnt flesh blowing in from the gateway gave Alex a pounding headache. She rubbed her temples and pulled a canteen of water from her saddlebag and splashed water on her face. "Although it's early morning, the light in the Chasm is fading. If you look over the canyon, darkness and storm clouds have settled in."

Beryl's donkey brayed. "Maybe we should camp here for the night and wait for the storm to pass," Beryl said.

Alex made a quick decision. "We need to go now if we are to make it to the other side before nightfall. Who knows what the interior of Moreland might be hiding?" She adjusted her breastplate and put on her helmet. "Put your regular clothing back on. We don't want to arrive in Old World looking like we're part of a traveling sideshow." She shifted around in her saddle and positioned her sword and shield to be ready to fight. "The remnant expects an army from St. Regents."

Alex took a spyglass from her saddlebag and peered across the strange terrain while she waited for her allies to change clothing. "The valley has an irregular shape," she called over her shoulder. "Although it looks empty for a distance, we can't be sure what is beyond the horizon." She knew from her schooling never to take a potential battlefield for granted. "We need to be vigilant."

Nyla finished dressing and mounted her camel.

Alex handed her companion the binoculars. "Have a look."

Nyla squinted through the heavy apparatus, making adjustments with a wheel mounted to the side. "The land looks devastated by a volcanic eruption, but there is no sign of a volcano anywhere." Goose bumps made the hair on her arms stand on end. She watched Alex attach a bow to her back and pull two daggers from her bags.

"Take this," Alex instructed. I have an extra weapon for

Beryl. Hide them in your clothing. We have no idea what to expect."

Nyla handed Beryl the dagger and eyeglass. She quickly put the sharp tool in her belt before adjusting her long hooded scarf. A strong wind was blowing in from the north, chilling the air. Nyla pulled her robe tightly around her shoulders, fighting chills that had more to do with uneasiness than cold.

Alex barked orders to her team. "Beryl. You will need to take extra care with the wheels of the cart. The ridges look deep." Without waiting for a reply, she dug her heels into Malak's side and they began the journey into the belly of the mountain.

Thunder rumbled in the distance. The sky overflowed with a canopy of dark bulging clouds that exposed the black moon and a strange red star. She prayed Malak was going in the right direction. The entry into Old World looked farther away than before they started.

They came into an empty valley that stretched for miles. The high peaks of Moreland surrounded them. A light fog, painted with a soft ruby glow from the red star, seeped into the air, exposing a savage carnage. Thousands upon thousands of discarded swords, shields, belts, and helmets littered the ground. Vultures flew overhead. Some came to rest upon the metal bones of believers who deserted. Alex felt heartsick. *I'm afraid, Lord. Help me stay strong.*

The vultures watched them as they rode through the rubble.

"Stay alert," Alex cautioned.

They rode for what seemed like hours. Malak was slow and steady. Alex was edgy and wanted to ride ahead and scout the place, but the horse refused. She felt mentally and physically exhausted.

She tried focusing her eyes on the chasm littered with ridges, rocks, and depressions. Thick black smoke spewed from craters in the earth, blotting out the small amount of sunlight. The smell made her feel lightheaded.

Particles of ash filled the atmosphere. Lightning pierced the darkness, throwing its daggers of voltage at the riders. Each flash sounded like a whip as it struck the ground. The landscape went from dark to light in quick repetition, adding a strobe-like effect to the eerie surroundings. Judgment of time and space became impossible. Tempera, tiny specks of dust, stung her eyes. Her breathing was slow and labored.

Alex turned to look at her team and saw Nyla slump forward in her saddle

"Nyla," she yelled.

The girl lifted her head for a moment then collapsed forward, her face buried in the billowing fabric of her robes.

Alex rode back and grabbed the camel's reigns.

"Beryl. Follow me!"

Malak balked, refusing her lead. Alex reigned him hard.

"This is my call, Malak. We need to take shelter." Gaining control of her horse, Alex led her team to the base of a plateau. She dismounted and grabbed clothing from within the donkey cart.

"Beryl," she yelled. "Put Nyla inside the wagon bed. Cover yourselves with blankets. I'll be there as soon as I tie some coverings over the animal's eyes." When she finished, she tethered the animals together and climbed inside the cart, pulling the blanket tightly over her head. "We will wait here until the fallout stops."

Alex woke up startled. *When did I fall asleep? How long were we laying here?*

She jumped out of the wagon and checked the animals. "Thank God you're alright, Malak." She hugged his neck.

"Get up!" she whispered as she shook the form under the ash-covered blanket. The boy pushed the covers from his body and sucked in the rancid air. In turn, he woke Nyla from her sound sleep.

"Where are we?" she asked.

Alex smirked. "In the middle of nowhere."

Looking around, she realized the plateau that gave them shelter was beside a lake that smelled rancid. Heavy clouds crept above her head and, with vaporous fingers, reached into the smelly mud pot, stirring the bubbling stew in its earthen cauldron. Black bands of smoke spilled from inside the basin and floated toward them.

"Let's get out of here and try not to inhale the smoke," Alex said. She looked over her shoulder at Nyla who was standing within a blanket of black vapor.

She was strolling around, casually picking up samples of berries from ghostlike bushes and putting them inside her satchel. "Nyla," Alex cautioned. "Don't inhale the stuff coming from the lake. Get out of there!"

Alex noticed a strange detached look on the girl's face. "Do you hear me?" She yanked off her helmet and pushed strands of wet hair from her forehead. "This is a battlefield. Your unpredictable actions are endangering the mission."

Nyla ignored the warrior with a wave of her hand. "Some of this stuff is interesting. These berries can be ground into a poultice and used medicinally." She continued clipping and storing items. "These particular trees have been extinct for centuries. I think I can use these compounds in my ointments."

Alex looked around for Beryl and found him digging stones from the hard earth.

"Stop this madness immediately," she demanded.

He looked at her with the same detached look in his eyes as Nyla.

Alex dismounted and prepared to give them a lecture on battlefield safety when a wide staircase appeared out of the fog. It towered for miles into the murky sky.

"Beryl," she whispered, "where do all these steps lead?"

He ignored her and kept digging while Nyla continued her search for berries, oblivious to Alex's hallucination.

Alex felt compelled to forget her assignment. Without looking back, she began to ascend hundreds of stone steps to reach the top of the staircase, hidden under a canopy of clouds. Her legs ached when she reached the pinnacle and her lungs burned inside her heaving chest. She fought for control. Alex hunched over, gasping for breath. Her pounding pulse made her feel as if she could gargle her racing heart. A dog barked in the distance and the thick cloud cover lifted. She forced her body to stand perfectly still and willed her mind to focus.

Looking around the compound, she found herself standing in the middle of a city. Shiny buildings stood like guards, protecting a forested courtyard that surrounded a beautiful temple with turrets that reached beyond the sky. The street was teeming with people of every color. Listening to the cadence of their tongue, she realized they were travelers from many lands. Multitudes were buying and selling trinkets, food, flowers, and livestock. The thick aroma of exotic spices, roasting meat, and fresh-baked bread spread through the air. The crowds seemed to be getting ready for a celebration. *I need to hide.*

Crouching down, she sprinted into a narrow alley. Her ears rang with the sound of cheerful laughter, the bleating of sheep, and the ruckus of shouting merchants. Flattening her body against the wall, she waited, hoping no one spotted her as an intruder. With her body tight against the wall, she inched sideways. Her armor scraped the building's exterior wall, betraying her presence. To her surprise, the building was not constructed with stone but of smooth polished steel.

She stood motionless for what seemed an eternity, sure the loud noise would alert the authorities of her presence. She waited until the sun slid behind the temple tower. In its wake, the entire city began to shine like gold in the fading light. Alex wiped sweat from her face and placed her gloved hand on her sword. Feeling it was safe to relax, she peeked around the corner and scanned the busy square. Built in a circle outside the temple gates were schools, shops, booths, and many churches. High elevation walkways connected one building to the other, all leading to the central shrine.

Something small and round, like a ball, clattered down the alley in her direction. It clicked and squeaked with each mechanical step. As it came closer, Alex realized it was a spider. Its eight skinny legs rotated in a clumsy clockwork circle, propelling the thing forward.

It clinked to a stop next to her foot.

"Shoo," she coaxed, pushing it with her boot.

It made a whirring noise and the top half of its body lifted into the air and hovered in front of her face. It rested, suspended in midair, before its many blinking eyes began flashing bursts of blue light around her face.

The light stung her eyes. Then in an instant, the lights and clicking stopped and it sunk back to its original position. With a few clicks and chirps, its clockwork legs began rotating away.

"You little devil," Alex whispered. "You're a spy." Her booted foot came down hard, crushing it. Screws, springs, and shards of metal shot out in all directions.

I must get out of here.

Keeping her body low, she sprinted across the square. As she approached a vendor's booth, she tucked her body and rolled behind a pile of large willow baskets. They swayed slowly but inconspicuously at her interruption. Peeking from her hiding place, she could see the merchant was a sculptor that sold terrapin, carved idols of the gods.

"This is a very rare statue of Astarte, the goddess of fertility," the merchant boasted to a wide-eyed couple that stood before his booth. "When you put her inside your home and worship her, she will bless you with many sons."

The young customer rubbed her swollen belly. "Yes, yes, Omri," she whispered to her husband. "We must add this one to our collection."

The young man pulled coins from his overcoat and paid the bearded merchant for the statue. The sculptor's turbaned head nodded and he smiled broadly. "Those who pray to the goddess have their wishes granted."

The couple left and the merchant took a necklace from inside his deep pocket. He held the crescent moon high to show the crowd. "Who will buy this treasure? It will keep away the evil eye." People pushed and shoved each other, fighting to claim the moon-like shape as their own.

From her hiding spot, Alex watched men in red hooded robes begin to walk into the square. They started to light torches that lined the busy streets. Her heart jumped when she saw that their faces were hidden behind ugly masks. Each disguise represented a different sacred animal. The first hooded man wore the mask of an ewe, another a cow, a few birds, and numerous reptiles made up the macabre torch men. In the windows, candles jumped to life, making the city glow like stars in the spreading darkness. Alex's skin tingled with goose bumps as the night wind blew its cold breath over the ziggurat.

The jarring screech of horns began to rumble through the air. The multitudes squealed with anticipation. The congregation parted, allowing a procession of soldiers ample room to march down the boulevard toward the stockyard. At least a hundred men and women in leather cloaks and leather helmets, trimmed in bronze, filled the main street. Alex could see the glint of light from their breastplates as they moved forward. The ground vibrated under their stomping feet and the sound of them beating their spears against their shields rattled her nerves.

The populace cheered as the procession marched toward the open doors that fed the troop inside the stockyard. The noise escalated. Worshipers began throwing flower petals, creating a colorful carpet over the cobbled ground.

The drumming stopped and the soldiers stood aside. A reverential hush settled over the crowd. A magnificent white bull, held at bay by warriors with pointed spears, shuffled toward the slaughterhouse. His immense head hung low and swayed back and forth. His hooves made their own beat as he clattered over the cobbled stones. Large golden horns curved outward in a flat arch above his head. He stopped and pawed the ground, throwing dust and stone over his massive body. The soldiers jumped back.

Sages, dressed in elaborate robes and feathered hats, began beating on drums, and girls in white togas danced while the sea of swaying devotees dropped to their knees to worship the animal.

> O mighty, Moloch
> Divine bull of heaven
> We offer you our children
> Upon your altar we sacrifice them
> Their bodies on the flames of your
> Burning altars
> Receive them we pray

Alex used the opportunity to flee. Her body trembled and her skin crawled at the thought of slaughtering children. She searched her mind for a scripture verse to help ease her fear.

"Open to me the temple gates of righteousness," she prayed, "and I will enter through them and confess and praise the Lord" (Psalm 118:19). Heat spread through her icy body.

She sprinted toward the gates of the courtyard. The guards, soldiers, and patrons swayed and sang songs of worship to the "divine bull of heaven." They knelt on the hard ground, chanting in religious ecstasy. Their torsos rose and fell like ocean waves and the whites of their eyes glowed like the moon while their faces burned like the fires of hell. Their trancelike state of mind made them oblivious to the stranger who snuck through the courtyard gates.

Inside the sacred walls, she found a magnificent grove. The sight of the ancient trees held her spellbound. A thick forest of oaks, birch, and pine spread their branches protectively over the pilgrims who made offerings to the tree gods. Garlands of flowers, talisman, and personal notes hung from outstretched tree limbs. Men, woman, and children prayed, sang, and wept beneath the canopy of green leaves.

Alex was shocked to see some men and women, wearing pieces of the Christian armor, worshiping idols alongside the unbelievers. Their presence among the pagans made it easy for her to blend into the crowd. She had no trouble wandering through their high places.

Alex fell in step with a procession of young girls in flowing blue gowns with crowns of wild flowers on their heads. They danced around wooden poles and bowed to the statue of Ishtar, the mother of the universe, praising her as their patron.

Boys in fur robes made their way to a large firepit. Officiating priests handed the novitiates bowls of water, oil, and milk to pour into the flaming mixture. They chanted and prayed until unclean spirits crept from the pit like thin tendrils of smoke and entered the human hosts. With fevered faces and glazed eyes, the boys ran through the glade, barking and howling like a pack of wild dogs.

Alex followed a wide path lit with naphtha fires and found her way to the temple entry. Tall pylons, one black and one white, flanked each side of the double doors like massive guards. The entry was carved with symbols of the all-seeing eye, triple moons, spirals, and circles. The heavy gold doors opened automatically, beckoning her to enter.

The interior was an immense labyrinth with many corridors, paved in white and gold marble, that led into a central chamber. There were sculptures of ancient deities in elaborate alcoves lining the walls. Each idol was carved in stone and inlaid with precious jewels. Some had human heads with animal bodies while others resembled the spirits of the underworld. Before each god and goddess were rows of votive candles to be lit by worshipers who asked their patron for favors.

Torches hung on the walls, like guiding hands, directing pilgrims through the maze of hallways toward the sanctuary. As she walked, Alex peeked into a large chamber where water gently trickled down the steep stone walls. Steam rose from the water that bubbled with heat generated underground.

Alex gasped. She quickly put a hand over her mouth, shocked to see handmaids and young boys, her age or younger, bathing with gray-bearded priests in luxurious tile pools. Strange women, with ram's horns instead of hair on their heads, served the bathers fruit and wine. Dread twisted in her stomach like a snake.

She hurried through the maze of quiet tunnels that ended at the inner sanctum, the house of joy. Alex looked frantically around the rectangular area. Her eyes came to rest on an elaborate altar with pillars of gold. It was clearly an offering table covered in fine white linen. She knew in the pit of her stomach the ornate monument was the building's core.

A statue stood guard over the altar. She tilted her head back, gazing up at the sculpture that was easily ten stories high. Her eyes took in huge claws, thick bronze legs, a massive body, and six serpentine heads. It was so tall she almost fell over backward gazing at the top.

Footsteps startled her. She turned around and saw a mysterious woman with deep-black hair, black lips, and black tattoos that surrounded beautiful azure eyes. She walked toward Alex with the skull of a large reptile in her outstretched hand.

Her clothing was revealing, showing the outline of her body.

She spoke to Alex in soft whispering tones. "I am Asmodeus, keeper of secrets." She paused and looked Alex over. "Your reputation precedes you, Alex. We never expected you to defeat two of our guardians. However, I must ask, what is a child of righteousness doing in my Valley of Pleasure?"

It seemed like an eternity before Alex could speak. "God sent us to teach the remnant how to have victory over the enemy." Her voice echoed like it was coming up from a deep well.

Asmodeus smiled and looked at the young girl patiently. "Look outside." She waved her hand and they magically stood outdoors in the sweet-smelling grove.

"Look at the pilgrims, Alex." She smiled. "All races, gender, and denomination worship the universe and all she birthed. She is the creator and center of all life."

The spirit took Alex by the hand and led her into a building full of books. "Watch how humanity rejoices over knowledge and self-fulfillment. Her wisdom will lead them on a pilgrimage to abundant living."

Asmodeus whispered more words of magic that transported Alex into the stockyard. They watched frenzied followers of the divine bull engage in acts of lust and debauchery. "Mankind lives to feed its flesh," she said. "The sons and daughters of the earth exalt sensuality and serve her demands religiously. The citizens of Old World bow in adoration to the spirits of lust. In turn, she encourages her followers to deny moral restraints, for without boundaries comes freedom."

Asmodeus clapped her hands and brought them back to the tabernacle.

"You must be mistaken. Surely God would not send you here where our borders are open to worship what we choose." She placed her hand on Alex's shoulder. "We strive to live in harmony with all people. Everything you see here is acceptable human behavior."

Alex shrugged the woman's hand from her arm. "These people worship idols that cannot speak, hear, or save," Alex said. "We must worship the one true God and him only."

"Nonsense, child. Many deities rule this present age. When we obey them, we find fulfillment and inner harmony."

Her words tried to find an opening into Alex's mind. Asmodeus realized the girl forgot a piece of her armor. "The very idea of only one God is so narrow-minded…limiting."

The bewitching priestess walked to the altar and began lighting candles. "Your God cannot be as powerful as these." She waved her arm in an exaggerated gesture, indicating all the statues that outlined the walls. "I understand his Son had to die. He could not even save himself. What good is a god that has no power over his own mortality?"

Alex stiffened. "He is not the God of the dead but the God of the living," she answered. "His blood was shed for all who believe he died and was raised from the dead. He died to set us free from the chains of sin and death."

The woman laughed. "Look around you, my dear. Does it look like we are in chains? Our devotees embrace every sensual pleasure available to man. We honor our own choices. We do not want or need some old-fashioned god to tell us what we can and cannot do." She smiled condescendingly. "Besides, your remnant, this insignificant few, are living in poverty and want. They hide themselves in caves, sneaking around the countryside, trying to gain converts to help them fight a losing battle."

Asmodeus kept her back turned as she prepared a sacrifice on the altar. "The few who still believe are indifferent at best. They have a form of religion but deny its authority. Be reasonable. A few cannot stand against the mighty power of this new age and our massive army of giants."

Alex clenched her jaw. "That is why we have come. It is our task to strengthen the believers' faith in the promise of our

Savior's return. We must help them ignite their zeal to continue fighting the enemy. We are to raise an army who will wrench the church from the control of King Apollyon and his forces."

"It is a foolhardy plan. No one is interested in your outdated religion with so many silly rules. It is stupidity," she said.

The priestess switched her tone. She reached out her arm and stroked Alex's face. Her hand lingered on the girl's cheek. "I like you," she whispered. Her breath rustled a strand of Alex's hair. "You are bold to come here and challenge our beliefs. I admire bravery. However, you cannot win this battle." Asmodeus walked around the warrior, looking her over. "I am going to give you a chance to denounce the God you honor and stay here in the Valley of Pleasure with me. I have wealth and power beyond measure. If I choose, I can make you rich and powerful, a leader within our army. Everyone will know and honor your name."

The spirit leaned forward and whispered in Alex's ear, "What high places are hiding within your heart? Everyone has a weakness they indulge."

Alex's body felt heavy, like she had fallen into deep water and her armor was dragging her down. Her heart raced, and her face felt flushed. Images of wealth and power attacked her thoughts. Her legs wobbled under the weight of the priestess's suggestions. Alex touched her head. Her hair was wet and plastered to her face. *I forgot my helmet.* Her heart jumped in her throat.

The spirit of lawlessness continued to speak, expecting to see the youth weakening. "In this house of joy, we embrace power, wealth, and immorality." She smiled inwardly, sure of her successful seduction. "We enjoy excess of every kind, along with all the pleasures that appeal to this generation. Surely there is something here to entice you." Her azure eyes were glowing. She knew it would not take long to infect the child with visions of sin.

The goddess moved aside and revealed her preparation. The altar was prepared for a health procedure. Medical equipment sat on the cloth smeared with blood. A young woman was laying there, in a trance, with a soiled sheet covering her body. In a basket, at the foot of the tabernacle, was an infant, mutilated.

"Like your God, we use human sacrifice to atone for our sin. You are free to indulge in sexual pleasure with no consequence." She held a bloody knife in her delicate white hands. Her face looked angelic, innocent of any wrongdoing.

With her other hand, she handed Alex a chalice of red liquid. "Drink from the cup of depravity," she coaxed.

Alex snapped to attention, standing tall before the beautiful woman and the brazen image. "I will worship only the Lord my God and serve him only. I will not worship your images nor will I practice these unholy rituals. It is written, 'Thou shall not kill.'" Her armor engaged, and her sword burst into flame.

The dark priestess became enraged and screamed profanities at the warrior. "Don't toy with me, child. You know I have the power to hurt you." Her human body shifted into black vapor. Men dressed in red hooded cloaks came from the chambers that lined the hallways. They escorted temple prostitutes into the sanctuary. Creatures that were half-man and half-goat led the procession toward the altar chanting, singing, and dancing in homage to the beast.

The stone monster erected above the altar began to breathe, its sides expanding and contracting to the ancient chants. Its eyes grew large and menacing, its muscles and sinews braced to attack. Asmodeus materialized once more and spoke softly to the monster while she stroked a massive neck. Alex could see it was angry by what the woman spirit was saying. It was bellowing and screaming, but Alex could not hear it because she felt like she was sucked backward, away from the noise and chaos.

She awoke sitting on Malak. He kicked and pranced, shaking his head, pulling against the bit. Alex felt she couldn't hold him and realized her body was soaked in sweat. "Where is the temple of sin? It's vanished."

The air around her smelled of death and disease. The little bit of light from the black moon and the red star cast grotesque shadows across the valley. A garbage dump appeared where the altar of innocent blood had stood moments before. She saw flies and maggots crawling among rotten flesh that smoldered with flash fires. The unnatural sound of people screaming, from somewhere within the earth, grew louder.

Nyla was still mulling about the site, oblivious to the vision only shown to Alex. "Look at this." She walked toward Alex, carrying something with two fingers like it was dirty, holding it away from her body. "It looks like a human bone." Nyla turned the object over in her hands, examining it closely. "Strange, it's so small like that of an infant." She walked a few steps further and found something else.

Nyla stooped to pick up the object. "It looks like a human jaw." Nyla gasped and dropped the small bone like she had burning coals in her hands. They made a loud clunking sound when they hit the ground. The echo resounded across the valley.

Alex's mind came back to reality. "Quiet! I think I hear something." She held out a warning hand.

Nyla wiped her hands on her robe, looking in the same direction as the other girl. A loud clap of thunder announced the arrival of rain. Water began to fall in vicious torrents, creating deep puddles of slime. The earth could not drink in the water fast enough.

"Get on your camel, now!" Alex's voice sounded alien;

it was full of fear and panic. Nyla froze. The camel bellowed in alarm.

"Beryl. Get ready now!"

The sound of scraping and scratching grew louder. Alex's hand moved to the sword in her belt. She heard sounds that made the hair on the back of her neck prickle.

Rats scurried from their hiding places within the piles of garbage. They advanced upon the intruders, looking for fresh meat to devour. The mutations were the size of large dogs. Dozens of rodents rushed at them.

Nyla tried to run but the soaking rain made the ground like glue. The mud sucked at her feet and swallowed her shoes. She struggled to free herself but the mire was as thick as quicksand. The sludge devoured her body, dragging her deeper into the belly of the wet soggy earth. She screamed as she looked around for Beryl. When she saw him, the boy had a large speckled creature skewered on his wooden staff.

One of the monsters jumped on Nyla's back. She could see its nose twitching and felt long coarse whiskers touching her cheek. Its breath stunk. It opened its mouth to bite her throat. It growled, pulling back its lips, baring sharp yellow fangs. The beast's thick saliva ran down her neck.

Alex pounced on the vermin, screaming in rage. Pulling a knife from her boot, she stabbed the creature repeatedly. Blood splattered over them while she used her arms and legs to push it away. Others were on the injured rodent as soon as it hit the ground, biting, eating, and chewing their victim. Screams of death spread across the valley.

Alex grabbed Nyla's hand and pulled her to her feet. She slashed at the enemy with her sword. A large male jumped at them, its teeth stained with blood. Alex swung her sword. The blade severed the monster's head and it hurled through the air. The bloody mess crashed to the ground with a sickening thud. Its lifeless eyes stared at them while warm black blood mixed with the pouring rain, feeding the thirsty ground.

"I can't run!" Nyla screamed. "My clothes, they are thick with mud." She tore her cape from her body and dropped it to the ground. Her soft caftan, wet and stained with blood, clung to her flesh like a snare. She ran but the fabric twisted around her legs, making her fall. She scrambled to her feet, but the weight of her clothing pulled her down again.

Alex whistled for her horse. He charged to their side. With strength she did not know she possessed, she grabbed Nyla around her waist and threw her up on the saddle. Malak whirled in circles as three beasts jumped on his flanks, throwing him off balance, knocking the rider from the saddle back to the ground.

Beryl sloshed through the mud and lifted Nyla from the slime and tried to beat the creatures with his staff. Alex stabbed and slashed the demonic hoard with her sword. The rats circled them, growling and screaming. Alex scanned the perimeter for Malak and saw him stomping on three beasts with his front hooves.

An exceptionally large rat noted her distraction and charged at her, making horrible rasping sounds. She caught the oncoming attack from the corner of her eye. She spun toward her assassin but lost her footing. Alex fell backward, hitting her head on a rock. She felt dizzy, and her vision blurred but she braced her sword in time to watch it impale itself on the blade. Beryl ran to her side and pulled the carcass from her weapon.

Alex stood on shaky legs. Blood and rain water spilled over her shoulders and began to run down the front of her chain mail.

Nyla gasped. "Alex, your head. You're bleeding."

When Alex touched her head, it was wet with blood. She felt no pain but her vision seemed dim.

Beryl handed her the sword. "The rats are running away.

What's happening?"

An earsplitting roar filled the air. Alex's arms went slack. "What is that?"

Nyla hid behind her partners. Everything went still and silent. The heavens closed, and the rain stopped. The mood over the valley shifted from fear to terror.

"Look at the ground," Nyla whispered.

Billions upon billions of black flies erupted from the wet earth. The black mass worked as a cohesive unit, constructing a demonic creation. In a matter of minutes, the loud buzzing stopped, and their conception lifted its massive reptilian head and opened its red bloodshot eyes. Black leathery wings unfolded from their creation's side and claws shot out of ponderous feet. Smoke that smelled of brimstone gushed from its nostrils.

Alex stood frozen. The beast towered above them, making rumbling sounds that shook the valley. Fear held her spellbound.

The dragon threw his head back. It peered up at the star in the sky and wailed.

Nyla covered her ears with her hands. She collapsed to the ground and curled into a tight ball.

Like a volcano ready to erupt, it threw its head up again and shot fire into the heavens. The entire ravine lit up like an inferno. Sparks fell everywhere. Burning cinders spilled like rain from the sky.

Alex tried to pull her armor off. "Nyla, help me, it burns."

Nyla struggled to stand. Her body would not obey. "I can't move."

Tears ran down Alex's cheeks. She wiped the water with her hands. Hot ash crusted her face and smeared over her features. Her eyes felt like they were burning in their sockets.

Beryl helped her to stand. "Alex," he whispered, "it's standing over us. Do something."

Alex faced the dragon, with her sword raised and ready, but an enemy more powerful than the dragon attacked her mind. Doubt found a way into her thoughts. *This enemy is too big for me.*

Alex dropped her sword and crumpled to her knees. Everything around her started spinning. She tried to focus her attention on the dragon, but something brighter than the creature's fire distracted her.

"Pick up your sword, Alex. Stand strong." The voice was firm yet kind.

She felt a surge of courage. With the last ounce of her strength, she stood and lifted her sword. Strong arms circled her from behind and steadied her. "Use your weapon," the stranger said.

With blurred vision, she looked up into the dragon's eyes. Its reptilian head bent to devour her. "God will keep and protect me from the evil one." Her sword exploded with fire.

The dragon thundered backward, dazed from the blow.

Before she passed out, Alex saw a warrior, an angelic being, standing over her. His hair was the color of a wheat field. He wore the armor of a soldier; his breastplate was aglow from the dragon's breath. He faced the beast, his sword white-hot and blazing. On his shield was the insignia of the cross. The angel's eyes were burning coals and his voice sounded like the roar of an angry ocean.

The dragon bellowed in rage, and fire gushed from its mouth. The angelic avenger stood his ground, averting the blaze with his shield. Sparks and flames bounced backward, hitting the dragon's chest and face. He roared, shaking the earth with his huge heavy body. His wings began a steady beat, lifting him into the air. The noise was like thousands of soldiers marching into battle.

The angel spoke but a word, spread his massive wings, and began to chase the beast across the valley. Alex watched until they were no longer in sight. Only the sound of thunder filled her ringing ears

After what seemed like hours, Alex heard voices, the shuffling of feet, and the clatter of the wagon. Someone lifted her into the cart.

"Easy, Malak." She heard Beryl's voice. "We need you to pull the wagon through the snow."

Alex tried to speak but her throat ached from coughing. "What is happening? Where did this snow come from?" She shivered as the cold flakes covered her body.

"Quickly, Nyla. Finish with her bandages while I make a tent with our extra clothing to keep her warm."

Alex could hear Nyla softly crying as she gently wrapped cloth around Alex's head.

"Hang on, Alex. Please hang on." Nyla tucked blankets around her body.

The cart began to move. With each turn of the wheel, pain shot through Alex's body. She knew it was snowing, but she was sheltered under soft blankets and could still smell the sulfur from the dragons' breath. She desperately wanted to cry out but was too weak. Fear clutched her heart, then only agony and darkness of spirit overwhelmed her.

CHAPTER 17

Feast on Souls

Malak pulled the wagon through the deepening snow, inching further away from the evil of the Chasm and through a narrow path into Old World. The cart lurched and bounced through the thick white powder. Alex groaned in pain. Beryl looked over his shoulder at Nyla who sat in the wagon bed, nursing their leader.

"Isn't there anything more you can do to help her? You are supposed to be a healer." He immediately regretted his words.

Nyla stiffened at the question. "I'm doing all I know how."

Beryl knew by her tone, his remark hurt her. "I'm sorry, Nyla. What I said came out wrong. I can't stand to think of her in so much pain." If she answered him, the howling wind drowned out her words.

He felt ashamed of his heartless remark. It wasn't Nyla and her abilities that bothered him. It was his lack of ability. What if there was another encounter with demons? What would he do? They needed Alex and her gifts to win these battles.

His hands and face felt numb from the bite of the cold. He was used to hot desert weather. Everything about Old World was worse than he imagined and he just arrived. Beryl left the reigns slack and tucked his hands inside his pockets. He hoped the horse would take them to safety, but his eyes darted through the whiteout, praying they would escape further danger. He knew once they left the Chasm, they were in enemy territory. Now they would face man *and* beast. He looked around at the frozen hellhole they called Mori. *How will we ever find the outpost we were assigned to?*

The countryside began to change from desolation to scattered evergreens and mountain peaks. The climb was uphill. He had only been able to harness one animal to the cart back in the Chasm. He chose Malak and hoped he knew the route to take them out of the canyon and into the plains. The donkey and camel were tethered to the back of the cart, making the burden heavier. The stallion grew tired and struggled to pull the weight alone.

It had been more than an hour since they left the Chasm and began this new journey. He could tell, by the position of the black moon, they were making slow progress. "You can do it, Malak. You can get us to safety." Beryl laughed at himself for thinking the horse could understand, let alone care, about their predicament. To his surprise, Malak stopped.

Beryl took a whip and cracked it over the horse's rump, but he refused to move. In exasperation, Beryl climbed from the cart to try leading him. His sandaled feet sunk into the snow, sending shivers through his body. "This is no time for stubbornness." He yanked on the reigns, but Malak stood his ground.

The black moon was high in the sky and the red star glowed a fierce shade, covering the countryside in a crimson glow. Beryl fought the urge to cry. He was cold, hungry, and their team was lost in a blizzard. *Abba Father,* he prayed silently. *We are defeated before we start. Why did this happen? You sent us. We carry your message of hope for the future.*

"Look," Nyla called.

His eyes followed her pointed finger. The wind broke a

large tree limb, exposing the entry to a cave in the mountain.

He fumbled through the mess inside the wagon bed and found his lantern.

"Wait!" Nyla said. "I'm not sure going in there is a good idea."

He swallowed hard. "If I don't go, we will be buried alive in this frozen place."

He pulled his dagger from the folds of his robe and walked inside. To his surprise, he found no demons, only three skinny horses and two camels. They were soaked from the snow and shivering, but they found a bed of fodder at the far end of the cave where they huddled together, getting warm. He raised the lantern and realized it was an abandoned hideout. The brigands left a firepit, kindling, and a pile of wood.

"Thank you, Abba Father," he said aloud. "Looks like we are not defeated."

He led the wagon inside and set up camp. With the dry kindling, he made a fire, and Nyla began to boil snow to brew an herbal tea for Alex.

"Her fever is high," Nyla said as she checked her field dressing. "I stitched Alex's head quickly on the battlefield. It does not look infected. But the burns she encountered from the dragon's fire are blistering."

Beryl lifted Alex from the wagon and put her on a bed of dry blankets near the fire.

Nyla put a cup of tea to Alex's lips. "She is in and out of consciousness."

Beryl looked at their injured leader and made the sign of the cross. "I'm surprised any of us survived that battle. She has a will of steel. She will overcome."

He had not yet cared for the animals. The stallion was still in the harness. The horse breathed heavily, and his black coat was frothy with sweat. Patches of dried blood, from numerous rat bites, sliced his flesh.

He patted the stallion's large neck. "I wish we could stay here and be warm and safe, but Alex needs us." He spoke softly as he unharnessed the horse from the cart and began to saddle him to ride. He turned to Nyla.

"Hopefully he can find the regiment these animals belong to. They are still wet, so the troop can't be too far away." He pulled on the synch and tightened the saddle. "If they are still alive in this storm, maybe they will have extra supplies and can direct us to our outpost."

Nyla gathered a pair of her gloves and a scarf from her belongings in her camel's saddlebag and handed them to the prophet. "I know they are not the color a monk would wear, but they are made of the finest wool and will keep you warm."

He looked at her and smiled. "They will look good with my lion skin."

She threw her arms around him, and they both began to cry.

Beryl felt like a dagger pierced his heart. He had never had true friends before and he could not bear to think of either one of them coming to harm. A new fierceness welled up inside him. He stood taller and wiped his nose on his sleeve. "Don't worry. I will find help."

"Hurry back," she said. "I will continue to pray, but she is very weak."

Beryl rode Malak through heavy drifts. The stallion pushed himself but Beryl felt him weakening. They had traveled for the better part of an hour when the wind stopped howling and the snow calmed down to a few flurries. The mountain was quiet, except for the sound of Malak's hooves crunching through the snow. The landscape was peaceful and majestic. Beryl watched Malak's breath turn to smoke in the cold air. *Maybe the worst of the attacks are behind us.* Before he had a chance to get comfortable with the thought, he heard voices up ahead.

Malak stopped in a small line of evergreens. From his vantage point, Beryl could see a desolate valley with a dilapidated tent in the distance. He felt like he walked into a nightmare as he watched a pack of demons prepare to devour two soldiers.

Big brutish creatures, neither man nor beast, closed in on the two men. One predator, with a horn on the top of its head, stood on two legs like a man. Beryl felt cold fingers of fear creep up his spine. The demon curled its lips into a sneer. In the moonlight, its teeth looked long and sharp like daggers. The demon unexpectedly charged into its own pack first and impaled one of its own with the horn. With unnatural strength, it threw the injured carcass aside. In a blood frenzy, the others dove on top of the injured creature, eating it like a pack of starving wolves. Clearly the leader wanted the soldiers for itself.

Beryl almost fell from the saddle at the guttural sound of the demon's voice. "I told you I would come for you."

He clutched the saddle to keep his dizzy body upright.

"I'm here to take you to hell." It roared its supremacy at the kneeling soldiers.

He heard the soldier's voice crack in fear. "God, if you are real save us now."

Beryl's heart froze in his chest. *Father God, what am I to do? I am like a grasshopper to these creatures. If I try to save the soldiers, we will all die.*

Beryl stuffed his cold hands into the deep pockets of his robe. He felt something warm buried inside. He pulled out his crucifix and made the sign of the cross. In his mind, he remembered the words God spoke to Joshua in the Bible. *Have I not commanded you? Be strong and courageous. Do not be afraid; do not be discouraged, for the Lord your God goes with you wherever you go (Joshua 1:9).*

Beryl knew that every word written in the Book of Life

was not only for the warriors of long ago but for every generation willing to believe. He jumped from the saddle and walked from his hiding place into the moonlit plain. In his haste, the long robe twisted around his ankles and he fell face-first in a cold dune.

The noise broke the beast's concentration. It heard a thud and rustling in the snow.

The demons who were feasting lifted their bloodstained faces and turned their attention to the new arrival.

Aza took a breath. Something or someone had distracted the alpha, saving him from death. He looked at his brother who cowered beside him. "Who is it? Can you see? Could it be reinforcements from our tribe?"

Sargo wiped tears of fear from his eyes. "I can't see anything."

Aza watched the dominant creature begin to pace. Its movements were erratic, agitated. He had never seen them act in fear of anything. The creature stood up then crouched low, like it was unsure what to do. It sniffed the cold night air, assessing the new target. "Why do I smell no fear?" the beast growled. "Don't you know who I am?" it boasted.

Aza stood to get a better view. He couldn't believe his eyes. *Did God hear my prayer? Is that thing an angel or a boy?*

Beryl froze unsure what to do.

The alpha huffed and bleated. "Bring the foreigner to me. I feel a peculiar power coming from the strange boy."

The pack of Soul-Sifters crept forward, slow to obey. They growled, snapped, and clawed at each other, pushing the weakest of them to the forefront as they circled the fresh victim.

"Prepare for attack!" Beryl announced. *What a stupid thing to say! Now they will attack me. What am I supposed to say? I wish Alex were here.* Beryl was surprised. The demons slunk back, eyeing him from afar. *Are they afraid of me?*

Aza watched the boy stand up. He looked ridiculous covered in snow. He seemed powerless. The boy steadied his body on a wooden staff he carried. He wore a gray hooded robe under a bulky lion skin that looked like it had swallowed his skinny body beneath its folds.

The alpha demon snarled, showing its teeth.

Aza could see him clearly. The boy's flesh was whiter than the snow. *Is it an angel?*

The stranger shook snow from his robe and hopped from one sandaled foot to the other. "Who goes there?"

Aza stood to his feet. "Help us!" he yelled.

The large predator stood to its full height. An eight-foot giant. "Can't you see? This small speck that has fallen from the sky is helpless," he lied, hoping to embolden his pack. "Look at it. This thing is sickly, pale, and vulnerable—like a newborn."

He took a few steps forward. "Don't you know who I am?"

"Get back!" Beryl warned. He shook his wooden staff at the beast. Skeletal remains that dangled from the neck of his shepherd's hook rattled. The demon backed up.

"Who are you?" it demanded. "I can smell you and you are no angel." He inhaled again to be sure.

The boy cleared his throat. "I am Beryl. A prophet of the highest God." He stood tall and pulled his cloak and lion skin around his shoulders, hoping he looked intimidating. "I was sent from Safehold to set captives free."

The demon laughed. "You're joking! We have seen many of your kind in Old World. Most of the heretics are dead or in prison."

Aza's heart sunk in his chest. *It's not of the spirit realm. This boy can't save us, no one can.*

The demon inched forward, taking quick shallow breaths.

It rose on two legs, considering the boy. "Don't you know who I am, shepherd boy?" he asked for the third time.

Beryl watched in horror as the creature came toward him. It moved more like an animal than a human. Its muscles bulged under its gray skin. He could smell its foul stench and gagged. He noted the creature's left eye twitching as it watched him. He hoped the demon would not see the sweat on his upper lip. He forced his quivering body to stand tall. "I told you my name, now you can tell me yours."

The beast was taken aback. It narrowed its eyes and glared at him with hatred. "I am Ketev, chief Soul-Sifter. My army and I are given the spoils of war. We take unbelievers, the weak-willed, and the lukewarm in faith. They are easy targets for us to destroy."

Beryl stood tall as the beast searched his eyes, as if the creature was looking into his soul.

Ketev snarled and growled like a feral animal. "I am sure you are just a boy. A human mutation. They call your kind albino."

Beryl rolled the crucifix through his shaking fingers. "They call your kind destruction. I call you destroyed."

The creature laughed. "You have no authority here."

Beryl's heart hammered in his chest. "We will not fear the terror of night, or the arrow that flies by day, nor the pestilence that walks in darkness, nor the destruction that lays waste at noonday" (Psalm 91:5–6).

The demon screamed. Beryl felt a wave of vertigo. Ketev lunged at him, its horn gleamed like a dagger in the moonlight.

Beryl raised his staff and spoke to the creature of darkness. "For my God will give His angels charge over me, to guard me in all my ways" (Psalm 91:11).

Beryl's staff burst into flames. The Soul-Sifters froze in fear. Ketev, the demon of destruction, backed away from the light. Aza put his hand to his chest, trying to quiet the hammering, certain his heart was going to explode. Sargo's knees gave out and he crumbled to the ground, shielding his eyes from the light.

"What is that thing?" Aza asked his brother. He stared at the ugly boy with white skin and the powerful staff. *The old man said three were coming. Where are the others?*

He saw the demons disappear like shadows into the darkness. Aza didn't know whether to laugh or cry. *Maybe there is a God.*

CHAPTER 18

The Tribe of the Remnant

Alex woke up with a jolt. She felt a stranger bending over her. Her hands shot out and seized his throat.

"Whoa! I'm on your side."

His voice sounded tense. Soft wavy hair fell over her hands. She released her grip and touched his face. He had a square jaw and high cheekbones. Even with her eyes bandaged, she knew he was strong and handsome. Prickly stubble pinched her hands. He smelled of leather and horses.

"You were injured in the Chasm," he said.

She thought his words were guarded.

"We had to bandage your head and eyes. You've been asleep for over a week. Do you remember us bringing you here?"

She shook her head. "Bits and pieces. Like a bad dream." Every inch of her body ached. She tried to move but shooting pain shot through her head, forcing her to cry out. She heard the shuffling of bare feet on the floor and the rustle of robes. She hoped it was the prophet.

"Beryl, is that you? What is going on? Where am I?" she asked. "How did I get here?" Her throat was sore and parched. It sounded garbled and strange to her ears.

The man with the stubble answered. "My name is Aza, the other is my brother, Sargo. We are soldiers in the army of the remnant. You are sheltered here in the mountains of Mori, known as Martic Forge." He paused and winked at his brother. "Your friend Beryl found us when we were trying to distract the Soul-Sifters from attacking the refugees in our care."

Beryl folded his arms. "You were running away. Deserting your men and the refugees."

Sargo pushed the prophet across the room. "Try to prove that and see what happens to liars."

Alex heard the two scuffle. Her gut tightened. "Beryl, are you sure we are safe here?"

A cold hand held hers. "We are safe and sheltered at the outpost we were sent to protect," he whispered. "I spoke with the elders and they are grateful to have us stay with them and their tribe."

Alex didn't need to see these two ruffians to know what they were about. They reminded her of Joseph, God rest his soul, and his team back in St. Regents. She knew, by the way Aza overpowered the conversation and his indifferent tone of voice, he wanted the upper hand. But why?

Beryl's presence made her feel secure. She was not alone. Her team was by her side. "How did you find them?"

Aza spoke up, "My men and I were on the brink of slaughter when Beryl burst upon the scene, out of nowhere." He paused, putting his hand on Sargo's shoulder. "He saved us from the Soul-Sifters, a band of murdering morphlings, hired by King Apollyon." He rubbed his chin. "He rescued us with that lightning stick he carries."

Beryl interrupted, "It's not a lightning rod," he explained. "The power is in the word of God, not in the stick."

Aza raised his voice, ignoring the boy's explanation. "It holds some magic that scares off demons." He looked at the dirt floor. "Don't get me wrong. We are grateful for the boy's help. He saved our lives…this time."

Alex's mind spun with questions. *Soul-sifters hired by the king?* She waved her hand, gaining their attention. "Nyla, where is she?" Dread shook her stomach.

"She's fine," Aza blurted out, more excited than he intended. His cheeks flushed. "She had a few scrapes and bruises, nothing serious." He lowered his eyes and faked a cough. "She's out administering medicine to the members of our tribe." He knew his tone of voice betrayed his infatuation.

Alex's voice hardened. "As part of my team, Nyla will have no time for romantic involvement."

Aza looked at Sargo and smirked. They both shot Beryl a look.

Beryl shifted his weight from one foot to the other. The prophet contorted his lips into a grimace, attempting to match the older boys' scowl. He pounded one fist into the other. "You heard her," his voice cracked. "Keep your motives in check."

Aza laughed. "What? You think you give the orders now?"

"We have our orders from St. Regents," Alex interrupted. "Nyla understands her duty to the mission and will act accordingly. And just for the record, my team is in charge now. Direct orders from Safehold."

She heard the two soldiers snicker. "Yeah. You look in control."

Alex ignored their remark. She had other things to worry about. Reaching out, she felt for the hem of the prophet's robe. "I can't seem to remember what happened after my hallucination in the Chasm. What is wrong with me?"

Beryl pulled the river rock from his pocket and rolled it through his fingers. "Don't you remember the rats and the dragon?"

Alex's voice shook. "The dragon? What happened? I remember an angelic warrior of God that chased the beast across the Chasm."

Beryl shrugged his shoulders. "For some reason, the dragon backed away from you, we're not sure why. I was hoping you could give us the answer to that question. There was no warrior, only Nyla and I."

Aza looked over his shoulder at Sargo who stood in the shadows. "Strange things are happening in Old World since the three of you arrived. The storm was abnormal, snow never falls on the flats. The wild magic and the dragon in the Chasm are new warnings. Not to mention the temple that appeared and vanished into the air. I can't imagine how we are to fight these new manifestations."

Alex touched her face, feeling the bandage that surrounded her head and eyes. "We were sent to teach you to use God's weapons of warfare."

Aza rubbed his neck. "You did a lot of talking in your sleep when we brought you in. You said you saw a ziggurat and child sacrifice. What was that all about?" he asked.

Alex sighed. "I can explain." She shook with the memory. Her mind pictured the ancient temple and the demon who called herself Asmodeus.

"I was taken to the temple of the moon god, Sin. Today we know it as the shrine of Pan, the god of lust. Both sites were dedicated to the practice of human sacrifice. The she-demon, who impersonated the temple priestess, is born to confuse and tempt us through seduction and deceit." Alex paused, trying to control her breathing. "This demon's followers generally worship the goddess Isis, Aphrodite, and Ashteroth. Jesus referred to her as Jezebel, the symbol of a false prophetess who bewitches believers into immoral practices."

Alex felt goose bumps cover her arms. "Asmodeus tried to get me to stay in the Valley of Pleasure and denounce God and our calling." She chewed her lip. "King Apollyon's army of darkness works on our weaknesses, trying to get us to surrender to temptation. They make evil look inviting and pleasurable. Then when sin has control over us, that false freedom turns into bondage and we become *his* prisoners."

She rubbed her head that was beginning to throb. "From ancient days, the evil one has murdered and coaxed others to kill the innocent because he cares nothing for human life. He never gets his fill of blood. Wicked kings and religious cults sacrifice their children to demons, thinking they can appease the beast and live a life of comfort and prosperity. They foolishly think they can buy favors from the master of darkness. In the process, they sacrifice themselves for eternity."

Her voice softened. "God redeems his followers with the blood of his Son. Satan uses blood, over and over, to kill and destroy."

"Why sacrifice the innocent?" Aza asked.

Alex sighed. "For many reasons, among them, it is acceptable to get rid of what is inconvenient. When a nation is ruled by immorality, greed, and rebellion toward God, the result is demonic control. People become like the gods they worship."

Aza's stomach lurched. "What is the point of trying to defeat these murderous fiends?" He sneered. "We may as well give in and give up."

Beryl looked the commanding officer in the eyes and discerned his unbelief. "Don't be afraid. Greater is Jesus who is in us than Satan who is in the world" (1 John 4:4).

"What do you know about any of this?" Aza shouted. "You're just a kid. I trained for this battle since I was your age. My men and I are the strongest warriors in our clan. I command my own troop. Nothing scares me!"

Sargo rushed over. "Who does this freak think he's talking to? We have fought this battle relentlessly for six years."

Beryl sputtered at their outburst. "I am a student of the Word of God. My training is useful and valuable regardless of my age."

Sargo's eyes blazed with hatred. He pushed the boy backward. The burley teen pounded his fists into his own chest, daring the prophet to attack. "Look at you. Your body is scrawny and weak. Life here is hard." His pulse throbbed in his neck. "You need combat ability if you are going to survive in this war."

Beryl planted his feet firmly on the ground. "Physical training is of some value, I admit, but you must add faith and spiritual discipline to defeat the king of Old World."

Sargo went after the prophet. "I'll give you a real lesson in warfare. I'm going to beat that childish faith out of you!"

Alex tried to get out of bed.

Aza grabbed his brother's arm. "Let it go. We don't want the elders to interfere. They already question our integrity since they spoke to the prophet."

Beryl settled Alex back in the bed. "I'm all right. It's over."

Sargo cursed and stormed out of the room.

Aza gathered his belongings and started to leave. "We will place a guard outside so nothing can get to your partner."

Beryl watched them leave. "What did I say to get them so mad?"

"You called them cowards," Alex said. "Great job making a good impression on our allies. Try a little diplomacy next time."

He scratched his head. "I was simply stating a fact."

"Don't worry about it. You can't let anyone think less of you because of your faith." She smiled. "If everyone here is like Aza and Sargo, we have our work cut out for us."

Beryl patted her hand. "Rest a while. I will stay here. You don't need to worry."

She squeezed his thin hand. "Promise me you will find my weapons and Malak."

Beryl waited until her breathing grew deep and sleep claimed the exhausted warrior. He put another tattered blanket over her and sat on the floor.

He prayed silently. *Abba Father, bring Alex through this trial with greater strength. Amen.*

CHAPTER 19

Dispensary

The morning sun rose over the mountains of Martic Forge. Long fingers of light chased the night from the floor of the dark forest. A sunbeam exposed the entrance to the tribe's headquarters. Nyla walked outside and away from the protection of the cave into the chilly air. She pulled a heavy wool cape around her shoulders and tucked her cold hands inside the deep pockets. Scanning her new surroundings, her heart thumped with a mixture of awe and fear. The trees were lush with leaves of gold, red, and orange, glistening in the predawn light. The sight was unlike her arid homeland, protected by a sapphire-blue sea, vast deserts, and balmy temperatures. This alien country was very different from the peace and security of Safehold.

She inhaled the scent of pine needles wet from rain. The new smell warmed her spirit yet the distant screech of a winged lizard chilled her blood. A flock of blue birds, the size of her hand, sang a lovely song in the trees that surrounded her. *How can Old World be so beautiful yet hide so many dangers?* She looked heavenward and shivered. *Will I ever be able to call this land home and these people family?* She sighed and a puff of smoke from her breath lingered in the morning mist.

Thick patches of fog began to lift over the nearby stream. Nyla made her way through the tangled tree limbs to the edge of the riverbed. The stream wound its way around twists and turns, like a giant snake, gliding peacefully over the river rocks. She bent down and splashed cold clean water over her face, trying to wash away the exhaustion of the past week. An unexpected thump, the fluttering of wings, and loud brutish chirps forced her to stop bathing. She slowly raised her eyes from the brook and looked left and right. A loud silence swallowed the forest. Looking back at her reflection in the peaceful stream, she froze. Large frightened eyes looked back at her from the clear river depths. Nyla's hand shot to her mouth to stifle a scream. The lifting mist exposed the reflection of a wooly carcass, twisting in anguish. The large animal's eyes were wide with pain. Its mouth gaped open, holding a silent scream. Covering the mighty beast with a blanket of blue feathers were the little birds.

She watched the beautiful vultures rip and tear the remaining meat and sinew from the injured beast's hide. The small carnivores peered across the water in her direction. She realized her presence at the water's edge distracted them from their morning meal. Nyla stood slowly, her focus never leaving the flock of savages, and backed away.

She ran into the forest, looking for the cave entrance she shared with the tribe for safety. A gusty blast of autumn wind tugged on her long hair. She whirled around and came face to face with a stranger.

"Why are you in the forest alone?" The girl glared at her with cold hard eyes.

"I'm sorry. The sunrise was so lovely and the..." Nyla's words fell away. "I forgot for a moment how savage your country is." She looked around frantically.

The unfamiliar medic ignored Nyla's remark and stretched. She bent from side to side, relieving the stiffness from her back. "Sleeping in the belly of the cave makes you feel old before your time." She raised her bushy eyebrows and grinned. "It's a good thing they gave you a suitable uniform.

At least you won't freeze to death." She smirked. "Or be eaten alive from sheer stupidity." She snorted and spit a wad of mucus in the bushes. "I'm your new mentor. We always go outside with a partner, never alone."

Nyla fumbled with her new cape. She felt naked without her head covering but her scarf lay in a ruined heap somewhere in the Chasm. Although her embroidered tunic and pants needed a few minor repairs, the clan replaced them with brown leather breeches and a coarse green tunic that tied at the waist with thin leather laces. Her comfortable soft slippers were lost forever in the miry clay within the belly of the Chasm. A female recruit gave her an ugly pair of brown leather flats that felt big and uncomfortable. Her ankle bracelet made it unscathed and jingled softly as she followed the stranger. *Thankfully I hid some of my trinkets before Mother confiscated all my jewelry.* Nyla looked behind them and felt her pulse race, knowing each step took them farther away from the protection of the cave into the shadowy forest.

Instructed by one of the elders upon their arrival, Nyla was ordered to shadow the girl who looked about her age. The medic had a round freckled face, brown frizzy hair, and eyes that resembled the mud puddles that pooled on the ground after last night's rain. She was tall, chunky, and clumsy like a trained bear. The legs of her trousers had ragged cuffs that dragged through the mud, and her boots were filthy. She was loud and disheveled. Nyla cringed.

She followed her mentor through a threadlike path, partially hidden by tall evergreens. Nyla stayed close to the medic, aware of the unfamiliar sounds and smells that surrounded her in the forest.

"Follow me and stay close," the girl ordered. She led her to a hidden grove where a group of women handed out supplies. "Fill a wooden bucket with bandages, ointments, and herbs," she told the new girl.

The other women looked at Nyla with suspicious eyes and few words.

Nyla rummaged through the piles of homemade remedies and made a face. "I brought my own pouches with medical supplies. Unless you have some laurel? I saw some growing under the trees by the creek."

"What plant do you speak of? Our tribe is unaware of any such species." Frances rubbed her chin and looked quizzically at the healer. "What do you use it for?"

"Snake bite," Nyla answered. "All of these boulders and crevices could easily hide poisonous insects and reptiles."

Frances drew close and whispered in Nyla's ear, "I carry the madstone." She fumbled around in her pocket and pulled out a white pebble. The girl handed it to Nyla. "It has power to heal. This one was handed down for two generations."

Nyla rolled the trinket around in her hand. "This piece of bone is the stomach of a goat!" Nyla chuckled. "You do not really think this holds any medicinal qualities, do you?"

Frances grabbed the charm from Nyla's hand. "We have used this as a remedy for many years." She put the treasure back in her pocket and untied a leather wineskin from her belt. The girl uncorked the lid and took a drink. "This is the juice of angelica. Many of us drink the elixir to protect us from poison and to build up our strength." She held the bottle out for Nyla to drink.

The healer shook her head. "I rely on prayer and a little bay leaf if needed."

Frances bristled. "You will have to show me this remedy of yours before I will believe it works better than our madstone and angelica." Frances felt her face flush as anger boiled in her gut. *She thinks she's better than me with all her education and uppity good looks.*

Nyla watched the girl try to smooth down her frizzy hair with dirty fingers. "I meant no disrespect," Nyla said. "I will look for the plant or a substitute in the forest. For now, I would like to collect some sycamore bark. The trees are everywhere but you have none with the supplies."

"I will help you collect some," Frances said, pretending to know what sycamore bark was, and followed Nyla to a grove of trees.

Nyla took a small knife from her belt and scraped bark from a tree. The medic fumbled around in her bucket, found a paring knife, and copied the new girl's way of gently chipping at the bark.

"We need to be going. There are many sick refugees in our camp." The medic hung the bucket from her arm and shuffled down the muddy path. Her mind fumbled for something to say as her boots made slopping sounds through the mud. "Things always look clean after the rain, don't you think?"

Nyla looked around at the dripping tree limbs and mushy leaves that had blown around before sticking to the wet dirt and soggy grass.

"This is your idea of clean?"

Again Frances felt her face redden and lowered her eyes. "I guess this is ugly compared to where you come from."

"An understatement," Nyla commented absently.

"By the way. My name is Frances." Her voice sounded like a clanging bell. "Which one are you?" She took a breath. "Wait! Let me guess." She stopped so suddenly, Nyla bumped into her. "Beryl. I bet you are Beryl." She turned and looked at the pretty girl who stood brushing off her tunic like she had been touched by the plague.

"Sorry. Did I get you dirty?" She came toward Nyla, attempting to help.

"No! Please! Do not touch me!" Nyla lifted her hands in protest. "I need no assistance. I'm fine…really."

Frances took a step back, annoyed by Nyla's abrupt tone. The medic cleared her throat. "Beryl," she asked, "do all of you stand and walk so straight and tall?" The cherub-faced nurse smiled and a dimple dotted her cheek. "You look like a princess or someone very important." Frances noticed the new girl's posture and fluid movements were graceful like a cat. Even though she wore the soldiers' uniform, it did not conceal her long limbs and womanly curves.

Nyla rolled her eyes. "My name is Nyla, and I am not royalty." She shook her head and long loose curls bounced around her body. She made sure her eyes shot unspoken daggers.

Frances put her hand on the healer's arm. "If you have a secret, it's safe with me." She watched the beautiful girl with coffee-colored skin tense.

Frances lowered her voice. "Let me give you some friendly advice." She waited for the stranger to object. When Nyla remained silent, Frances whispered, "You changed your clothing but the ruby nose ring, the necklace, the ankle bracelet are not something we see in these parts. Only the very wealthy or royalty can afford such luxuries."

Nyla bent over and unclasped the trinket from her ankle and thrust it into her pocket

"I will not remove the ruby." She cocked her head defiantly. "Many of the girls here have piercings." She laced her fingers around her neck, loosened the clasp on the necklace, and secured it in a pouch on her waist.

Frances shrugged her shoulders. "Suit yourself, but the tribe already has questions about the three of you."

Nyla tensed. "What questions?"

Frances looked Nyla in the face. "How can we believe you were sent from God to help us battle the enemy of our souls when the warrior is defeated?"

Nyla looked down at the mud that sloshed over her shoes. "She will recover."

"I hope you're right. Most of us have lost faith in those

who say they come from Safehold." Frances licked her fingers and tried to smooth down the top of her frizzy hair. "You all look different… but can a princess, a beaten warrior, and an albino prophet deliver what you promise?"

"Stop calling me a princess. If you tell anyone, I will incite a riot against you. I will make sure they take your livelihood and everything you own."

Frances shrugged her shoulders. "I own nothing. I am hiding here like everyone else. The king's henchmen will come for us, and after that…" She paused and made the sign of the cross. "My fate is anyone's guess."

Nyla was speechless.

Frances grinned. "I will not tell anyone because I'd like to be your friend."

Nyla sighed. "Why? I have no authority here. I was sent as your servant."

Frances scratched her head. "I want to be special. The others will think you have something they need. You're pretty, and Aza already has his eye on you. The leader's affection will make you popular. I want them to see I'm with you. That will make me important in their eyes."

Nyla smirked. "What people? I do not care what these people think of me."

Frances ignored her remark and began to walk toward the infirmary. "When you meet them, you will care."

Nyla silently followed her new friend, her mind formulating a plan. *She reminds me of Abada. I might need an informant while I am in this hostile place.* Her heart squeezed within her chest at the thought of home, friends, and family. She hated to admit she was already homesick. She missed her mother and the many comforts of home. As quickly as the feelings attacked her emotions, she pushed them away. *I will never admit defeat.*

The thin muddy path began to open into a wide grassy

glade. The sound of children crying and people coughing broke the silence that surrounded them. When they rounded the corner, Nyla's eyes widened. She saw people of many nationalities, waiting for medical help. Young and old sat on tattered blankets on the cold wet ground. Her eyes welled up with tears. This was what she prepared for, helping and healing refugees was her purpose and passion. She quickly wiped her eyes with a trembling hand and shifted her focus to the other medics who were treating patients.

Nyla walked through the open area and felt every eye staring at her. Her heart pounded in her chest.

Frances stopped near a boulder and set up her station. She motioned to the next woman waiting in line. A frail girl pushed a thin child ahead of her. Nyla watched Frances gently unwrap a shirt used as a blanket from the shivering toddler's shoulders.

"How long have you been here?" Frances asked the child's mother, never taking her eyes from the shaking child.

"We were brought in by Aza after the snowfall in Mori." She glanced at the healer. "The boy who is one of your partners from Safehold saved us from the Soul-Sifters."

Nyla shook her head. "He is the prophet. His name is Beryl."

The healer reached out to touch the woman's hand, but the refugee quickly drew away. "Don't be afraid," Nyla whispered. "I am a healer, and I want to help you."

As Frances ministered to the child, Nyla continued her conversation with his mother. She noticed the woman tried to keep her face and body hidden within the folds of her blanket. Her voice betrayed her pain.

"May I look at your injury?"

The woman tensed. "No. I am fine. I am not injured."

Nyla took the toddler from Frances and held him out to his mother. "Hold him," she demanded.

Frances's mouth dropped open. "What do you think you're doing?"

The woman stepped away from her crying child. "I cannot." Her voice was a whisper.

Nyla softened her tone. "I will not hurt you."

The blanket slid from the young woman's head. She tried to cover her lips. A red rash splashed across her face and ran down her neck, shoulder, and arm, leaving a trail of raised lumps. Her hand and fingers were swollen under thin white fabric she used as a bandage. Nyla could see a volcanic abscess that was black, yellow, and festering with pus.

Frances gasped and made the sign of the cross. "She has the devil's claw."

Other refugees who waited in line whispered and backed away. The commotion created a large circle of curious onlookers.

"This is the work of a warlock who put a spell on her," Frances yelled.

"No!" Nyla put a comforting hand on the woman's arm. "This is not the work of sorcery. It is an infection."

Frances grabbed Nyla's arm and spun her around to face her. "You do not understand the ways of this world. Look at the amulet she wears on her neck. It is the Eye of Horus. She is trying to protect herself from harm. It is definitely the work of demons."

Frances turned on the woman. "Tell her the truth. You have the red bumps all over your body, and you wear the charm to ward off the evil spirits."

The woman dropped to her knees and wept. "Yes. I am under their magic."

Nyla yanked her arm from Frances and faced the gaping crowd. "If this is a spell, my medicine will not help her. If it is an infection, the medication I carry can heal her."

The sea of faces stared at her, and the crowd mumbled.

The refugee held out her hand. "What is your name?" Nyla asked.

"Gemma," the young mother whispered.

Nyla began peeling back layers of fabric sticky with dried pus. She held her breath. The infected blister smelled of rot. The woman groaned and tried to pull her hand away, but Nyla clung to her wrist.

Many patients who gathered to watch groaned in disgust.

"The boil is very hot to the touch, but it is draining so that is good." Nyla kept her voice soft and even. Opening a gold velvet pouch on her belt, she took a red vial and poured a drop of liquid on her patient's wound. The fabric separated from the festering abscess, and the woman cried out in pain.

From a larger pouch, the healer scooped out some dried herbs. Wetting them with another drop of liquid, she spread the balm over the infected area.

Nyla finished and held the woman's hand. "That was not so bad, was it?"

The refugee shook her head and wiped a lone tear from her cheek.

Nyla squeezed her hand, hoping to reassure her. "May I pray with you?"

The young mother hung her head. "I have spent my days hating God for inflicting people of faith with so much pain. I stopped praying many years ago." Tears spilled down her cheeks. "Will God forgive a sinner like me?"

Nyla patted her hand. "When you ask for forgiveness, Jesus is quick to forgive. It is not our heavenly Father who has brought this suffering upon us. The enemy of our souls wants us to doubt God's love and faithfulness. Our Redeemer's plan is to save the lost." The healer cleared her throat and raised her voice so those who pressed close to see the spectacle would hear her prayer.

"Lord of all creation," she prayed, "you came to earth

to forgive our sins and heal our brokenness. You died that we would have life. By your power, heal the infection that has crept into Gemma's soul. Grant your healing touch to my sister's body, mind, and emotions. We ask for your healing power, in Jesus's name. Amen."

When Nyla opened her eyes, the woman smiled. "I felt peace that I cannot explain come over me. I was very afraid before you prayed. I was sure the evil spell would make me die and leave my son an orphan. Now I believe Jesus has forgiven my sins because he cares about me, and I know I will live."

Nyla put her medications away. "In a few days, the physical evidence of the infection will begin to fade away."

The woman touched the boil. "It no longer burns."

Nyla handed Gemma some sycamore bark. "Boil this and let it steep. Drink it a few times a day. The red bumps on your lips and body will dry up and fade away."

"Thank you," Gemma said and lifted her child from Frances's arms. She walked away in awe, whispering to other patients who waited. "She has healing power."

Frances looked at Nyla in wide-eyed wonder. "Can you teach me to do that?"

Nyla smiled. "A prayer said in faith is something Jesus tells us all to do. I act in obedience and our Lord does the rest."

A quiet rustling in the surrounding forest broke the moment. The soft murmuring of the patients ceased, along with all movement. Every eye turned in the direction of the approaching noise. Like shifting shadows, the soldiers entered the camp, snaking their way through the underbrush. With uniforms of layered leaves, pine needles, and tree bark, the soldiers resembled the surrounding forest. The troop crept into the infirmary with tar-streaked faces and bodies dirty and bruised.

Nyla noticed their expressions were tense and strained. A youth of about fourteen, with slanted black eyes and long dark hair, tried to make light of the situation. "Did you see Bear land his ax between the eyes of that creature?"

A few of the men laughed. "The blood shot out like a waterfall. I think we are all wearing some of the black ooze."

Nyla could not help but wonder at their unique differences. Some of the soldiers were young, barely in their teens, yet their eyes were full of hate and hopelessness; others were heavily muscled with tattooed heads and bodies, hardened by the trials this life offered. The regiment consisted of both male and female, each a different nationality and from different tribes.

It was at that moment, Nyla realized these men and women were the center of everything. The tribe members reverently made room for them to pass and made comments about them as if they were gods. The elite group was venerated, loved, envied; but more importantly, they were watched. Every male and female, who was not part of their group, stood a little taller, hoping to be seen and admired by one of them.

Aza spotted Nyla watching. The distraction made him fall over a rut in the dirt. His smiling face turned red, and he punched Sargo in the bicep. "You tripped me."

They pushed each other good-naturedly.

Sargo glanced in Nyla's direction and scowled. "I see Her Majesty is up and around. You would do us all a favor if you stayed away from this one." He nudged his brother. "She's the type who will draw you in like a spider into a web."

Aza stood glued to the spot, his heart pounded in his chest. She was more beautiful than he remembered. He had carried her to their headquarters after the rescue on the Plains of Mori. At the time, she was disoriented, dirty, and tired; yet even then, she was unlike anyone he had ever seen.

A soldier bumped him hard from behind. "You act like you've never seen a girl before," Ravenna teased. "Pull yourself together. Your gawking is embarrassing." She shoved past him with the rest of their team.

Aza regained his composure and walked over to Nyla's station. He pulled open his shirt, revealing a long gash across his midsection. Nyla's green eyes flashed. "You must wait your turn in line, sir." The black ooze that covered his uniform smelled putrid.

He flashed a smile. "It is customary, in time of war, to look after the soldiers first."

Frances began to scurry around like a mouse. She quickly poured fresh water into a basin and gathered clean bandages. She placed the items in Nyla's reach. Aza sat on a large rock, facing the healer.

Nyla ripped a piece of cloth and threw it to her mentor. "Frances," she commanded, forgetting her new rank. "Clean the soldier's wound."

She turned to storm away, but Aza grabbed her wrist. "No. I want you to attend to my injury."

Nyla fought the urge to slap his face. Pulling the cloth from the other girl's hand, she faced him ready to verbally attack. One look into his gray eyes disarmed her. She stared at him, unable to look away. His eyes mirrored the confusion in his soul. An odd mixture of hatred, lust, murder, and vulnerability made him seem all the more attractive. Red heat spread across her cheeks. Nyla felt disgraced by her thoughts and actions. Looking into a stranger's eyes was a bold gesture in her culture, but he held her captive, like a moth to a flame.

Instead of the slap she intended, she gently blotted the blood from his muscled abdomen. The soldier flinched and took her small hand in his.

"Your hands feel like ice."

She looked into his eyes and could see his raw hunger.

He reached out and touched her cheek. "So beautiful," he whispered.

Nyla slowly pulled her trembling hand from his and

forced her eyes from his face. "This cut will need stitches." She backed away; a feeling of vertigo made her weave. Regaining her balance, she barked orders to Frances. "I need some warm water and clean bandages."

Nyla took leaves from her pouch and began to grind them with a stone. Her hands shook while she attempted to crush the herbs; again she flushed, cursing her emotions for making her feel excited under his stare. Frances returned with a steaming pot of water and fresh linen. Nyla placed the aromatic leaves into the boiling liquid, the vapors smelled clean and sweet.

She willfully calmed herself and worked carefully, heating the rag in the antiseptic and cooling the bandage before placing it over his long cut. She let the bandage sit on the wound while she took silk thread from her bag and prepared the sutures. She could feel Aza's eyes burning into her body. She squirmed under his gaze. Inside her belt, she took a vial and opened it. Holding the flask under Aza's nose, she forced her quivering lips to speak.

"Inhale deeply." Her eyes avoided him.

The soldier smiled. "What witchcraft is this?"

Nyla bristled. "Unless you want to squeal like a pig as I stitch this wound, I suggest you cooperate."

Their eyes locked.

Aza leaned toward her, never taking his eyes from hers. He inhaled hard and the acrid scent filled his nostrils. Within seconds, his eyes rolled in his head. The soldier laughed. "Am I supposed to feel like I'm flying?"

Nyla watched his head drop forward and his breathing become shallow.

"What have you done to him?" Frances asked.

"I made him comfortable. He will awaken soon, prideful as ever." Nyla began to stitch his wound, her hands working skillfully over the deep gash. She chided herself for lingering to admire his muscled body, surprising herself with these bold actions. She stood back and appraised her work. "He will have only a slight scar," she said absently while putting another compress over her work.

Aza slept comfortably, his chest slowly rising and lowering, his body relaxed.

"You are so fortunate to have him attracted to you," Frances whispered. "Don't you find him handsome and brave?"

Nyla rolled her eyes. "He is an arrogant fool." She snapped her fingers repeatedly in front of the sleeping soldier's eyes. He remained unresponsive. "When he regains consciousness, tell him you will remove the sutures in a week's time."

Nyla packed up her bags and started to walk back toward the camp with a group of medics.

"Where are you going? Aza will want to speak to you when he awakens."

Nyla huffed. "He will be fine. Let one of the other girls tend to his needs."

Frances's eyes narrowed as she watched Nyla walk away. "You are the arrogant fool," she said.

"Where is she?" Aza asked.

Frances almost jumped out of her skin. "I thought you were still sleeping," she stammered.

"Where is she?" he repeated.

"The elders needed her back at camp," she blurted out the lie without thinking. "Nyla told me to tell you she will meet you after dark."

Aza's eyes widened.

Frances faked a cough. "To…" She wrung her sweaty hands. "Check your bandage."

Two soldiers helped Aza to his feet.

He groaned. "Make sure she shows up." He stumbled and the men repositioned him over their shoulders. "I'm counting on you."

Frances watched until they were out of sight before she

put her supplies away. *I must find a way to get Nyla to meet with Aza or I will be out of his circle of trust before I have the privilege of being one of them.*

CHAPTER 20

Friends and Enemies

Alex slept fitfully. Memories and dreams seemed to keep her locked in constant fear. Beryl wondered if she would ever get over her mental injuries. When she did sleep, he left her under constant guard. He wandered the corridor of caves, trying to clear his head, and realized a small segment of the mountain became home to different tribes and their families.

Beryl estimated there were about three hundred people living underground, including the refugees. He walked with his head down and his hands in a prayerful position. He learned early in life that people shunned him because he looked different, but it enabled him to listen to quiet murmurings and pick up bits and pieces of information. It appeared that many people here were looking for asylum, and all were welcome regardless of religious or civic apostasy toward King Apollyon. However, the few who held onto belief in the Baptism of Fire made the compound high-risk for attack. He understood why this tension created divisions.

He discovered that the cavern he shared with Alex and Nyla housed the hospital, kitchen, and sleeping quarters for everyone, except the soldiers. Beryl followed his nose to the mess hall and made friends with Anat, a chef for her kinsmen.

"You are tall as a willow and thin as a twig, young man!" She made clucking sounds with her tongue and shook her gray head disapprovingly. "Don't they feed the youth where you come from?"

Beryl's eyes watered as they adjusted to the smoke that hovered like a light fog around the cave. He watched Anat heap boiled root vegetables, watery rabbit stew, and barley bread onto a wooden dish. His mouth watered. He hadn't sat down to eat a meal in days.

She handed him the plate. "Eat! Eat!" she said as she smiled and patted his arm.

Beryl sat cross-legged on the floor and got comfortable. This portion of the cave felt warm and inviting. As he ate, he counted many pottery jars that held water and noticed onions, garlic, and herbs hanging from pegs in the wall. The aroma filled the room with a hominess that made him homesick.

"This meal tastes so good. How can I thank you?"

Anat turned to look at him. "Eat every drop. There is plenty more in the pot."

Beryl knew this kind woman would give him her portion if he asked for more. His stomach growled. "No, thank you, Anat. I have had more than my share."

He stood and returned the plate, noticing cooking pots sitting in numerous firepits around the large rectangular room. "Do you share this space with others?"

Anat wiped sweat from her brow. "Yes. A few other clans. This corner is my space."

She had a large iron kettle simmering with enough stew for her people. On the dirt floor, rocks outlined a pit, smoldering with hot ash where she cooked flat disks of barley bread, on broken pieces of pottery, to feed her faction of survivors.

"My flat cakes are finished," she announced while she carefully organized them on a narrow wooden platform. "As soon as they cool, you can be the first to taste."

He smiled to himself as he watched her scurry about her space. He could sense the love and pride she put into the preparation of the meal. White flour dusted her dimpled cheeks and her threadbare wool tunic smelled of woodsmoke. The belt around her waist had faded and the wimple that covered her hair was missing a tie, yet she seemed to make the most of her life of freedom within the belly of the mountain.

"My husband, Simeon, is tending one of the small gardens that supply our clan with vegetables and herbs."

Beryl raised an eyebrow. "Aren't you afraid the enemy will spot the crops and confiscate your harvest?"

Anat shrugged her shoulders. "We have little choice if we want to feed our families. We try to make our plants blend into the natural vegetation. It has worked for over a year."

"How did you end up here, in these caves?" he asked.

The old woman sighed. "We are born-again refugees. Before Aza turned…" She coughed and changed her tone. "He and the soldiers rescued us from the slums of E'Doom after we were turned over to the authorities for our belief in Jesus and the Baptism of Fire. Many in our village were being saved, healed, and delivered from evil spirits."

Beryl sucked in his breath. "Aza turned, you say?"

Anat tucked strands of gray hair into her cap. "Shush. I hear Simeon coming." She smiled and brushed off her apron and smoothed down her hair.

"Anat," he called warmly as he entered the kitchen. "I have something special for you." He kissed her cheek and whispered in her ear. "Watch what you say. Some of our accusations are unproven." He winked at Beryl, and from behind his back, he handed his wife a bunch of yellow daisies and sunflowers.

Anat clapped her hands. "I love fall flowers. The colors are so vibrant. No time of year can come close." She smiled and her beautiful gray eyes misted over. "They remind me of the flowers in our homeland."

She lowered her voice. "I was telling our young friend how we became part of this tribe of survivors." She sighed and looked Beryl in the eyes, ignoring the warning look from her husband. "Aza shows signs that he has been initiated into a secret cult, along with many of the youth here." She folded her arms over her chest. "I will not cover for him. The elders of each clan should be aware."

Simeon took Anat's hands in his. His voice was soft and sad. "Hush, my love. We no longer have a homeland, and if the wrong ears hear your suspicions, we will be banished from this tribe." He looked at Beryl. "We are no longer free. Old World is under the heel of Apollyon."

He reached out a dirty hand to Beryl. "You must be the prophet."

Beryl shook the elder's hand, grateful he didn't pull back at the pallor of his white flesh.

A few women, shrouded in black, walked into the cooking area and sat on the stone ledge to peel carrots and slice onions to season their stew. They nodded vaguely to Anat and Simeon, looked suspiciously at Beryl, and then whispered to each other.

Simeon escorted him to a corner of the room and lowered his voice. "We are willing to fight as soon as the warrior is better." He removed his cap, revealing sparse white hair. "Many in our group have been waiting for this moment a long time. We are ready to take back our land from Old World's king and his army of locusts."

Beryl put his hand on the elder's shoulder. "What about the others and the soldiers who inhabit the cave?"

Simeon looked over his shoulder. "There are many clans that live together under this mountain's roof. We are all waiting for liberation." He pounded a right fist into his palm. His agitation brought on a momentary coughing fit. "We serve the same God but have different backgrounds. For this reason, we have not been organized and are losing ground in this war."

Anat broke into her native tongue and her voice escalated. Simeon shook his head and put a finger to his lips, cautioning her to keep her voice low.

"Many within the new generation of warriors believe the lies of the enemy. This new era promises freedom from old rules and values. Wisdom is belittled and the one God and his precepts are forsaken."

Simeon continued, "Our people are offered wealth, position, and influence if they join with the army of destruction. Many have flocked to the city of E'Doom, embracing the new Aeon. Our countrymen flaunt their power as they lead enemy troops against their own people." He paused to make sure no one could overhear. "Some, within the compound, are recruiters for the enemy. We must be careful at all times that no one hears us speaking about rebirth."

A clatter of hooves and the noisy bleating of sheep interrupted the conversation. Six lambs scurried through the narrow hallway and into the kitchen, followed by a handful of giggling children.

"Sorry!" One little boy giggled. "We were chasing each other, and somehow, they got out of their pen."

The workspace became the hub of chaos as the rowdy children knocked over water jugs, vegetables, and bread in their wild pursuit of the frightened sheep.

"Oh my! They will ruin our supper," Anat said.

Beryl joined the commotion. "Don't worry. I'll get them out of here."

He helped the children corral the escapees and secured them once more within their stable, next to the chickens and goats.

A cherub-faced boy snuck up behind Beryl and stuck him in the butt with a wooden sword. "Want to fight, ugly ghost?" he asked. The others laughed and pointed at the prophet.

"Why is your skin so white?"

"Can you see in the dark with those creepy eyes?"

A small girl sniffed his cloak. "You smell!"

The children laughed and started teasing, "You stink, you stink…"

Beryl ignored their remarks. *I guess some things will never change.* He picked up a wooden sword and acted like a swordsman sparring with his challenger. In no time, the play drew the attention of other little warriors. What was once a fair fight quickly became a war with wooden weapons. Beryl lifted the first soldier off his feet and held him upside down as his prisoner before there were any accidents or tears.

"I will run you through with my weapon unless you can answer me a very important question," Beryl said as he gently put the laughing child on the ground.

The group formed a circle around him.

"Who knows where they keep the big black stallion?"

The children giggled. "There are lots of black horses here."

Beryl tried again. "I mean the one that came from the Mountain of Evermore."

The children jumped up and down as they tried to talk over each other. "He is in another cave where the soldiers train."

A girl, about Beryl's age, pushed through the chattering children. She was dressed in leather breeches and wore a padded vest, used for weapons practice, over a white shirt. A well-made sword hung from her waist. Tucked inside one knee boot, he saw the handle of a dagger. Her brown hair sparkled with auburn streaks and her porcelain skin was dotted with freckles.

"You're one of the three messengers from Safehold," she said.

Beryl was not sure if she was asking a question or making a statement.

She glared at him with one hand on her hip, looking him

over. "Everyone is talking about the three of you. Most of the soldiers think you are too late to help us. After all, the warrior is defeated."

Anger boiled within him, but he kept his thoughts to himself. *These people have no idea what Alex has already accomplished. I'm sick of hearing that word.*

She scratched her head. "Not too good with a weapon I see."

He didn't answer.

"If you're not mute, I'll take you to see the horse."

He nodded his head.

Beryl followed her through dark narrow hallways that snaked their way through the cavern. Torches sputtered and smoked. The faint light lit a trail to follow. After a long silent journey, he saw the promise of light and could smell fresh air. They came out into a bright yard where warriors were sparring and practicing military maneuvers.

The combat field was large and grassy, sheltered by the mountain range that enclosed it like a stronghold. Tall evergreens and thick forest circled the perimeter creating an arena completely hidden from enemy eyes.

Beryl watched the combatants spar and marveled at the soldiers who were capable of fighting six to eight opponents at once. He was fascinated by their use of footwork as well as their ability to utilize shield and armor as part of their defense.

"They're practicing counter cutting," the girl said, noting his distraction. "These are advanced movements that are both offensive and defensive. A soldier must be extremely proficient with his weapons to engage the enemy with these maneuvers."

He wondered if Alex was familiar with this form of combat. A punch in the bicep brought him back to reality.

"Let's go!" she insisted. "We're wasting time." She led him past the training yard and inside a cavern that was hot from the blacksmith's fire. Hundreds of tiny sparks flew around in the darkness. They stepped over piles of swords, battle-axes, and war hammers waiting for repair.

A sweaty muscled form was bent over a curved anvil. "Hand me the other hammer," he shouted without looking up from his work. His accent was thick and his voice was loud.

The girl immediately went to a bench. She picked the tool from a pile of rasps, files, and chisels. After handing him his desired utensil, she hauled a pitcher of water to a basin and poured the extra liquid into a large wooden barrel sitting next to him. Without further instruction, the apprentice lifted the sword from the blacksmith's large dirty hands and plunged it into the cold bath. The immersion created ribbons of steam and loud hissing. She pulled it out of the water and handed it back. The huge man held a mallet and pounded skillfully on the metal, reshaping and remolding the blade. The thunderous hammering echoed around the room.

Beryl watched him slowly raise himself from his bent position. He wore no shirt and down both sides of his massive back were scars and rows of thick gold rings pierced into his flesh. Fierce black eyes under thick hooded brows bore into Beryl's face. Dark curly hair, like a lion's mane, surrounded his head, and he had a thick grizzled beard. Beryl thought he resembled a wild animal.

The man's gaze strayed to the girl. "You learn quickly." He smiled, holding up the creation he was working on.

"Thanks for finishing my sword for me," she said. "Hammering it out after the steel is soft is a little out of my league, for now."

"You possess a gift like the others in our family." He smiled broadly. "You make me proud." He patted her lovingly on top of her head. "Now you must polish the blade on the stone wheel until you see your reflection." He wiped his hands on a dirty rag and shifted his hawk eyes to Beryl.

"Who is the monk? He must be from far, far away." He made mocking gestures with his big hands. "I am sure of this for I have never seen such hair." He chuckled under his breath.

"He's a mute from Safehold." She smirked at the boy, then looked innocently at the giant of a man.

Beryl quickly thrust out his hand. "My name is Beryl. The young lady and I have not formerly introduced ourselves."

"Is that right, Tika?" He paused, looking at her under his bushy brows. "That is no way to treat a stranger." He took the young man's hand and shook it vigorously. "My name is Baccus. This young lady is my daughter." His hawk eyes turned soft.

Beryl smiled. The man's gruff exterior and soft heart reminded him of Brother John. He immediately liked him. "Tika brought me here so I could find the warrior's horse and armor."

"Yes. I have both. Aza gave them to me for safekeeping." The big man looked Beryl over. "There is much talk throughout the tribe concerning you and the other two messengers. Some good talk and some not so good." He winked at the boy. "I save judgment until I get to know you."

He lumbered across the room, his heavy boots crunched over the dirt floor. He stopped at a workbench and pushed aside snakeskins, animal claws, and buffalo horns until he found a key among the bizarre clutter. He blew dust from the object and bent over a large ornate chest, unlocking the clasp. He lifted Alex's sword from within.

He held it up, admiring it in awe. "Every line is straight. This weapon is perfectly balanced. No measuring tool or human eye could achieve this," he whispered. "The steel of the blade is of the highest quality. Nothing like this material is mined anywhere in Old World. The elaborate detail of the vine and fruit is exquisite. King Apollyon's bladesmiths have not acquired skills like these." Out of habit, he wiped the blade with a soft cloth.

"Don't misunderstand. This work of art is a weapon capable of disembowelment, lopping off heads, *and* pulverizing bones."

Beryl made a sick face.

"The breastplate, shield, belt, and helmet are of the same quality. They vibrate with power." The big man was clearly impressed.

"Yes," Beryl whispered. "This is the full armor of God."

Baccus respectfully put the weapon away and locked the case. "Come. I will take you to see the stallion. We have stabled him away from the other horses for now."

He led them to the far end of his shop; a fur rug partitioned his work area from his sleeping quarters. He took Beryl through the sparse room and out into the sunlight. A wooden shed with a corral stood a few yards from his room. Inside Malak lay on a mound of grass. He snorted quietly when the humans approached.

Beryl was shocked. "He doesn't look too good."

Baccus shrugged his shoulders. "The healer comes every day to take care of him. She says he is improving."

Tika knelt beside Malak and stroked his nose. "I think he misses Alex. How is she?"

Beryl was surprised that Tika knew their names. After the shock wore off, he realized they were within the cave for a little over a week. In such close quarters, word spread quickly. As Baccus said, some of the news about them was good and some not so good.

"She is getting stronger, but her spirit is weak." He sighed.

The tree branches above their heads swayed and creaked. A loud screech announced the arrival of a winged lizard. Beryl looked up at the raptor and shuddered. "I'm not sure I like the large birds of prey," he said. "In the desert of my country, we have only feathered birds."

Tika looked up at the lizard perched on the tree branch. "This one is small, unlike others here in Old World."

"How's that? I have only seen the small ones."

Tika smiled. "There are other raptors here that are huge almost dragon-like. They are worshipped by the king's army and ridden only by his elite troop."

Baccus folded his arms across his chest and looked the prophet up and down. "You have much to lean before you take to the highways and byways of this country." The big man frowned. "A few times out in the field with a scouting team should help you understand what we are up against."

Beryl's stomach lurched. "I must get back. I don't like to leave Alex too long. Aza posted a guard, but I like to be there when she is awake."

Baccus slapped Beryl on the back. "Come see us again," he said jovially. "Tell your partner we are praying for her."

Tika led him into the training yard. "Can you find your way back without me?" she asked.

Beryl looked around. There were many openings into the belly of the mountain. "Is it the one to the east that is oval in shape?"

"Your memory is better than your swordplay," she joked. "By the way." Her tone turned serious. "One of the soldiers said you were starting to teach from the Book of Life."

"Yes." He beamed, glad the word was spreading through the camp.

"I'll teach you to use a weapon if you show me how to use one of those lightning sticks they say you carry."

He chuckled. Lots of news was spreading through the tribe. "Please come. And yes, I do need some lessons on wielding a sword. We meet tomorrow at noon, on the southern slope."

"I'll be there with a few of my friends." She turned and jogged away.

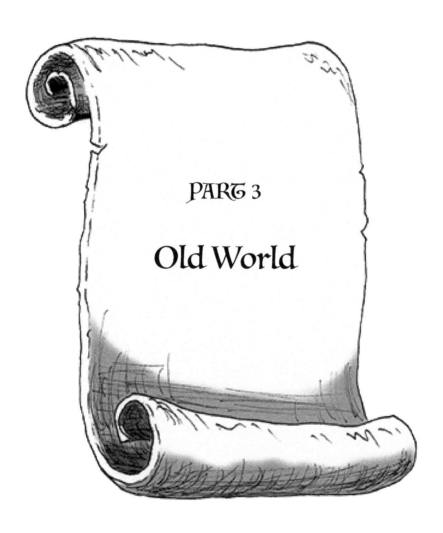

PART 3

Old World

CHAPTER 21

Shaken or Proven

Beryl got back to Alex's room as the sun began to set over the mountain range. It was a warm evening with clouds gathering in the distance. He walked through the partition that separated her room from the tunnel.

"What are you doing?" he asked.

Alex was sitting on the edge of the sleeping pallet. "I'm tired of the bandages. I want them off as soon as Nyla gets here."

Her tone surprised him. "Is something wrong? Nyla thought maybe by the new moon."

She sighed. "I have been wrapped up like a corpse long enough. I want to get started training the soldiers. Enough time has been wasted."

Beryl cracked his knuckles. "Nyla should be here soon."

He was glad she was ready to begin her duties, but her spirit did not seem right.

Alex coughed. "I hate the smell of this cheap oil. It makes my throat burn."

He hadn't noticed it before, but a torch on the wall burned a smoky oil that lit the room with a soft glow. "Yea, I hadn't noticed. It doesn't really bother me." Out of habit, he sat on the floor and busied himself, sketching a quick rendering of Tika.

Nyla walked through the partition. "Alex, good to see you up. I take it you're feeling better."

Alex tried to keep her voice level and calm. "I want the face and head bandages off. Now."

Nyla looked at Beryl and shrugged her shoulders. "I will do it right away, but if the burns are not better, we may have to wrap you again for a while."

Alex could sense Nyla's hesitation but didn't care.

Nyla tried to ease the tension. "I had an eventful first day in the field," she said while opening her bag, setting up numerous bottles on the cold stone floor. She looked over at Alex who picked at the bandage, trying to find an easy way to rip it off.

"What do you think of this group?" She asked as she used a mortar and pestle to prepare medication. "And what about this alien frontier we have entered?" She looked away from her injured leader and locked eyes with the prophet. "This is not what I expected. I get the feeling some members of the tribe don't really wants us here." She stood and crossed her arms over her chest. "Most of the soldiers I've met are arrogant fools."

Beryl nodded his head in agreement. "They don't trust us yet. We need to give them time." He cracked his knuckles. "I have a small group who meet each day to learn the Word. I am also making some progress with a team of musicians."

Alex noticed when Beryl spoke again, his voice was low, tense, and on edge.

"The frontier is deadly. I will feel better when Alex is up and around." He made the sign of the cross and looked at the ceiling. "*Deo volente.*"

Nyla pushed her braid over her shoulder. "I heard some of the elders talking. They say the plains of Mori are flooded after the unusual snowfall, and many cannot cross the flatlands and get back to this camp."

She inhaled some frankincense oil to calm her fears.

Alex felt their stress and noticed the sound of Beryl's

scratching of pencil on paper was loud and abrasive.

The clinking of glass as Nyla collected her bottles seemed unusually noisy, rattling her nerves. "Please! Stop the small talk and help me with these bandages."

Nyla and Beryl joined her at the bedside. "Stay still," Nyla cautioned. "Let me do this carefully. I'll use my paring knife and it will fall away quickly without pulling skin with it."

Alex let her friend slowly cut the bandage until she couldn't stand it anymore. She looped her fingers under the fabric and yanked it over her head, ignoring the protest from the healer.

Nyla gasped. "You pulled off some new skin!"

Alex blotted sweat from her face. She tried to open her eyes but they were stuck.

Nyla handed her a damp cloth. Alex blotted her eyes and opened them to blackness. She felt around her face, hoping to feel something still covering her eyes. Her face went pale.

"Alex are you all right?" Nyla asked.

Alex tried to stand. "What is happening?" She rubbed her eyes. "I can't see! I'm blind." She fell back against the bed. Tears began to roll down her cheeks.

Beryl felt like he couldn't breathe. He searched Nyla's stunned face for answers.

Nyla felt her throat go dry. "Blind?"

Alex felt their shock like a slap in the face. "Somebody tell me this is a dream."

Silence hung in the room like smoke. Alex felt sick and dizzy. In the pit of her stomach, she knew this was her nightmare, but she would never wake up to see the light of another sunrise.

She felt like she had just died and there was nothing left.

Nyla's heart was like lead in her chest. She motioned Beryl to leave them alone.

"I'll leave you for a moment with the healer," Beryl said softly. "I'll just be outside."

Nyla sat down and tried to clean the raw skin on her face, but Alex pushed her away. She stood up, next to the bed and tried to think of a way to soften this blow. "Your wounds are healing quickly, considering how terrible they were when I first saw them. I was sure you would be badly scarred."

Alex stiffened. "You have healing gifts. Why can't you cure my eyes?"

"I have a gift. It is not magic." Nyla watched the look of disappointment on her friend's face. " I did learn that sometimes, healing takes place inside a person, a spiritual maturity."

Alex pounded her fists on the bed. "To hell with spiritual maturity! I want my sight."

Nyla swallowed the lump in her throat. "I was taught trials and illness can produce trust and…" her voice quivered.

Alex turned her back on the healer. "Go away, Nyla. I want to be alone." She pulled the blanket over her face. "Just get out."

Nyla's voice shook. "God cares about you. He will not abandon you."

Alex heard the uncertainty in her voice. "Stop lying to yourself. You don't believe a word you're saying."

Nyla looked around the austere cave and shuddered. She had met some of these survivors. Most were lukewarm in their belief in the power of the cross at best. They were on the verge of giving in to the pressure of the new aeon of rule.

"I told you to get out!" Alex yelled.

CHAPTER 22

Temptation

Night began its slow descent over the mountain range. The rumble of thunder growled in the distance. The soldiers who were in the forest to gather firewood began to scramble, hoping to collect enough of the kindling to keep the night creatures away.

Frances paced uneasily at the mouth of the cave. She mindlessly rubbed the madstone in her hand with sweaty fingers while watching the fire from the soldiers' torches weave in and out of the trees. *I can't believe my good fortune. Aza noticed me. That's great, but now, he is counting on me to make this rendezvous with Nyla happen…tonight!*

She realized she had run out of ideas. *I have to figure out a plan to get the healer outside and to the campfire where Aza and his team hide from the elders.* She stifled a scream and dropped the stone when someone appeared from the trees.

The camouflage-clad recruit saluted her. "I have come to escort the healer through the darkness to check Aza's bandage."

Frances stood mute. *Am I dreaming this?*

"Did you hear what I said?" he demanded.

"Yes," she stammered. "I will beckon her right away." Frances bent down and scooped up her talisman before running into the cave.

She found Nyla, lost in thought, distracted. It looked like

she might have been crying.

"Are you feeling all right?" Frances asked sheepishly.

Nyla shook her head. "I just received some very bad news." She paused and looked at her mentor who looked flushed, like the devil was after her. "What's wrong with you? Why are you here?"

Frances swallowed the lump in her throat. "You have been summoned to check on Aza's injury." She chewed on the inside of her cheek, dreading the healer's answer.

Nyla shrugged her shoulders. "Why? The medication I used will keep him comfortable until the stitches need to be removed."

Frances avoided the other girl's eyes as the lie dripped from her tongue. "They think it's infected."

Nyla looked stunned. *Why is this happening? Everything I touch is falling apart.* She rose quickly and checked her medical bag.

"Did they say he has a fever? Is he having pain?"

Frances shook her head. "He did not say."

Nyla threw a lightweight cape over her shoulders and followed Frances into the humid night air.

The soldier who waited gave a quick nod of recognition before he took off into the forest. Nyla accelerated her pace to keep up with Frances who seemed to have grown wings. They traveled in single file with only one hissing torch and its flickering light to guide them through the tangle of tree limbs.

Nyla hated the forest at night. "Why do we need to go so far from the main camp?" she asked, not really expecting Frances to answer. *If I were honest with myself, I would admit how much I despise Old World and its barbaric people and customs. I'm stranded!*

She laughed to herself as her thoughts continued to taunt her. *Alone by my own choosing. Adrift in a world far away from peace and security, everything I took for granted. Did I make a mistake coming here? Will I find what I'm longing for and what has been missing in my life?*

Thunder rumbled over the mountain, and the humidity made her flesh feel sticky. Everything about this frontier was inconsistent. One minute, she was shivering beneath a heavy cape, and the next hour, she felt like throwing off her clothing because it was hotter than the desert. Her thoughts tormented her. *Worst of everything is Alex. How can we go on? Why did God let this happen? Everything I thought I knew about the God I serve seems like a lie. He abandoned us, and I'm stuck here.*

The tall oaks, elms, and pines towered above her and crowded the path, sucking every breath of light and shadow from the forest floor. Owls hooted, wolves howled, and the wind rattled the leaves like dry bones. The sound of crying made Nyla's heart jump. She listened but the crash of thunder drowned all other noise. Frances and the soldier sped down the path, unaware or undisturbed by the noises that circled them. Once more, she heard the cry. Like someone in pain. She paused and strained her eyes against the darkness that devoured her, looking in the direction of the sound. The black abyss distracted her while Frances and the soldier moved completely out of sight.

"Frances!" she yelled. "Wait." She took a few steps forward. "I hear someone crying. They may need help."

A threatening growl answered from the darkness. Nyla felt her heart drop to her feet.

She swallowed her fear and stood tall. "I will not run," she said to the stalker, hoping to sound brave. "I carry a weapon, and an army is coming for me." She gathered her courage and crept forward, hoping her legs did not collapse beneath her. She used her hands to keep branches from slapping her face.

A dark form jogged behind her, she could hear it following her, circling the area until it was on the path ahead of her. The creature waited.

A large shape blocked the path. Nyla stopped and tried to make out the image that stood in the way. It resembled a man but it hunched over like a dog, beaten and broken. One eye glowed red in the inky blackness. She stared in amazement at its size. It easily weighed three times as much as she did. Its fangs gaped from its jaw. The sheer power it had over her was evident by the way it toyed with her, watching and waiting.

Nyla pulled her dagger from her boot. She felt foolish holding the weapon; it was not as large as one of the predator's fangs.

"Come and get me," she taunted and locked eyes with the beast.

The Soul-Sifter hissed but showed no sign of aggression. Nyla's heart pounded. Her eyes tried to adjust to the darkness, to make out what the creature was doing. She prayed for it to go back into the forest, but the lumbering monster crept closer. She could hear it and smelled its stench. It stood barely inches from her; the creature's breath blew her hood off her head and over her shoulder.

Nyla kept her eyes down. "What do you want from me?" she whispered.

The morphling sniffed her. A garbled weeping was all the sound it made.

Nyla lifted her head and looked into its face. The creature was so ugly, she felt dizzy with fear. The face was half-human, half-skeleton. It seemed to be dying a piece at a time. The beast's flesh was ashen and discolored like a living corpse. The nose on one side of what was once a face was a gaping hole and slightly higher than the nostril that was still flesh. The eyes were like nothing she had ever imagined. It was like seeing into hell itself. On one side, the deep pit was red, like burning embers, while the human eye was vague, empty, and totally hopeless.

Nyla could not look away, fearing the worst. "Who are you? What are you?"

It held out a scaly clawed hand. "Help me," it whispered.

Nyla flinched and backed away. "How can I help you? What do you want?"

The thing sobbed. "I want to come back."

Loud noises came from inside the forest. Torches glowed in the distance, closing in on them. A figure of a man jumped in front of her, shoving Nyla to the ground. He yelled and waved his torch at the stunned creature. More men ran from the trees, torches in hand, banging their swords against their shields. The beast screamed and spit at the intruders. Aza moved in with his sword. The morphling swiped at him with a huge front claw, throwing him through the air. Aza hit the ground hard. He touched his torso, looking for blood, surprised that he was not ripped open. *Why did it spare my life?*

Archers closed in and rained arrows into its body, piercing its flesh. Drops of blood dotted the ground.

"No!' Nyla yelled. "Don't hurt it."

A soldier ran forward and buried his sword in the creature's side. It grabbed him with clawed fingers and flung him to the dirt, pinning him.

Nyla watched in horror as the beast severed the soldier's arm from his body. The screams from the injured boy turned her stomach.

The morphling screeched in fury before bolting into the forest.

Nyla crawled on her hands and knees toward the injured soldier. Her mind felt numb as she watched his blood pooling in a dark circle on the forest floor.

A man's voice spoke from the darkness. "Are you hurt?" Strong arms pulled her from the dirt.

Her body weaved and she fell against him.

"Why did you attack it?" she demanded. "Your boy should not have attacked it."

Sargo grabbed her roughly around her waist and scooped her into his arms. "That boy was trying to protect you."

Aza ran forward and knelt over the bleeding soldier. "Help me lift him," he ordered. Four soldiers helped to lift the mutilated boy and carried him back to their camp.

Sargo followed the procession with Nyla thrown over one of his broad shoulders.

"Unhand me immediately, you ill-bred pig!" Nyla pounded his back. Her words dripped with the authority that came from royalty.

Sargo dropped her to her feet. "Is that better, my lady?" he asked with sinister gentleness.

Nyla brushed off her cape. "The creature was no threat. The loss of that soldier's arm was unwarranted. All you seem to want to do is kill!" She saw Sargo's body go rigid.

"You know nothing about life here. We kill to survive." He picked up his pace. "Stay close. If I lose you to the forest, you may not be as lucky next time."

Nyla could smell the fires long before they entered the camp. The encampment was a secluded enclave surrounded by a thick grove of evergreens. Soldiers quieted their conversations, stopped sharpening their weapons, and stared at Nyla as Sargo led her into their site.

"Why did you bring her here?" a recruit asked as he downed his last bit of ale. "I thought we agreed to keep our business here secret. Don't tell me you believe they came from Safehold with power to free us."

Sargo grabbed the youth by his collar and pushed him to the ground. "Aza's orders."

"My apologies, sir." He crawled out of Sargo's way like a whipped dog.

"Watch her until I come back," he said to the whipped

dog of a boy before he walked away to follow Aza into a cave with the injured youth.

Nyla watched a girl with dark spiked hair and a revealing gown lead a procession of females to the cave entrance. One carried lit candles, another a brazier of incense, and the third a large leather book. The whipped dog poured more ale and sat on a log, staring at Nyla as if she was some circus freak.

Nyla let her cape fall from her shoulders. The night was hot and steamy. Beads of sweat collected under her thick braid.

"We have plenty of ale." The boy smiled. "A drink will help you forget about the heat."

Nyla gazed beyond the fire ring. Drunken soldiers caroused with scantily clad girls, as if they were in a brothel, hidden within the cover of the trees. The girls were out of uniform and were comfortable with very little clothing. Nyla's face flushed and she lowered her eyes.

"You don't seem to care about the young soldier who was injured tonight," she accused.

He grinned. "War has many casualties." He tried to hand her his cup. "Have a little, it will help you relax."

Nyla pushed the cup away. "How much longer will your leader be detained?" she demanded.

The boy shrugged his shoulders.

As she waited, she watched a group of soldiers sitting by the fire with a strange weapon. It had five sharp spikes, laced together. They dipped it into the soot and made markings on a girl's forearm. "Be easy!" she moaned. "I want a tattoo, not burnt rotting flesh."

The soldiers laughed and handed her another tanker of ale.

The boy with the spike looked at Nyla. "Look. She's watching us. I think the lady of Safehold wants to take the mark."

They all laughed.

"You can be next," he said.

Nyla pulled her cape around her shoulders and covered her head. She felt confused. There was something intoxicating about this place. Her heart beat faster.

"Why sit way over there?" they called to her. "We will make room for you. Come get a drink." They laughed again and continued to mark the girl's flesh.

Aza and Frances walked from the cave in her direction. As they got close, she saw his clothing was covered in the injured soldier's blood. Aza pulled his shirt off and threw it into the fire. She watched small beads of sweat trickle down his throat. His sweaty chest glistened in the firelight.

"Let me see your wound." She felt tongue-tied. Her heart fluttered in her chest, and she tried to cover up her racing hormones. "Will the soldier be all right? I am a healer. I can help." Nyla stood to examine his wound. She realized his forearm had a tattoo. A triangle with a circle in the center. Small Xs formed rays of light that spread outward from the symbol. She forced her attention back to his injury as her hands traced the line the stitches made down his muscled abdomen. "There is no sign of infection."

She turned to face Frances as anger replaced confusion. "You lied to me."

Frances could not meet her eyes. "No…we just—"

Nyla's pulse raced. "You both lied to me." She paced in front of the fire. "Where did you take the boy? Because of you, he must live without his arm."

Aza looked away. "Those demons are not common to these woods. It must have been displaced because of the flood on the flats." He rubbed his chin. "This happened because of the wild magic you started in the Chasm. Even the weather has changed since you arrived."

"Are you seriously trying to blame me!"

He winced. "I did not mean for it to sound that way."

He raked his hand through his hair. "The Soul-Sifters never back down or leave without a kill. They generally travel in packs, following the warlords and their armies. The mutations are changing. Growing stronger. I have never seen one alone."

Nyla shook her head. "It spoke to me. It wanted help."

Aza laughed. "You're mistaken. This creature is a killing machine."

Loud screaming came from the belly of the mountain.

"Then why didn't this killing machine finish the job? This is your fault, not mine. If the boy dies, you killed him. The morphling was at the wrong place at the wrong time." Nyla pushed past Frances and marched toward the cave.

Inside candles glowed softly, illuminating the walls with painted symbols and ancient writing. Small winged lizards ran across the high ceilings, clicking, chirping, and clucking softly as they moved.

A brass brazier burned incense that smelled of balsam wood. The girl with black hair sliced her palm with a sharp blade and mixed her blood into a bowl of belladonna. She turned and faced Nyla. Colorfully painted bird wings surrounded her deep charcoal eyes, accentuating a thin scar that crossed her cheek. Her hands and body were covered in the boy's blood.

"I am a healer," Nyla said. No one responded, so she took a step forward. "Would you like me to pray?"

The girl chuckled, but it was midnight laughter. "We have healing power stronger than yours." She turned her back.

"That is not healing power, it is sorcery." Nyla felt the hair on her arms stand on end. "It is forbidden by God."

Ravenna turned on her. "Ignorant fool. Your heritage kept you sheltered, locked away like a child. You will never make it in our world," she said. "Watch and learn." She stood over the injured soldier and used the mixture in the bowl as an ointment to cover his wound. The boy moaned and writhed in pain. Two females, dressed in flimsy robes, softly chanted and dropped pieces of his ripped flesh into the fire.

Nyla walked over and lightly touched Ravenna's shoulder, hoping to change her mind. "Please allow me to pray. He has lost so much blood."

"No!" the boy screamed. "Keep her away from me." His eyes were wide with fear. "I want nothing to do with her God!"

"You heard him," Ravenna said icily. "You are not the only one in touch with the spirit realm."

Aza stormed into the cave with Frances. Sargo trailed behind.

Ravenna faced him. "Why did you bring her here?" she screamed. "This place was to be a refuge for all who reject the God of our ancestors." She turned to Sargo. "Get her out now!"

Ravenna's stomach lurched as she watched Aza staring at the beautiful girl from Safehold. She hated his blatant desire for this innocent. In a fit of rage, she threw the bowl against the wall. The noise frightened the lizards. They jumped from the ceiling, flying around in a blind panic, screeching and wailing. A large female landed in Nyla's hair. She screamed and began to swat it away. The creature hissed and bit her finger, drawing blood.

Nyla watched her blood drip down her hand and onto the ground. She felt dizzy and began to have difficulty breathing. She turned toward Frances and tried to reach for her friend, but her legs crumpled beneath her.

She felt Aza lift her from the ground and heard him yelling orders.

"Ravenna, get me the antidote quickly."

Antidote? Nyla tried to push him away, but her body refused to move. She watched Frances who looked frantic. Her lips were moving but Nyla could not understand her. As she spoke, her mouth became a gaping black hole. Spiders crawled out and swarmed Frances's face. Nyla screamed and kicked but only in her mind. Her body lay limp in Aza's arms.

"Use the madstone." Ravenna laughed. "You have one, don't you?" She smiled mischievously at Frances.

Aza laid Nyla on the floor. "Use the stone, Frances. Quickly!"

Frances knelt next to him on the dirt floor. "No!" She fumbled in her coat pocket. "She said sycamore bark and prayer is what she uses for venom."

Aza stared at the girl. "I should kill you for being useless."

Nyla felt herself begin to spin. Aza's handsome face began to grow long and thin. Streaks of black and purple spread from his forehead to his chin while his ears stretched into long black points. His beautiful gray eyes turned red and evil. Nyla fought the arms that held her like a vice.

Ravenna laughed. She bent over Aza and glared into Nyla's face. Her hair began to grow out of her head like tree roots. Yellow snakes slithered through the branches. Nyla wanted to close her eyes, but they focused on the frightful apparition.

She felt Aza stroke her face. His breath was hot on her cheek.

"I do not have the healing gift," Frances whispered. "But she said to obey and pray."

"Do you have the tree bark?" he asked.

Frances shook her head.

Aza grabbed her throat with one large hand and squeezed. "Pray," he demanded. "Pray hard or I will kill you."

Nyla's eyes fluttered open. She heard soft rain falling, washing the forest trees. A cool breeze blew over her body, reminding her of her bathing area in the palace. *Thank God. I'm home. Abada...Mother.* She looked around and her heart broke. She realized she was still in Old World. *What am I doing here?*

She turned her head and saw Frances sleeping a few feet away, sitting with her back against the rock wall. Aza's chest rose and fell under her head. Her memory of the night flooded back to her. She reached up and touched his face. His eyes fluttered, and he looked down at her with concern in his eyes.

"Nyla." He smiled. "How do you feel?"

He looked over at Frances and chuckled. "I did not believe her prayer would reach the ears of God."

Nyla held back tears. "How long have I been here?"

He lightly touched her cheek. "The sun has not come up yet. We had a nasty storm last night, but it has blown off."

Frances stretched and wiped the sleep from her eyes. "You're alive!"

"Lucky for you," Aza said.

Nyla tried to sit but Aza restrained her. "Rest a while. You are in no shape to leave yet."

Her body relaxed.

"It's my turn to take care of you," he said.

"How is the boy?" Nyla asked.

"He will live." He pulled Nyla close. "Old World has many dangers. These soldiers are aware of the risk. We understand the law of this land, and we are making our own rules. We have decided to try something different than our ancestors." His tone changed and his eyes narrowed. "The elders and the other clan members must never know about this place. Do you understand?"

Nyla considered his words.

She looked away and let her mind linger on how this secret camp made her feel free. *Maybe they are right. Maybe it's time for a change. I need to form a strong alliance to survive in Old World. I can't make it here on my own. I can't go home. Who could blame me? I left my home and family for a new life, and now, everything has changed. Alex is blind! The mission is over.*

She looked at his handsome face, staring at her, waiting for an answer. She nodded. "I think I understand." She pushed a long curl behind her ear. "I left my home for the same reason. I wanted to make my own rules. Live my own way."

Aza smiled. "I'm glad we have your allegiance."

He eyed Frances.

She lifted the sleeve of her tunic. "I took the mark to become part of his secret society."

Nyla inhaled hard. It was the tattoo of the triangle.

He looked down at Nyla. "I will take you back as soon as you're ready. Frances will make up an excuse in case you are discovered sneaking back into camp."

Nyla felt a tinge of guilt. She wanted to protest. Take a step or two back.

"I don't want to lie."

Aza traced her lips with his finger. "You look like a woman, but you talk and think like a child. I thought you left Safehold for adventure."

Nyla's cheeks burned. "I am a woman."

He shrugged his shoulders. "Then act like one. Make a choice. Do you want to live free or live up to someone else's expectations?"

Nyla felt her emotions pulling her in a million directions.

She looked into his eyes and her heart melted under his gaze. She heard herself whisper, "I guess one lie can't hurt."

CHAPTER 23

Never Alone

Alex lay on the soft blankets, her hands behind her head staring at the ceiling, eyes wide open. She was engulfed in total darkness. Her stomach churned at the thought of this new reality. Her mind demanded an answer. *Why? What did I do wrong? Why has God abandoned me?* She wiped a tear from her face. *I wonder what Reverend Mother would think of her champion now? I've let everyone down. I'm a failure.*

She sat up in the bed and rubbed her eyes hoping maybe this was just a bad dream. Her disappointment brought on more tears. *I never thought about my eyesight before. Who could even imagine something like this happening to a warrior of God? I can't do anything without sight.*

Distant footsteps down the cave tunnel distracted her. She held her breath. Listened. Strangely, she could tell if the person walking was wearing boots or sandals and could identify a man, woman, or child and believed she could guess their size and height. Her acute hearing made it hard to rest. She heard words plainly through quiet murmurings and found it easy to make out most sentences spoken during private conversations. The flutter of a partition down the hall became a disturbance. She felt restless and edgy.

She heard Beryl approaching. She knew it was him by the flip flop of his sandaled feet. She heard him stop, and a voice spoke to him quietly. "Even if she overcomes this, she will be of no use to us."

Alex pushed her body forward on the bed, straining to hear.

Another voice, deeper than the first, spoke. She recognized his voice. It was Aza, the leader of the warriors. "She is a blind guide, it's impossible."

For some reason, she found herself desperate to know what Beryl had to say.

She heard nothing.

Alex imagined the prophet must have shrugged his shoulders or shook his head with a response. The other voice laughed. Then heavy footsteps stalked away and both men were gone.

Beryl shuffled through the partition.

Her body tensed. "Go away and leave me alone."

Beryl ignored her. "I brought you supper," he said in his whimsical upbeat voice. "And I have good news! Nyla thinks you should start some light exercises to help you regain your strength."

"Me? Exercise? I'm just a useless blind guide." She rolled over in her bed and turned her back to him. "Why did this happen to me and not Nyla! And why are you up and around? How is any of this fair?"

Alex pounded her fists on the bed. "I am young and strong. This should not happen to someone my age," she swore, venting her anger on her friend. "Why would a loving God let this kind of thing happen to one of his own messengers?"

She fought back her tears. "Was that Aza I heard you speaking to in the hall? Does everyone think I'm a useless blind guide?" She waited but Beryl didn't answer. "Tell me! What did you tell him? What do you think?"

Beryl touched her shoulder. "I won't pretend to understand how you must be feeling." His voice was soft and kind. "I have asked God many times why I was born the way I am, with pallid skin and strange eyes." He looked at her, lying with her back to him, and felt her pain. "The Word of God tells us that even if our father and mother abandons us, the Lord will hold us close." He took the river rock from his pocket and rolled it through his fingers. "I am sure of one thing. God has a great plan for your future, and he never changes his mind toward you. Continue to trust him and this trial will work for good in your life and those he sent you to serve. God always has a plan for our healing and restoration."

She was silent. She did not know if she wanted to laugh or cry. "I know that." She turned to face him. "That's not what I asked. I want to know what *you* think."

Beryl smiled. "I think you better start a recovery program. The soldiers need an infusion of faith."

He cleared his throat. "I have a favorite verse from Scripture that may calm your anxiety. Do you want to hear it?"

She smiled. "Do I have a choice?"

Beryl placed his right hand on her forehead. "Don't cheer over my tragedy, my enemy! When I fall, I shall arise; when I sit in darkness, the Lord shall be a light to me" (Micah 7:8).

His words were like a spark that ignited her emotions as a flame lights a fire.

Beryl watched her lift her chin a little higher and detected a slight curve on her lips. "Satan wants you to crumble under this pressure. If defeated thoughts keep you down, you will no longer be a threat to him or his legion."

Alex pushed a wild strand of hair behind her ear. "I will not be bested by the deceiver. I'm resilient and will do more than just survive. It will take more than this to keep me chained." She forced herself into a sitting position.

"Thank you, Beryl, for reminding me to trust God and not my situation. The Word says, 'I am more than a conqueror'" (Romans 8:37). She smiled. "I might not look like a conqueror or feel like a conqueror, but God says I am *more* than a conqueror through Christ who loves me." The scripture verse empowered her. "I am ready to get well and pick up where we left off, right in the middle of the enemy's camp!"

Anat came to check on the patient. "Are you eating the food I sent?" She scanned the room, looking for the plates; in her arms, she carried extra rations. "Beryl," she scolded, "you are allowing her meal to get cold!" She clicked her tongue. "What are you thinking? She needs her strength."

Anat picked up a slice of bread and handed it to Alex, hovering over her like a mother bear. "Don't you worry, my cooking will have you up and around in no time." She took the wooden bowl of soup and handed it to her.

Alex was amazed. *This wonderful woman is treating me as a person with sight.*

"Anat will fix you up."

Beryl looked at the old woman lovingly. Strands of her gray hair fell across her forehead from the braided bun on top of her head. He smiled at her menu. It was as threadbare as the older woman's clothing. Watery soup seasoned with roots, a small slice of flat bread, and goat cheese.

"Food is necessary for someone coming through such an attack," she said.

Alex was starving. She said a quick prayer of thanksgiving then dug in, slurping as much of the hot liquid as she could with the wooden spoon. "This is better than any meal I could have imagined."

Anat sat on the edge of Alex's bed, studying the young girl's face. "Faith is a spiritual force," she said in broken English. "It is a weapon. Use it against the enemy's attack on your mind which will come many times before faith has the final victory."

She took Alex's hand in her own. "I have learned many lessons over the years." She paused, pushing a stray hair from her eye. "We will have many troubles in this life, but God delivers us from them all."

She stood to leave and smothered Beryl with a hug that knocked the air from his lungs. "Simeon and Anat will take good care of God's warriors."

The next morning, with the sun still low on the horizon, the team began their new routine.

Alex had washed and dressed without help.

"Beryl, where is Nyla?" she asked.

Before he could answer, she arrived like a leaf blown in with the wind.

"Your late," Alex said.

Nyla tried to steady her voice. "Sorry. Have some new orders." *What excuse can I give this time?* "Orders from the elders. They expect certain things from me." Her heart pounded in her chest.

Alex heard a tremor in the healer's voice. "You answer to me first from now on. This war for souls is raging all around us. We are a team, remember?"

Nyla put her hands on her hips. "Got it. We are a team," she said sarcastically.

Alex ignored the feeling that something had changed within Nyla. "I feel stronger than before the attack. I can't explain it, but I know we can defeat King Apollyon and his legions." She tried to stand but her legs were weak. Beryl quickly grabbed her arm and helped her to sit back down on the bed.

"I said light exercise! Not get up and leave the room!" Nyla gasped.

The prophet shook his head in disapproval. "I admire your zeal, but you might want to consider a day or two more of rest before we head outdoors."

"No!" She pushed him aside and tried again. This time, Alex made it to her feet before collapsing on the pile of blankets. "I'm telling you, I'm unstoppable."

Beryl considered tethering her legs. "I can see that, definitely unstoppable, but I think you need a little more time." He hoped his words were sinking into her stubborn head.

During the days that followed, Alex regained her physical strength. She found she had new abilities that compensated for her lack of sight. As she recovered, Beryl sent for her weapons. She realized her helmet, sword, and shield were changed. The fire from the dragon had forged a stronger, more durable metal. She felt in her spirit, the more she used her faith, the stronger her weapons would become.

"Beryl, Nyla, come here quickly! I want to show you something." She picked up her sword and flung it around her room, practicing her attack stance. Her long quick strides and accurate thrusts with the blade were fast and sure. A few times, she heard Nyla gasp when her sword tip stopped short of the cavern walls.

Alex laughed. "I can see better with this new inner eye. I'm invincible." She had a sense of victory and purpose.

Finally, her team allowed her to go outside the cave. She felt free, as if she had been buried alive and was now returning to life. There was a gentle breeze and she could hear the leaves moving overhead and the wind dancing around her in the October sunshine. It was beautiful. She had never paid attention before. She felt like she could taste the fresh air, inhale the sunshine, and write a song to the sound of falling leaves.

The soft wind blew strands of hair into her face. She dropped to her knees and rolled in the grass, throwing pine needles over her head. "Everything feels so new. Flowers, pine needles, and grass... I never realized they were so wonderful."

Nyla scanned the camp. "Alex! If someone sees you, they will think you have lost your mind."

Alex jumped to her feet. "It feels good to be alive. I don't care what people think. Let them watch. I'm free!"

Alex took off jogging. She could feel in her spirit where the trees were, where the path turned, where the stream made its way through the forest.

Nyla tried to keep up with Alex's long strides. "How are you feeling so far?"

"If you and Beryl would give me a little breathing room, I'd be great." She shrugged them off and walked ahead of them. "I can feel and hear air pressure, like sound waves. I know where objects are around me." She danced in circles. "I can't believe this. It's amazing!"

Simeon was outside in the garden and joined his new friends. "It's hard to believe she is so sure and steady on her feet." He watched her. "Look at her. She can maneuver easily around the vegetable garden." He stopped and listened. "What is that clicking sound she is making with her tongue?"

"I believe it's something like bats use," Beryl said. "I don't know about you, but she's making me nervous."

Nyla huffed and put a hand on her hip. "You better leave her alone."

She spoke too late. Alex turned and walloped the prophet in his arm. "Back off. I can handle this. I'm not useless. I'm not a defeated blind guide as Aza said."

Alex sat on the ground, too excited to continue. "I need a minute." She felt tears of joy coming and couldn't stop them.

"I'd like a little time to sit and enjoy the remainder of the day," Alex said.

Nyla stood over her friend. "Aren't you tired?"

Alex made a face. "I just spent weeks in the belly of a cave. I need time in the fresh air to clear my head."

"Well." Nyla thought for a moment. "What do you think, Beryl?"

He rubbed his head. "Just until sunset."

She listened to their footfalls trail off into the distance and settled on the ground in a pile of leaves, resting her back against the tree trunk. The world around her pulsed with life.

Her thoughts wandered back to the Chasm. *I have crossed*

a personal gorge in my life. Little pieces of my old self I left behind, broken and shattered yet I feel renewed.

She sighed. *Lord Jesus, use my pain like a tool to chisel and reshape a stronger soldier. I want to come through this trial with faith that is proven.*

She relaxed under the tree silently praising God for her new gift of sight until she felt night setting in. The air was cooling, and the chirping songs of the forest changed and quieted. She could hear a new noise, the clatter of people and children. Alex heard the prophet's sandals slapping the grass.

"Are you ready to turn in?" he asked.

"Why are the people leaving the shelter of the cave?"

"They are preparing to relax in the cool air, taking advantage of the balmy night. It is a nightly ritual while the weather permits. Each tribe sits around campfires, close to the cave entrance, eating and sharing stories about their day."

Alex stood to her feet. "Let's go mingle with the troops."

Beryl led her toward the clearing in front of the cave's hidden entry. She heard men and women talking and children playing and squabbling. The vicinity throbbed with life.

All of the voices made Alex feel like an interloper. For a moment, she considered turning back and hiding out in her room. Instead she steadied herself. "Tell me what you see," she whispered.

Beryl cleared his throat. "We are approaching about thirty soldiers and night watchmen, preparing to take their post."

"Seems like a lot of watchmen? Are they anticipating trouble?" she asked.

"A week or more ago, a soldier was attacked by a morphling, a Soul-Sifter some call them. The half-human ripped off a soldier's arm. They have stationed more guards since the incident."

Alex stiffened. "After what you told me about them, it seems odd that it would not go for the kill."

Nyla ran up behind them. "What are you doing?"

Alex paused. "Visiting." She inhaled. "You're late again."

Nyla huffed. "I had some last-minute things to do. You know...pack supplies for tomorrow."

Alex crossed her arms over her chest. "You smell different. No lavender or jasmine in your hair."

Nyla faked a cough. "I'm trying to fit in."

Alex let it drop. The sound of the people was getting louder.

The guards had their backs turned, forming a solid barrier ahead of them.

Nyla tapped a man on his shoulder. He turned to face the distraction.

"What the—" his eyes widened.

He elbowed a fellow officer. When the others became aware of the warrior's presence, a whisper went through the crowd like the wind.

Beryl and Nyla nodded their heads in greeting. Quiet murmurs returned from everyone they passed. They were met with questioning stares and suspicious eyes.

A girl pulled Nyla aside. "What are you doing with them?" Frances whispered.

Nyla's face flushed. "I am still one of them."

The medic shook her head. "You can't be part of Aza's group and side with the outsiders. Our friends expect our loyalty."

Nyla pushed past her. "Shut up. I haven't cut the ties yet."

Frances huffed and walked away.

Alex could feel the tension building. "What was that all about?"

Nyla feigned ignorance. "She is one of the medics I met while working with the tribe. I'm not sure what she is talking about."

Alex nodded and fell in line with Beryl and walked steadily through the sea of strangers. The site became eerily quiet with only the sound of crackling campfires.

A booming voice broke the stillness. "Beryl, Nyla, over here." Baccus waved his big arm, motioning them to his group. Alex breathed a sigh of relief.

Within minutes, the tribesmen went back to their conversations, planning strategies to release captives taken during this War for Souls. Group members congregated with family and friends, children began their games, and women distributed food among their own people.

Baccus introduced Alex to Tika and many of the elders from the different clans. They sat in the twilight mist, sharing stories of the early erosion.

"It was written by our ancestors, many years ago, that erosion began in the city on the hill. The city we now call E'Doom." Kaspar shifted himself into a more comfortable position, enjoying the attention he was receiving from the strangers.

"They say we began to let the demons inside Old World little by little." The fire crackled and sparks flew beyond the fire ring.

"That's right," Ravenna interrupted from the darkness that descended upon the camp. She shoved past the group of elders and the small clan that spoke to the messengers. By her side were her friends; all seasoned soldiers, agitated and on edge because of the messengers from Safehold.

"I hate her," Nyla whispered to Beryl who sat by her side. "They criticize my heritage." She straightened her spine, sitting up straight as an arrow. "I tried to fit in." She pushed her thick braid over her shoulder. "Instead it made Ravenna and her group more hostile." Nyla elbowed the prophet. "Are you listening?"

He flinched. "Of course I am." He shifted his position and looked at his friend. "Have you been with them when Alex was recovering?" He felt betrayed.

Nyla rolled her eyes. "Of course. I thought I needed to take Alex's place while she is..." She paused. "indisposed, for lack of a better word." She tapped her foot impatiently. "Enough questions. I'm talking about me." She looked around suspiciously. "Aza said she was Sargo's woman, but I can tell she wants Aza's heart."

Beryl was not used to the romantic intrigues of the female world, and he felt uneasy.

Nyla's enemies strutted into the circle as if they owned the place. Ravenna made sure to bump into Nyla, knocking her off balance. Her friends followed, led by Frances, who deliberately pushed her and silently bullied her.

"What's wrong with them?" Beryl asked.

Nyla's face flushed. "Revenna's mad because she's an ugly, jealous, spiteful piece of—"

Beryl squeezed her arm.

She yanked her arm from his and smoothed her shirt. "She *is* ugly," she whispered.

"I don't think she's unattractive," Beryl whispered back. "She's kind of pretty."

Nyla's eyes narrowed. She pinched his arm and puckered her lips into a pout. She stood tall and placed her hand on her hip. "Tell the truth. Next to me, she is a toad."

"Okay, okay." He smiled. "She is not as pretty as you are."

Nyla unbraided her hair and let it fall free.

Beryl stared at the group of soldiers. "Ravenna must be important. It looks like she is one of the first to go into battle, judging by her clothing and the sword strapped on her belt."

Nyla shrugged her shoulders. "Maybe she'll be one of the first to be killed."

Beryl's eyes widened. "Nyla!"

She huffed. "Just a thought."

Ravenna took center stage before the campfire and gained the attention of the tribesmen. "My grandfather used to tell me stories, when I was a child, about the early infestation." She warmed her hands over the fire. "He said when the demons first settled in our land, we fought against them, keeping them away for centuries. With each generation, we strayed farther and farther from the words of wisdom in the Book of Life. The ancient God said, "Come out from among them, and have nothing to do with them or their evil practices."

The sound of crunching footsteps on dry leaves brought another into the circle. "Instead of obeying God, we saw there were good things we could acquire from these beings. They brought with them the ability to mine gold, silver, and many precious stones. They also brought trade with kings and nobles from many lands. They had armies capable of keeping our borders safe. Most of our people decided to trust in their power instead of relying on God to protect us and lead us to victory."

An elder stabbed the dirt with his staff. "Treason!" he muttered.

The youth continued, "Their wealth and power began to increase, and they found favor with those governing Old World. After decades of compromise, King Apollyon became the ruler of the entire world."

Alex listened. She heard a common thread in their testimony. Compromise.

A familiar voice whispered in her memory. *Reverend Mother always said compromise was a silent demon. An evil born when believers let their zeal for truth conform to the world's standards. Once grown, compromise always distorts the Word of God.*

"Over time, we forgot the past and the battles fought against the enemy. We mixed with them, married them, and became comfortable with their way of life, their religion, and their gods. Eventually we began to live and act like them."

Clouds drifted over the moon, and shadows lengthened across the face of the camp. A dark form spoke from inside the gloom. "They became strong and began to despise Christians, especially those who refused to accept their way of life." Aza walked from the darkness and joined his comrades around the firepit. Every tongue quieted at the sound of his voice. "Some of the demons who married our people produced giants, mutations. This breed became the army we now must face and overcome."

A tall warrior, with many tattoos covering his muscled body, spoke up. "These goliaths have stolen our city from us. Our children are leaving the protection of our camps and are embracing these new beliefs. The youth believe this new order has all the answers to life's questions. Besides, even the leaders of the church have aligned themselves with the king."

He looked at the sky and pointed to the star known as the Red Dragon. "An omen of what is to come," he said. "As soon as a church starts to have any glimmer of hope in the Baptism of Fire, the warlords slaughter the converts and frighten any who might think about rebirth. They make us their prisoners unless we decide to conform to their thoughts. Most of us have gone over to their side like the youth of this generation. It's not worth it to fight on the outskirts anymore, too few victories."

An old man spoke from among the elders. "My name is Nickodemus. I was sent into Old World by our Savior, many years ago, to establish truth and fight the good fight. Sargo and Aza rescued me from the jaws of the scavengers because of rebirth." He stood and faced the group. "Would I do it again?" He paused and nodded his head. "Yes! I would risk my life again and again to save our people and our faith from extermination."

The old man's voice shook with passion. "If Apollyon

does not kill us, his reign on this earth will tempt us away from God's truth. He misleads us! He infects us with hatred! He seduces us with his lies! He contaminates us with his impurities and his abominations!" His eyes were ablaze. "We must fight the enemy with the help of the Holy Spirit of God. The Baptism of Fire is the only way."

His words started an uproar within the camp.

"You are a fool, old man! Fighting is now more a matter of principal." A warrior spoke out in a loud aggressive voice. "Most of us fight for revenge, not because of some religious purpose. God is not here to avenge our murdered loved ones. No one cares that our homeland is overrun with profiteers. Where is God when the enemy plunders our homes and stalks us at night, taking us prisoner?"

Wolves howled in the distance. Children ran to their parents and hid beneath their robes.

The conversation continued, and the tribe was oblivious to the spirit realm that surrounded them. Asmodeus materialized in the forest, like mist over water. She hid outside the torch line of the camp and strolled among the growling wolves, listening to the chatter of the clan.

She felt a demonic presence. "Come down from the tree, Shadim. You can't hide from our master. I heard from the spirits of the air that you have been demoted. No more, General Shadim. You failed him, and he will find you."

He jumped from the branch. "If it hadn't been for the boy with the staff, the Soul-Sifters would have killed the soldiers and left their remains as evidence of our supremacy."

Asmodeus scanned the compound for a means of entry. "Nonetheless, your failure to stop this invasion of faith began at St. Regents. You are to blame."

Her inhuman eyes were cold and hard, turning Shadim's soul to ice. "Yes, that is true," he stammered, "but it was you who failed to stop them from crossing the Chasm. They are in Old World now because of you. It was a total failure when the dragon couldn't stop their little show of faith. I heard from the spirits of the air the warrior is blind, but it has made her faith stronger, a greater threat to our master. To make matters worse, your sister, Aether, botched your chance to annihilate the small army crossing the flatlands. King Apollyon will not be pleased with your service. You will need to do something extraordinary to regain his trust."

With her mind, she lifted Shadim into the air and threw him into a tree. "Shut up and watch. I have a better plan to rid Old World of the infidels."

She exhaled a vapor into the air, giving birth to an embryo. Like a newborn baby, the germ nestled in her arms. "Envy," she cooed. Asmodeus held the seed gently against her body and gave the deadly sin her orders. "Go into the camp and lodge within a willing host." The seed squirmed with anticipation. "You are invisible to the human eye and can easily infiltrate the group. Find an insider, a member of the clan with influence, make them stir up trouble and keep everyone agitated and angry." She smiled. "Evil has taught me a valuable lesson. No man can withstand the wrath of jealousy."

Asmodeus held the seed close to her lips and blew it into the air. It floated, undetected, on the gentle breeze and into the camp. The wicked germ tested one individual after another, probing the condition of the human heart. Finally it found the perfect home within one who had been playing with the occult. The girl opened a door into the demonic realm. The insidious vapor embedded itself within the flesh of its victim. Ravenna swatted what felt like a mosquito from her neck. The welt itched and she scratched the wound until it bled.

Asmodeus smiled at her victory. "You see, Shadim, in time, the seed will grow and ripen while its host leaves a legacy of confusion and every evil work."

She rubbed her hands together. "Listen. She is already

stirring up strife.

Ravenna ranted, drowning the other voices. "We are tired of watching our lives go on, year after year, in unrest because we are holding on to some old laws we don't agree with anymore." She picked up a stick and stoked the fire. The flames jumped and sputtered, illuminating the girl's features. Her cold hard eyes locked on Nyla. She assessed the healer with a look of hatred, malice, and resentment.

"God's own churches are full of corruption. No one really lives up to these Ten Commandments your kind preach."

A few prepared to fight. "Heresy! You speak blasphemy."

Aza took the position of mediator, hoping to stop a brawl. "We are grateful that you came with healing ointments and the powerful staff of light that did save us from death. However, we cannot rely on small victories anymore. We know when we are defeated." His voice became hard, and he looked away from the three ambassadors. "We are tired of waiting for old legends to be fulfilled."

Sargo burst through the group, pushing some aside. "Belief in the Gospel of Christ gets us killed! King Apollyon's army flays our skin from our bones and throws us into his prison. They toss us into the arena with killers who rip our bodies to shreds. The world laughs at the Book of Life." He stabbed the ground with his sword. "The Baptism of Fire only brings more trouble upon us."

Alex walked forward. The light from the fire made her armor glisten. "We are not ashamed of the Gospel of Jesus Christ."

She raised her voice, wanting the entire tribe to hear. "We were sent into this war zone with a message of hope. The Messiah *will* return. Before he comes back, there will be trouble and temptations we must face and overcome so we don't fall away from the faith. He gave us instructions in the Book of Life on how to live and how to fight as we await his return."

Many clans stood with the messengers, mumbling their agreement.

"Stories!" Ravenna growled, throwing a stick into the fire, sending sparks flying. "Stories no one believes anymore. We are tired of waiting. There is new power, occult power, that is stronger than the Baptism of Fire."

An elder scoffed. "You are deceived! Satan comes to kill, steal, and destroy. Look how he has turned us against each other."

"It's time to break this up!" Aza ordered, frustrated with the tension the messengers brought into the camp.

"You don't understand," Alex said. "The Baptism of Fire will help you fight the enemy and win."

The soldiers turned their backs on the messengers and went back to their duties. They set a new guard over the perimeter of the camp. The moon shifted in and out of cloud cover, playing a game with shadow and light. The Red Dragon pulsed, like a beating heart in the heavens. The countryside seemed hypnotized under the eerie glow. The surrounding area fell into a peaceful and quiet sleep.

Asmodeus was relieved her seed took root and was creating trouble. "Look, Shadim." She motioned heavenward. "My sister in the heavens is riding the Red Dragon. The two glow feverously in the night sky, signaling success." She paused and tapped her foot nervously. "To be certain of success, I will call upon the horde to coagulate my triumph. I will not fail my master again."

She began to chant and whine, conjuring creatures from the dust of the ground. A multitude of spirits, born of unbelief, answered her from beneath the earth. They clawed, dug, and crawled out of the soil, anxious to do her bidding. Vicious creatures erupted from the dust. The wolves howled and whimpered in fear as they hid behind Asmodeus.

"Infect the believers with unbelief," she ordered. "Suck

the life-giving words of faith from their minds and replace it with doubt. Let them bite each other like snakes, with venomous lies, that kill and destroy the knowledge of God."

She smiled. "Go now!"

CHAPTER 24

Not Ashamed

The horde crept undetected toward the encampment. The scent of new converts aroused and excited them. Shadim applauded her.

His praise fed her excitement. "These demons can smell a fledgling believer. They know the one who will try conversion for a time but will turn from the truth at the least sign of trouble. It can sniff out those weaklings who will allow their own pleasure on earth to rule over their heart."

She strutted around the glade, lost in thought. "I need this small army dismembered, scattered, and weakened before the Word of Life spreads and takes root. The insignificant three have become too much of an opponent for Apollyon's legions. Their beliefs could catch on. An army could rise and ruin my lord's kingdom."

She stopped pacing and looked Shadim in the eyes. "If they want the supernatural, we will give them King Apollyon's magic. We will infest Old World with black occult magic, and when we are finished with this deceit, the master's harvest will be ripe with lost souls." She rubbed her chin. "Come, Shadim. Let us watch the destruction that is to come."

"Wait!" Alex called to the tribesmen who were leaving the campfires.

"I thought I came from Safehold ready for battle." She swallowed her pride. "I came with a gift that needed to be tried and proven. I have come to realize that through my trial, I am stronger. We need to use and exercise our gifts to win these battles." She walked through the crowd, showing them she was able to function without physical sight. "We need to believe we can win despite our circumstances."

Alex understood their doubt. "I just spent days fighting thoughts of abandonment by the God I love and serve". She could feel the clan looking at her with dull unbelieving eyes.

"I have a different sight now, a spiritual sight. Fear will destroy what God has anointed us to accomplish."

Sargo stood with Ravenna. "These losers are good for a laugh!" They heckled them, instigating others to follow their lead.

Alex spoke over the insults. "I know the feeling of being abandoned. I thought I had failed and would never triumph again." She spoke directly to the warriors who tried to ignore her. "We all go through trials and suffering. It's part of life. We must stand strong and steady in faith and not let Apollyon or his minions intimidate us. This will be a sure sign, to him and his army, of their defeat."

She walked over to her friends. "You all know Anat and Simeon." She draped her arm over their shoulders. "They lost their home and countrymen yet still stand strong in faith." She walked through the circle, pointing out others. "Baccus lost his wife and Tika her mother. Nickodemus lost his congregation. Some of you have lost loved ones to the teachings of this new aeon. We have all lost something. Yet we are here together for a reason. We are part of a growing army of warriors, ready to take back the land Apollyon and his armies have stolen."

Ravenna laughed. "You are too late. Many of us want no part of religion. We have found a new god. One who has been overlooked for centuries. A god who indulges our desires, dreams, and fantasies." She spit into the fire. "We will destroy Christianity and implement something better. Something more appealing to those with a higher intellect so we can lead others down the path of enlightenment."

Alex felt gooseflesh cover her arms.

Ravenna loved the attention. "More and more clan members are interested in the occult. They come to me to tell them their future. I conduct séances in the woods and call forth the spirits of the dead." She stood inches from Alex, directing her words at the warrior. "My following is growing."

Alex felt a spirit of foreboding envelope her mind.

Ravenna chanted mystical words. She called out names of deities Alex had not heard of in St. Regents.

"The god of this new Aeon is so powerful, few can withstand the spiritual pull of self-worship and the lure of immortality under a master who sets forth no rules to bind us."

Beryl leaned in and whispered in Alex's ear. "She wants to distract those listening to this message of faith in God."

"I am not afraid of her misuse of power," Alex answered.

Sargo stormed past the laughing onlookers. "Why should we believe God? So we can end up defeated like you?" he seethed. "I want to see victory."

The crowd cheered their agreement.

"How long do we have to wait to see results from this God of yours?" Ravenna said.

"We are tired of old clichés and unanswered prayer. We want more. We want what the demons offer." The girl's voice was husky and resonated with a disturbing purpose. Her black deep-set eyes sparkled with an unholy radiance.

Alex stepped forward. "The freedom you seek is found in the words within this book. It is time to repent and take back the territory lost to the devil."

Sargo shook from rage, clenching his fists. Aza stood beside him and tried to usher him away before a battle broke out. "Let's go, she is not worth the trouble of an aching fist."

Beryl placed himself directly between Alex and Sargo.

"What she says is the truth. All of you have been doing things your way and have gotten nowhere with the enemy." His white skin glistened in the firelight. "This war you are fighting can only be won if you believe and obey the instructions God gave us."

The entire crowd burst into laughter. "The prophet's words are big for a freak."

Aza clasped Sargo around his shoulder. "Back off, brother," he warned. "We can't afford to alienate our own men. Stay put. I'll take care of this."

Aza confronted Alex. "You better weigh your words or you will lose the little bit of respect they have for you and your partners." He watched Alex stand taller.

"We'll see about that," she said.

He bristled. "You may be too late to pull some of them back to the faith. It's been a long time since they have had success."

Aza scowled at Nyla and stormed away with his fellow officers, whispering and laughing.

Nyla grabbed Alex's arm and spun her around to face her. "What do you think you're doing? We are supposed to win them over, not push them further away from the truth." She folded her arms across her chest. "I know what you're saying is true, but they are not ready to accept this fact yet." She stomped her foot like a child. "The leader of the soldiers has walked away with the mockers. We needed him as our ally to pull this army together."

Alex smirked. "If they are going to be ready to fight, they need to grow up spiritually." She pushed past her friends and sat before a firepit. "We were sent to get them ready to fight this war."

The light from the glowing embers reflected concern in her blue eyes.

Beryl rolled the river stone through his fingers. "Many

in the crowd believe what you said, Alex. The Holy Spirit is moving within the tribe." He looked around. "A few are standing with Ravenna and the soldiers, but most of the clans want to hear more from the Book of Life."

Nyla looked away. She felt her face flush. Guilt churned in her gut as she thought about all her lying and sneaking around with the soldiers. She had dabbled in magic along with them and felt that it was already a part of who she had become. She looked up and saw Aza staring at her with a look of disgust on his face.

This can't be happening. Her mind raced. *I'm just starting to get close to Aza. There is no way I'm going to lose him now. I no longer care about this stupid mission. It's a lost cause anyway. I'm happier with my new life. I need to regain his trust and confidence.*

Beryl interrupted the moment. "Music has a way of bringing peace to bad situations." He gathered his small following of elders, musicians, and new converts that he taught daily. He hummed a playful melody while they set up their instruments.

"Nyla," Beryl said. "Why don't you get a tambourine from your backpack and join us?" He remembered how much the villagers enjoyed her singing and dancing. Alex followed along and picked up a lute, a type of guitar, form the instruments the musicians were using.

Why now? Nyla thought. *Wait. Maybe Aza will soften his attitude toward me if I distract him with a dance.*

As the band keyed up and rhythm began pulsing through the air, Nyla started to dance as the musicians played. She seemed able to float on the music as she beat her tambourine to the tune. She hoped she could bring Aza back to watch her perform. She was confident in her beauty and enjoyed how some of the boys looked at her and admired her. She surprised herself when she realized how much she wanted Aza's attention. His beautiful gray eyes were always on her and made her feel excited.

She played her tambourine, swayed, and twirled freely to the music. The young girls who watched tried to emulate her graceful movements. She grabbed Tika from the crowd and a few of her friends and brought them into the center of the circle, coaxing them to dance with her as the group began to sing.

> Stand strong
> Stand firm
> Stand up and proclaim
> Salvation is found in no other gods' name
> Stand strong
> Stand firm
> Stand up and proclaim
> We carry the Gospel in our frail human frame
> The enemy surrounds us we're pressed in on all sides
> Fear won't stop us we have Christ on our side
> We are scorned and rejected, pursued and condemned
> Yet Jesus the Savior fights for us to the end
> I'm not ashamed
> I'm not afraid
> The power in my life
> Comes from his name
> The enemy deceives with temptation and lies
> Doubt won't defeat us we have Christ on our side
> We were bound in fetters and held tight in sins chains
> Yet our Savior released us from Satan's domain
> I'm not ashamed
> I'm not afraid
> The power in my life
> Comes from his name
> We carry the Gospel in our frail human frame
> (Song based on 2 Corinthians 4:8).

Beryl's voice, accompanied by the instruments, was fun and catchy. Nyla and Alex mixed with the teens, dancing and singing, as they continued to praise.

The music was contagious and brought Aza back to watch and listen.

The group clapped and danced. Despite their torment by the enemy, many of the young tribesmen were beginning to enjoy the three that came into their dismal world. The music was powerful. It gave them hope and a purpose.

Aza watched. *I want to believe things can change.*

The blanket of night covered the glade, hiding everything outside the torch line of the camp. The horde that came to dismember them cringed at the sound of the sacred music. They tried to escape the ambush. The music was a ferocious weapon they were powerless to fight.

Aza heard a commotion in the forest and looked in the direction of the noise. He thought he saw a demon, his heart jumped, then nothing. He strained his eyes, trying to focus into the black mass of trees, but the light from the moon played tricks on the forest floor. The singing became louder, and he looked back at the camp; all was well. He gave the perimeter one last look, his body pumping with adrenaline, and saw nothing. He settled back into his unbelief and retreated into the cave.

He failed to see the horde that lay dead on the forest floor. The song of praise to God had brought them down with no one, but Asmodeus, the wiser.

"No!" she screamed. "How dare they sing in homage to God?"

Shadim climbed back into the tree. *Another failure.*

Asmodeus paced the forest floor. "I must find a way to stop these agents of truth," she chanted in desperation.

Send into the forest, O great sister earth,
the slithering and crawling creatures of the dust
to devour the remains of the walking dead.

The last thing I want is the remnant of believers to find the carcasses and become aware of this powerful weapon called praise. She ran into a clearing, fearing her king's wrath over this new failure. Her form exploded into vapor that rose into the sky to confer with her sister and the Red Dragon.

When the music ended, all memory of harsh words forgotten, the group prepared for bed and a new day. For tonight, they would sleep peacefully; a spark burning in their stony hearts warmed them from the cold and dangers of their world.

CHAPTER 25

Fellowship

Beryl rose early the following morning. He loved to watch the sunrise break through the darkness. Taking his backpack with the Book of Life, he sat quietly under a large oak in the cool morning air. He inhaled, savoring the scent of wet campfires from the previous night. He settled into his front-row seat and watched the sun paint the inky sky with wide strokes of pink, orange, and purple until the clear light of day erased all traces of night.

From the thicket, a deer crunched through fallen leaves in the high grass, stopping now and then to look in his direction. Squirrels hopped across the glade, gathering nuts. Birds began their morning songs. He yawned and stretched his long limbs as he got to his feet and followed the sound of trickling water. *Ah yes. Fresh clean water for a bath.*

He hung his robe and lion skin on a tree branch, kicked off his sandals, and stooped at the edge of the stream. He splashed the cold water on his chest, under his arms, and washed the sleep from his eyes. He gazed at his reflection in the water and stroked his chin. *I think I feel a little stubble.*

He turned his attention inward and prayed to his Heavenly Father. "I feel spiritually refreshed after the night's success," he spoke aloud. "Thank you, Abba, for this victory. Many in the tribe are anxious to hear more about salvation, and some are ready to rededicate their lives." He slipped the robe over his head and continued his conversation with God. "A few of the elders are instrumental in overseeing the afternoon classes. Nickodemus offered to be my mentor. Things could not be going better in that respect."

The prophet tied the leather belt around his waist and sat down to fasten his sandals. "However, there is one problem." He sighed while repositioning himself under the tree. "The soldiers are leery of Alex's ability to lead in battle. They need proof she is physically capable. For the time being, they are unable to understand they need to use your weapons, not their own might, to defeat Apollyon and his legions. They have set up a sparring match for her. Please help her succeed so we can show them your plan."

He turned and looked at the sound of footsteps and watched Alex walk toward him. "How did you know I was sitting here?" he asked.

"I could smell your breath," she said, plopping down next to him. Her mood turned thoughtful. "I heard you talking to God."

Sunlight spilled through the trees, promising a beautiful day. A ray of light rested on Alex's face. Beryl thought she looked radiant. "What made you come through this trial so quickly?" Even after last night, he was unsure of her state of mind.

"I decided not to wallow in self-pity," she said simply. "One of my teachers said you can't be pitiful and powerful at the same time." She twirled an autumn leaf in her hand. "We need to be firmly rooted in faith when hardship comes. You can be sure trouble of some kind will find every one of us. Yet the Book of Life says, after we have suffered a little while, God will make us what we need to be."

"I can't argue with that," he said.

Nyla walked toward them from the opposite direction. She looked disheveled and sleepy.

"Where were you?" Beryl asked.

She wiped her tunic sleeve over her lips, hoping the rouge had not smeared when she and Aza kissed. "I was in the forest, meditating. I needed time to focus on our mission," she lied.

Alex stiffened. "Has everyone lost their minds? There are creatures in those woods capable of mutilating you."

Nyla looked at her defiantly. "Who are you, my mother?"

Alex folded her arms over her chest. "What's different about you?" she asked. "Besides your attitude. I don't hear your bracelets jingling or smell the jasmine in your clothing."

"Oh that…" she said. "I already told you they weren't practical. Some of my friends did not understand my heritage. I decided it was better to fit in. Besides I like these clothes much better." She looked down at herself and wiped dirt and leaves from her tight trousers and skimpy shirt.

Alex stood. "What do you think of her new look, Beryl?"

He faked a cough. "Well, she looks like she is from Old World," he said honestly.

Alex ran her hands through her hair, praying for the right words. "I'm not your mother, but I am the leader of our team. A change of clothing doesn't bother me but a step into the ways of the world can lead to rebellion." She paused and listened to Nyla's body language. She could hear the girl fidgeting with her clothing.

Nyla snickered. "You're right. My clothing doesn't mean anything. My loyalty to this mission is the same as when I left Safehold. Believe me. I'm totally committed to the cause."

The tone of Nyla's voice left little doubt she was being defensive. Alex changed the subject. "After the morning meal, we are going to the paddock to see Malak and meet with the soldiers. I'm told they want to spar with me to be sure I can lead the army into E'Doom. It's time for me to take over. Are you still coming?"

"Yes. Of course I am. I will meet you back here after I eat," Nyla said.

Alex listened to her rush away toward the cave entry before beginning some stretching exercises. "What's going on with her?"

Beryl shrugged. "I don't know. She spends a lot of time with the soldiers and has been moody."

Alex felt heat rise to her cheeks. "She probably thought she needed to take my place. Now that I'm up and around, I will reclaim that position and she can once more visit the sick." Alex took a deep breath. "I'll see if I can talk to her later when we're alone."

Beryl rolled the river stone through his fingers. He decided to keep quiet about the rumors of her infatuation with Aza for the time being. He hoped that once Alex got involved, the healer would stop her foolishness.

"Maybe she is missing her home and family. This place has a way of getting to you," Beryl said.

Alex jumped into a plank position and began doing push-ups. "Don't let me find out your covering for her."

Beryl's cheeks reddened. *Can she read minds too?* He put his things away. "I'm going to root around for some protein."

"Knock yourself out but please do it somewhere else. Just imagining the protein you eat makes me sick."

Alex picked up some food from Anat and ate leftover bread, goat cheese, and seeds on their way to the paddock.

Nyla pulled Beryl aside. "Are you sure she is going to be ready for this?"

He shrugged his shoulders. "She has to try sooner or later."

They hurried to keep up with Alex's long strides.

Beryl broke the silence. "I brought a cane along to help you find your way around," he said. "Not that I think you need it but just in case you feel a little unsteady since this side of the compound is new to you."

Alex stopped abruptly. "Get out of my way, prophet! How often do I have to explain this to you?" Beryl plowed into her. "I don't need help!" Alex's words were sharper than she meant them to be.

She pushed the prophet away and took off jogging. "I love the scent of grass and horses," she yelled over her shoulder.

Nyla placed her hand on Beryl's arm. "Just let her go. If she fails, it's her own fault."

As soon as Malak heard his master approaching, he began to whinny and prance around the paddock. Alex sprinted toward the gate when she heard her faithful friend. Without any hesitation, she placed her hands on the top railing and jumped the fence in one easy motion.

"And you worried about her walking to the paddock," Nyla said sarcastically.

Beryl threw the cane in the bushes.

Alex ran her hands over the horse's body. She could feel his new scars where the rats had taken chunks out of his hide. She examined his right flank with gentle hands and felt pieces of bone that were jagged, uneven, and bumpy. "Do you think his injuries are healing properly?"

Nyla looked over the fence. "He will have scars, but it shouldn't hinder his ability as a warhorse."

Alex stroked his rough muzzle and kissed his nose. "We're better for the wear and tear, aren't we, Malak," she whispered. "These few wounds are our medals of honor in the service of our King. Just watch what we can do now."

She carefully held a lock of his thick mane in her hand and mounted him. His muscled body quivered slightly and he pranced sideways. She relaxed her weight until she felt comfortable without the saddle. She clicked her tongue, and he walked forward. She envisioned her lower body becoming one with her horse. The mental image helped her create a natural sense of balance.

She breathed deeply, relaxing, and felt his muscles stretching and contracting as he moved. She focused on the sound of each hoof as it hit the ground. Placing her hands gently on either side of his neck, she cued him into figure eights and circles around the paddock.

"How about a saddle and your bridle, don't you think you might need…" Nyla's words trailed away as she watched Alex take the horse into an easy trot.

"A great warhorse is controlled with limited use of the reins," Alex said. Her hands rested lightly on his neck. With gentle pressure from her fingers and thigh, she pushed right and he turned obediently to the left. She kept her body erect and perfectly balanced over his back, and mentally, she was calm and focused. Malak sensed her confidence and eased into his paces. She used her legs and weight to guide him.

She worked out a command, making clicking sounds with her tongue, letting the horse know she wanted him to jump a hurdle. He would need to trust her new instincts. She took him into an easy canter. They approached the fence. Alex compacted her body to absorb the charge of takeoff and clicked her tongue.

Malak easily cleared the fence and galloped into the surrounding forest. Nyla and Beryl watched in awe.

"Where do you think they went?" Beryl questioned. "What if she falls off?" He wiped sweat from his brow.

"She will be fine. You worry too much. Besides aren't you the one with faith in her new abilities?" Nyla snapped. "We can't both doubt her new skills." She cupped her hands over her eyes and scanned the perimeter of trees but saw no sign of them.

They waited. Nyla began picking herbs, nuts, and berries

to pass the time. Beryl dug around rotted logs, selecting protein. When they didn't return by noon, he practiced rolling his stone for what seemed like an eternity.

He stomped across the meadow toward the healer. "She has been gone too long."

Nyla shook her head. "I will get Aza and have him ride out with me to find her."

Beryl grabbed her arm. "Wait! I see them."

Her voice shook. "I thought the enemy captured her."

Beryl grinned. "She looks confident and ready for action." He lifted Nyla off her feet and spun around with the girl in his arms. "We're back in the race."

Alex galloped the stallion back to the paddock. Her cheeks were bright red from the cold and her eyes danced with excitement.

"I can hear the echoes from the trees and mountain boulders as we near them and I can judge the distance accurately." She felt empowered. She slid off his back and the old stallion nuzzled her playfully, following her across the paddock.

She found his brush and began to groom him. "He seems fine." She patted his large neck. "But I don't want to push him too hard right away." He nudged her with his nose.

"I think he's trying to tell you he's ready to get back into the battle," Beryl said. "He has your personality."

Malak's black coat glistened in the sunshine. He shook his great head and his mane fell like a waterfall over his neck.

Baccus and Tika joined them. "You both look like warriors ready for battle," Baccus said. "You would never know you are…" His words trailed away.

"It's all right to say it. I'm blind." She put her hand on his broad shoulder.

He looked away. "Forgive me. I was not thinking."

Alex shrugged. "My disability does not define me. I am a child of God, an heir of the kingdom and set apart for good works as we all are. I'm focused on the job set before us to rid Old World of Apollyon's evil."

Baccus clasped her shoulder. "You give us hope, young defender. I am ready to march as soon as you give the order."

Tika took a carrot from her tunic and offered Malak the treat. He took it gently. His soft nose tickled her palm. "We were not sure what special needs he required, so we treated him like one of our own horses."

Alex lifted his foot and ran her fingers over the V-shaped groove under his hoof. "He was specially bred to serve in this harsh terrain under dire conditions. He does not require anything special. You've done a good job." Alex smiled. "He seems comfortable and protected here." Her stomach lurched when she thought of the rats and the dragon that had attacked them.

"Don't worry," Baccus said, noticing the look of fear that crossed her face. "The other horses we use are corralled at the foot of the mountain under a heavy guard. Malak will stay here until you are ready to lead the soldiers into battle. Someone may be tempted to steal such an animal as this. He would make an excellent gift to King Apollyon. The thief would be heavily rewarded."

Alex finished his grooming. "I'd like to stay longer but I better go and show the soldiers I can still fight. Beryl tells me the men want to see how gifted I am without sight. I'm anxious to show off a little."

Alex and her team walked across the training yard toward the colorful mass of trees that edged the forest. Groups of soldiers stopped their drills and followed.

"Aza told me to take you into the forest," Nyla said. "Are you sure you're ready for this? I'm certain they have something difficult planned."

"I'm ready."

Nyla glanced at Beryl but could not see his face buried

within the folds of his large hood.

"The soldiers are setting you up. They want to defeat you," Nyla confided. "I heard them say they wanted to see how you will react in battle." She knew more but did not want to double-cross Aza or her new friends.

Nyla stopped when they reached a narrow game trail. "Aza told me to leave you here."

Beryl protested. "I'm not leaving her anywhere." He gazed at the jumble of trees and vines that snaked their way across the path. He knew even a sighted person would have a difficult time maneuvering through the underbrush.

"Quiet!" Alex commanded. She listened. Birds took flight at the sound of their approach, rustling the treetops. She motioned to her team and the group of spectators to follow.

Nyla gasped. "I warned her. Why can't she ever listen?"

Alex picked up a long stick and gently tapped the leafy ground cover and proceeded into the forest. Small animals scattered. Winged lizards jumped from tree to tree in the high branches, causing leaves to rain down on them.

The path was narrow and vines crisscrossed the trail. She smelled pine needles mixed with a stench she could not identify. She sniffed the air. The hair on her neck prickled. The scent was faint yet distinct. A rustling sound caught her attention. She lifted her hand in warning. A vine caught hold of her ankle and began to climb her boot. Her adrenaline pumped. Another vine, thicker than the first, raced around her thigh, knocking her to the ground. She severed it with her sword. The crowd around her laughed.

Nyla screamed, "What is that?"

Alex jumped to her feet. "Watch these." She pointed to the thistle vines that littered the ground and wound their way around the trees. "Our friends here are well aware of these natural traps. Keep your weapons ready. This stuff has thorns like fangs. If bitten by one of these carnivorous plants, you will experience an oozing sore."

They walked on, taking care not to disturb the vines. The path was thick with saplings, fallen logs, and blankets of fallen leaves. As they walked into the belly of pines, the forest got darker.

"Watch your step," Beryl whispered over his shoulder to Nyla.

The path began to open into a clearing. A hush fell over the forest as if every creature was holding its breath. Alex held up her hand. She motioned for the group to wait. She dropped the stick she carried and slunk, like a predator, into the sunlight.

"Watch me get her with this one," Sargo whispered to Frances, stationed in the huge tree that hid them.

Like a lion, Alex crept through the glade, amused that she could hear them whispering and could sense exactly where they were hiding.

Sargo pushed his sandbag from the tree top. The weight and momentum of the sack tied with rope to the tree branch careened toward her. Alex hit the moving target, severing the rope with her sword. It crashed to the ground and set off a hidden trap. The sapling sprung upward, the empty rope thrashed around like a whip. The force was enough to pull its intended prisoner by a dangling foot into the treetops. This trap remained empty.

Another bag followed the first, coming at her from behind. She spun around and hit it with uncanny accuracy, surprising herself. The third bag whirled toward her. When it got close, she lunged forward and jumped on top of it and rode it as it swung back and forth in the clearing. The soldiers who followed laughed and cheered her on.

She dismounted her sandbag swing and followed her senses. She crossed the glade and ran deeper into the woods. Her soft boots crunched lightly atop dry autumn leaves. Her new friends scurried behind.

The soldiers prepared their final ambush. Ravenna was to give the cue so all five bags would be let go at the same time. Everyone was in position.

Alex jogged down the wide path into a grove of sycamores. "I wonder how they are going to surprise me this time," she whispered to Beryl. "I hope it's more of a challenge."

Ravenna waved her hand and the team let the targets fly. She was caught off guard by a snake coiled around a branch in the old tree. In her surprise, her foot slipped forcing her to lose her balance. She had no choice but to hang onto the sack as it flew from the tree. Ravenna screamed while the sandbag she was riding spun out of control under her additional weight.

Alex braced her body. She swung at the targets that sped toward her, turning right, left, forward, and backward, deliberately missing Ravenna's body.

Alex's sword impaled Ravenna's bag, allowing the sand to flow to the ground. Her timing was perfect. She never missed a beat and hit all the other targets as well. Her adversaries cheered.

Her attackers climbed down from their positions. Nyla, Beryl, and all the soldiers who followed ran forward to congratulate her.

"I have to admit, I didn't believe in you or your gifts at first," a young recruit admitted. "Coming from Safehold, we expected something else, a team more warlike. All of you are a bit weak." He tried to soften his words. "I hope you're not offended. I mean, we have waited a long time…never mind, you can fight by my side anytime." The soldier laughed and clasped Alex's shoulder.

Ravenna stomped forward. "She's an idiot! She could have impaled me with her sword."

Alex heard some of the soldiers laugh.

Ravenna muscled through her teammates and stood in

front of Alex. "Were you trying to kill me?"

Alex smiled. "If I wanted to kill you, we wouldn't be having this conversation. Admit it. Not bad for a blind woman."

Ravenna's band of followers cheered.

"Following these misfits will get you all killed," Sargo yelled before following Ravenna into the forest.

Alex shook some hands.

Aza had stayed in the background, watching. When the games were over, he joined the group. "You are far better than I expected," he said. "We still have to win the confidence of a few who doubt your ability, but after what I saw, I don't think you will have any trouble." He shook her hand. "When we go back to the training field, I will have you spar with a few of my best swordsmen."

One of the soldiers interrupted, "I guess we made a real mess out here, trying to outsmart you."

She laughed. "I'll stay behind and help disassemble the traps."

Nyla agreed, "I'll help too."

Beryl threw his arm over Alex's shoulders. "You are amazing. Almost as amazing as I am." He laughed. "Sorry I can't stay to help, but I have some business to attend to back at the camp."

Alex shrugged her shoulders. "Whatever that means."

The group went to work, cleaning up the debris from the afternoon's test. Shadows lengthened as the sun made its downward slide. Aza shivered and realized that the air was turning cool as the sun dropped and clouds moved in. "We should head back. The path will be dangerous in the dark." He gazed into the forest. "We are still not sure where the Soul-Sifter is hiding."

Alex felt edgy. This forest was more alive than any she had ever encountered in Safehold. The sounds of the approaching night made her skin crawl. Everyone in the group stayed together in a tight line as they maneuvered their way through the trees and back to camp.

When they reached the clearing that led to the cave, they heard laughter and cheers.

"What do you think that's all about?" Alex asked. She wiped her wet forehead on her sleeve, glad to be clear of the towering trees and vines.

The sound of the laughter was contagious. "I'm afraid to imagine. We haven't heard this kind of fun since we arrived," Nyla said.

"Chug, chug, chug, chug," voices yelled in unison.

When they reached the clearing, they saw the training yard had become a sports arena. Beryl was the center of attention, surrounded by a dozen young soldiers, cheering him on. They watched in idle fascination as he swallowed slimy slugs and worms effortlessly.

He entertained the troops by allowing parts of the half-eaten creatures to hang precariously out of his mouth. Sometimes he would chew with his mouth open, loving the response he received. The girls in the crowd screamed and ran, covering their eyes. Tika clung to a friend who gagged and choked in disgust.

"Okay. Who is next? Who wants to sample some of these beauties?" Beryl held up a four-inch cockroach. The creature hissed and wiggled its tiny legs. "They taste and crunch just like a bird's egg. When you bite into one, it explodes with a creamy texture." He smiled. Black fragments discolored his teeth.

Before the contest, he collected a plethora of mealworms and night crawlers from a nearby pond and placed them in a basket, along with some crunchy beetles. There were so many larvae they seemed to be pulsating and writhing as one giant beast.

"I'll do it, prophet. What's the big deal?" A handsome youth pushed up front and the crowd cheered. "I can eat twice as many as you." He flexed his muscles. The crowd roared. They wanted to see more. Children were coming from the cover of the bushes to watch the entertainment. Some of the older teens were placing bets on who they thought might win this competition.

"Beryl, just what do you think you're doing?" Nyla snapped.

He looked up in surprise, his cheeks burning red with embarrassment that he was caught gambling.

"Hey, who is in charge of the wager?" Alex demanded in a harsh voice. "My money is on the prophet." She took coins out of her tunic and handed it to the young girl taking bets.

Beryl looked up at her and grinned. Aza quickly followed her lead, betting on Ogden, the youth from his clan.

Nyla chided Alex. "I can't believe you're going along with this."

Beryl ignored her and handed his opponent the hissing beetle.

"This thing is strong," Ogden said as he struggled to keep the bug from jumping out of his hands. "Its legs are all bristly, and they pinch."

"We're all waiting," Beryl said. He shook the basket of chattering insects. "There are plenty left. Time is wasting."

Ogden took the first lightning-fast bite. The crowd of girls screamed, and the boys cheered.

"Right now, he feels like he is tearing into a juicy overripe fig," Beryl explained, speaking from his own experience. "His second bite will shoot the creature's insides out of the hard outer shell. It will feel like thick egg yolk." He licked his lips and winked at Tika.

A few of the spectators ran to throw up in the bushes.

Beryl got close to the boy and listened. "At this point,

there should be no movement in Ogden's mouth at all. The chattering wiggling arthropod should be quite dead."

Ogden nodded his head, confirming Beryl's explicit explanation.

"The most difficult part will be grinding down the exoskeleton into a gritty glue, ready for swallowing." He overemphasized his words.

The group watched, in horrified fascination, as Ogden chewed and crunched and chewed some more. For effect, he opened his mouth so the audience could see he was really eating the entire bug.

The group screamed and cheered.

Ogden made a huge show of swallowing by making loud gulping sounds. Like Beryl, he was enjoying the response he was getting from the onlookers. When he finished, he smiled, showing tiny prickly particles stuck between his teeth.

Beryl handed him a flask of water to wash the remainder of the creature down. "Hand me some of those mealworms," Ogden demanded once he caught his breath. "The beetle wasn't so bad."

The group was in a frenzy, watching the nauseating antics. Beryl filled two earthen bowls with worms. He handed one to Ogden and took one himself. "The first to finish their entire portion, without puking, is the winner."

The boys were in a large circle of spectators. They waited for the signal. The plump little mealworms wiggled around inside the bowls.

"Go!"

Beryl put the vessel to his lips. He chugged them down.

Ogden picked them up, one or two at a time, and swallowed without chewing. When he saw how Beryl downed his, he began pushing them into his mouth by the handful. The crowd cheered.

"Chug, chug, chug, chug…" The spectators continued to

chant as they waited to see who would win the contest.

Ogden was first to speak. "Delicious! Great nutty taste," he announced. He wiped his mouth on his sleeve.

Beryl let out a loud burp. "It was like eating peanuts. Not bad at all."

"Our champion," Aza yelled, holding Ogden's arm up in the air. The audience circled their clansmen, congratulating him. Within minutes, Ogden felt sick. He pushed through the crowd and threw up in the bushes.

Beryl winked at Nyla as they handed him the purse with the winnings.

"I guess I should have told him to chew."

The fun ended with the shadow of night spreading over the horizon. Aza wanted to finish the day by letting Alex spar with some of his best men. He called Ravenna and Sargo, along with a few of his favorites.

"She's blind! What the hell can she do against the giants?" Sargo said. He ripped his sword from its sheath in an angry burst of passion. "They're all fanatics, and most of us, except the elders, know it! If we leave things as they are, the demons won't care what we do. They will never find us or look for us. You see what's happening here. As long as we don't start playing with the rebirth, they leave us alone."

He stormed alongside Alex, glaring at her with so much anger his face looked distorted. "Most of us saw our parents and grandparents slip away from the faith. Those who continue have to watch constantly for an attack. We don't want to fight anymore. We want to enjoy the new life the chief priests and authorities created in the capital city. Why should we continue to hide out in these caves?"

Alex was sick of his attitude. "Why don't you just give your negative opinion a rest? You have free will. From creation, God gave man his own mind. You can go to E'Doom anytime." She faced the crowd. "I know a lot of you have lost parents and siblings to this new teaching and way of life, but you must press on. Some of your friends and relatives, we can win back."

Sargo spit on the ground and began to leave.

Alex grabbed his arm. "Don't walk away from me!"

"Get off me, you freak." He yanked his arm away from her.

Alex stumbled.

Aza grabbed his brother. "What do you think you're doing?"

Sargo laughed. "Don't pretend you believe these clowns can help us." He clenched his jaw. "She's no warrior. She is a nun, a nobody, straight out of the convent. Her sidekick is a bug-eating prophet, give me a break." He roughly pushed away from Aza's strong grip. "You're just going along because you're interested in making it with the healer. Everyone knows you have been sneaking off with her every night after curfew." Sargo swallowed hard. The look of betrayal on his brother's face crushed him.

"Shut up!" Aza bellowed. He pushed his brother into the crowd. "Watch what you say, if you know what's good for you." He hoped his threat would be enough to quiet Sargo's loose tongue.

"I told you she was a whore." Ravenna exploded, inciting the others who stood with her. She had her suspicions about the two of them but wanted to believe Aza was still in love with her.

Nyla's face flushed. She tried to hide behind Alex, hoping no one would directly question her.

"What do you have to say for yourself?" Ravenna asked, looking at Nyla with a frigid smile. "We all knew we couldn't trust any of you with your holier-than-thou attitude and special message." Her eyes narrowed while her mind wrapped around a plan to get rid of them so things could go back to the way they were.

"This is getting us nowhere," Alex said. "We don't have time to quarrel among ourselves. I don't need to prove myself to you or anyone else. You will have to accept me or leave the group." Her voice was firm and final.

Sargo clenched and unclenched his fists. "You can't shut me up, Aza." He motioned toward Nyla with a look of hatred in his eyes. "She has made you forget our plans to desert this mission and follow the new order. You're just playing up to that slut!"

Aza lunged at his brother in a fit of rage. Sargo jumped back, missing a direct punch. His twin was able to grab hold of his tunic and rip the garment from his shoulder. With a flash of indignation, Sargo drew back his fist and landed a right hook to Aza's nose.

Aza put his hand to his face, felt blood gush, and watched it cover his fingers. He went after Sargo with a new vengeance. Like a madman, his punches flew out of control and rained fury on his opponent's face and upper chest. He grabbed Sargo around the waist and hoisted him up off the ground. Aza threw him to the dirt, jarring his spine, knocking the wind from him. Beryl and Ogden tried to restrain him but his anger gave him brutal strength.

Sargo stood on wobbly legs, his strength weak with the surprise of his twin's obsessive rage. His brother lunged at him, knocking him to his knees. Aza grabbed his hair, jerked his head forward and kneed him in the face. Sargo groaned. Blood squirted from his mouth.

Alex, along with some of the men, pulled Aza off his injured brother.

Ogden shook his head. "I have never seen Aza act this way to anyone in the group."

Alex tried to help Sargo to his feet, but he pushed her away.

Ravenna rushed forward and helped him up. "You will be sorry you broke us up like this."

Sargo spit a bloody tooth into his hand. He glared at Alex. "I will never follow you or the God you serve."

Alex stood tall and proud in front of the soldiers. "Anyone who wants to desert the cause and chase the others into Apollyon's death squad…go! Follow Sargo and Ravenna. They are already traitors at heart."

She confronted Aza. "You can leave and join your comrades if that is your purpose. I'm not asking for anyone's approval or disapproval of us anymore. God gave us our orders, and we are ready to take back Old World with strength from the very hand of God's Spirit."

Beryl came forward with the elders and a group of new converts. "We need men and women of character, of courage, and of compassion who are not afraid to stand up for their belief in the Savior. With his weapons of warfare, we have authority to put the enemy under our feet."

To their surprise, only a few of Ravenna's small group of renegades left their circle. The other soldiers stayed with Alex, excited by this new hope. The buzz of conversation turned to visions of victory.

Nyla took Aza aside and began to minister to his bruised cheekbone and swollen nose. Standing next to him made her heart race with desire that was consuming her every thought. "We better be more careful," she whispered as she gently stroked his face. She covered his bruises with ointment. Her gaze strayed to his gray hypnotic eyes.

He squeezed her hand. "We will meet outside the perimeter tonight." His eyes met hers, exposing his own arousal. "No one ever ventures out that far." His voice was low and seductive.

She pushed a long curl behind her ear. "They have guards watching everywhere."

"One of the guards owes me a favor. I'll relieve him of his post at midnight. Meet me by the south entrance." He squeezed her hand again and walked away.

CHAPTER 26

Seeds of Deception

Ravenna fumed. *I knew she was a whore. I felt their deception in my heart. How could I have been so stupid to think I could win him back.* She felt dizzy with pent-up anger. She put her hand to her face that was burning hot. *I will make them pay for this.* Her body shook with rage.

By the time she got back to the cave, she could barely contain her feelings. She ransacked her cubicle.

Where is that book? I need my spell book. She deserves to be cursed. It was here yesterday. I saw it. She reached inside the recesses of the rock wall. *I always hide it here.*

Simeon's face flashed in her mind. "Damn him!" She grabbed her sack containing her collection of charms and dried roots, stuck a dagger in her boot, and stormed outside. *He must have spied on me. That old busybody is always warning me about consulting with demon spirits.*

Her adrenalin pumped a mixture of hatred and murder into her soul. A feeling of power overwhelmed her, and like an animal on the hunt, she sniffed out her target. The old man was in the garden. She stalked him from the cover of the trees. She watched him stand to stretch his back.

Ravenna smiled. *He's frail and vulnerable. An easy target.* Her mind shut off. Something dark from deep within her heart urged her on. She wanted to attack him like a wild beast. Her breath came in short bursts. Ravenna panted like a wolf;

her lust for blood forced her out of the woods into the open.

"You stole my spell book. Give it back!" she snarled.

He looked at her and cringed. "Ravenna, you must stay away from the black arts. It is idolatry. I do this for your own good." He wanted to reach her, to reason with her. "I will not tolerate you dabbling in the occult, it will surely cause your death."

She shoved him backward, making him stumble and fall to one knee. "You can't tell me what to do, you old fool. I like how the demons make me feel." Her body shook with aggression. "Now give me my book."

He struggled to his feet, his hands shaking, his heart frantic. "Can't you see how you have changed since you started using the spells. These ideas are confusing you."

Simeon looked at her and shook with fear. Her smile was menacing and her black eyes were red-rimmed and held a cruel stare. She seemed chillingly detached, heartless. He noticed, for the first time, how thin and drawn she had become. Her black hair against her pale skin made the dark circles under her eyes more pronounced. She had the look of someone troubled or possessed.

Her voice was pitiless and brutal. "Give me the book now!"

He saw a flash of silver. Ravenna loved the look of fear on his face. She tossed her weapon from one hand to the other, taunting him.

Simeon clutched his heart and fell backward, gasping for air, his chest squeezing. The world around him began to spin. Ravenna slashed through his tunic with her knife, frantically looking for her tome.

"Please, child. Have mercy."

She found the book hidden under his bulky robe and secured it inside her bag. "You brought this on yourself, old man," she said as she crouched over his body like a hungry wolf. She saw a red stain spread over his tunic and watched blood trickle from his body.

Ravenna ran into the forest. *No one can stop me now.* She felt empowered, and the feeling urged her forward. *Nyla will not have Aza! I will do whatever needs to be done to get rid of her.* Her breathing was labored but she continued to run. Her heart hammered in her ears. *I can easily kill her like I killed Simeon. They deceived me! Aza had her behind my back.* Her thoughts enraged her. "What if my friends knew and kept it from me? What if they chose her friendship over mine?" She spoke aloud to the woodland surrounding her.

Her anger propelled her forward. She ran as fast as she could, slowing her pace long enough to jump fallen logs that blocked her path. She bolted through the underbrush. Tree branches and vines scratched her face and arms. A thistle vine bit her neck when she stumbled and fell face-first on the ground. Her body felt no pain.

She ran into her secret place, a thick grove of evergreens, where she went frequently to be alone to practice her witchcraft. She fell to her knees. Her chest heaved; her lungs burned as she struggled for breath. With shaking hands, she dumped the contents from the sack she carried onto the ground. Her book, along with pigeon guts and bones, roots and fungus, spilled onto the ground. Flint and stone were among the contents. She struck them together savagely. Sparks shot out around her. She started a fire under the altar she erected from the specifications in the book. She used the altar stone on numerous occasions and began looking through the undergrowth for a sacrifice.

Asmodeus suddenly appeared in the forest. She watched and listened to Ravenna from afar. *I love the way jealousy gives birth to hatred.* The vibration of evil made the forest quicken. The wolves joined her. They growled and drooled, anxious for a feast.

"No," she whispered, stroking one predator's furry skull.

"I am not finished with her yet. I have a better plan."

It was twilight, the time of evening when the dying light makes everything look intense and indistinct. The last of the sun's light reddened and faded. Misty shades of gray crept around the trees. Asmodeus shifted her human appearance into a creature of deception.

Ravenna mumbled incantations and a prayer. "God of death, take Nyla's life for the pain and embarrassment she caused me." A rattling of leaves and snapping branches startled her. A beast, unlike any she had ever seen, charged toward her. It came at her like a mad dog. *By the gods of hell, what have I conjured?*

Ravenna fell to her knees. She watched in awe as the creature slowed and came close. Its mouth was in a perpetual snarl, like a rabid dog, but it was a human face. From the waist up, it had the body of a woman. A woman twisted and savage; a disfigurement that came from an internal seething and loathing.

The demon's legs were short and powerful like a bear full of brute force. Long disheveled brown hair grew from her head and covered her chest. Coming out of its back were leathery black wings. They seemed heavy since the beast needed to stay somewhat hunched over. Ravenna jumped to her feet and prepared to run.

"Do not fear me, child of iniquity," it said. "I am a messenger from King Apollyon. He left you the spell book that you found by the stream. The one you are using now."

Ravenna felt dizzy but watched and listened; frightened yet fascinated by the creature's power.

Asmodeus reveled in her authority over the girl. She growled and snarled dangerously. "It was our king who left the book of secrets from hell that has already taught you much about revenge and hatred."

Ravenna felt hypnotized by its voice.

"I was sent to bring you into our master's presence. His worship heard you summon him and the cries of your heart. He knows the terrible humiliation you have suffered at the hands of your tribe." Asmodeus tried to contain her smile but her lips twisted into a grin. "His Reverence is aware of the way the healer and her faction are taking your friends from you. He knows they broke up your relationship with Aza."

Ravenna watched its body quiver and contort as it spoke.

"It is plain to everyone you are a leader." Asmodeus paused, letting her compliments entice the novice. "We can see you are a born sorceress with great power."

Ravenna held her sword up, ready to fight, but the creature's suggestions burned like fire in her mind.

Ravenna shook the sword in the creature's face. "How can King Apollyon know all this about me? Speak quickly, disgusting beast, or I will cut you in two."

The demon sneered. "You summoned him yourself. Prayed to him and worshiped him at the altar you erected in the forest. He knows who belongs to him and who will heed his words." She crept closer. "Besides, those three who entered your tribe from Safehold are outrageous, to say the least. They act like they have authority to ruin your hard work." Asmodeus sat in front of her and continued.

"If you allow them to keep going on this way, especially that healer, your position will be seriously compromised." Asmodeus magnified her words. "Some of the soldiers, Satan's devotees, are faltering. They joined your circle of power and were initiated into your fold, but they are starting to believe in these Words of Life."

Ravenna jumped to her feet. "No one can take my position from me. I saved Aza from the sword in our last crusade. I talked them into leaving the clan to join the new order. I showed them how to worship dark and dangerous spirits."

She savagely stabbed her sword into the soft ground.

"They can't afford to use those girls or that prophet in my place." Ravenna began to pace. "My group mixed their blood with demon blood. They prayed to the hordes of hell. They can't just walk away. Satan won't let them."

Asmodeus pulled herself along after Ravenna, using her wings as a type of crutch. "Of course, you're right. You are in charge. But it is the healer who has Aza's ear—and heart, I might add." She cringed at her own words, like a dog waiting for a kick, knowing what was coming.

Ravenna drew her sword and put the blade on Asmodeus's heart. "He loves me, not her. I used the spell book, and I'm sure the magic worked. I felt it."

Asmodeus considered the girl's dark empty eyes. They held so much hatred it made her shutter with pleasure. The demon responded quickly, adding fuel to the fire burning in the teen's unforgiving heart. "You should act immediately to get her out of your camp. She is stealing him from you. For that matter, before they steal the entire group from you. Only a handful of friends followed you today, and they were only halfhearted about mutiny."

Asmodeus pushed for a violent response. She was not disappointed and felt Ravenna's wrath through the blade of the girl's weapon. Small drops of liquid dripped from Asmodeus's chest. *Good. Her anger is making her take unsafe risks.*

Ravenna forced the blade into the demon's flesh and drew more blood. "How dare you lie to me. This group is my family. They are my friends. Aza loves me. He needs me."

The demon took an amulet from a pouch around her waist. From inside, she took powder and blew it into the girl's eyes.

Ravenna waved her hand in front of her face, trying to blow the powder away. "Don't use that stuff on me." She felt dizzy and stumbled against a tree trunk. She rubbed her burning eyes and forced them open. With blurred vision, she saw a illusion, her friends making a pact. She could hear them whispering.

"What are they saying?"

Asmodeus crept closer. "They are saying they don't need you anymore because you have limited power," she lied. "They plan to strip you of your rank."

Ravenna wiped an angry tear from her eye. "What is Sargo doing? Why is he with them? He left with me."

Asmodeus shook her head. "He betrayed you."

Ravenna heard someone say her name. They were laughing and whispering. She could not make out the words, but it was plain they were talking about her.

"Look," Asmodeus said. "Is that Aza and Nyla?"

She watched as Aza embraced Nyla and put a crown of wild flowers on her head to symbolize his love.

Ravenna dropped her arm with the sword to her side and slumped to the ground. She felt like someone had ripped the life from her. "I hate them. I hate them all."

"As you should," Asmodeus soothed. "For this very reason, my master wants to offer you a deal. A deal which will give you power, and authority, like you could never have imagined."

Asmodeus smiled, knowing the girl believed her lies. "Aza will admire you, appreciate you, and honor your accomplishments. You will have power over those who hurt you so you will never have to feel excluded or deceived again."

Ravenna's slumped shoulders straightened like a puppet on a string. "I will do whatever it takes."

Asmodeus witnessed the birth of a new sin spring to life in the girl's eyes.

Revenge.

The demon smiled at the thought of the stupid girl's immolation. "The plan is simple, just summon me with information on how to capture any one of the messengers."

Ravenna scratched her neck. "I want them punished but punished with impunity. Can you arrange that?" Her heart pumped frantically. "If I'm caught, the soldiers will put me out of the group forever."

"I can arrange whatever is needed." Asmodeus stroked her chin, acting like she was lost in thought. *Does she really imagine I have left any detail unfinished? Her betrayal secures my promotion.* She pulled her attention back to the girl. "You can still sneak into the camp and act like you are sorry for the way you acted today." She paused. "No one saw you kill Simeon. You will act horrified that someone would stoop so low as to attack a vulnerable, innocent elder."

The creature smiled inwardly. She was a liar who understood liars and saw her plan taking shape. "Trust me. The plan will work." She took a deep breath before she continued. Asmodeus wanted her words to persuade Ravenna to commit this crime of betrayal without hesitation. "My king will have you evacuated as soon as the deed is complete. He will want to honor your success and give you your just reward."

Ravenna turned her back on the beast for a moment and contemplated her situation. Envy, malice, and revenge, her new friends made the decision for her. "Nyla and Aza have been sneaking out of the camp at night into the forest." She blurted out the traitorous information. "They are consumed by desire for each other." She turned and looked Asmodeus in the eyes. "On the south slope at midnight."

"Consumed by desire. Perfect." She shook with excitement. "You have done well, child of iniquity. The deed must be carried out without delay. Our king will want his victim as a sacrifice for the Feast of the Blood Moon. As soon as my lord secures the healer, you will receive your payment. Go back to the camp, spin your web of deceit, and await your escort."

Asmodeus disappeared like liquid shimmering in the air. For a moment, Ravenna thought she might have dreamed the encounter. However, on the tip of her sword was a chunk of its supernatural skin.

She ran to her hidden altar which was blazing hot. The flesh was fresh and had an aura of unholy life within it. She wanted to use it quickly. She began to chant and sing. Her body swayed and her eyes rolled in her head as the sensation of evil overwhelmed her. Ravenna placed the meat on a grate over the fire, using the flesh of the demon as a sacrifice. She grabbed her knife and began to cut her forearms in random patterns. Blood drained from her body, into the fire, and joined with the beast's sizzling tissue. After a prayer, she devoured the sacrificial meal.

A young fox scampered from the bushes. She hunched over like an animal and snarled.

Without thinking, Ravenna pounced on it and slashed its throat with her dagger. She held the quivering carcass in her arms and drank its warm blood. She felt alive and powerful. In her spirit, she felt something new living inside her body. She felt lust for murder spring to life in her stony heart.

CHAPTER 27

The Prince of Darkness

It was harvest time in the city of E'Doom. Multitudes came from all over the nation to celebrate the Feast of the Blood Moon. The king opened his borders to the rich, the famous, and the poor from every continent.

Booths and tents lined the streets with colorful goats'-hair canopies. Merchants sold peppercorn, nutmeg, mace, and cinnamon; spices that were rare delicacies, harvested in remote areas of Old World. Traders sold fine silks, velvet, and fur cloaks that were highly prized by the nobility. Tables were laden with finely cut diamonds, sapphires, and emeralds to entice wealthy buyers. Blacksmiths competed with artisan's who sold swords, knives, axes, and armor at this time-honored festival.

There would be a week of festivities with parades, feats of magic, plays, and food. The countryside was dotted with amusement of all sorts. Many came to participate in jousts and tournaments while others preferred to test their skills hunting wild game in the dark forest that surrounded the Castle E'Doom.

The first day of the feast was bright and sunny, bringing out more people than expected. Flocks of worshipers flooded into the city gates. The air was electric with excitement and anticipation. The roads and alleyways were filled with rowdy patrons ready for a party. Performers in colorful costumes roamed the streets. Jugglers entertained the crowds, throwing multiple knives, balls, and rings into the air. Like skilled acrobats, they caught the various props with their hands and feet.

Magicians with white-painted faces and black cloaks teased the crowd, making children appear and disappear inside elaborate boxes. Young assistants, bound and chained, were placed into barrels filled with water, daring time and death. Witches set up shop in colored wagons and hung herbs, animal claws, powders, and charms from the carriage rooves. Women with gaudy jewelry and multicolored scarves tied around their heads cast spells and sold amulets to eager shoppers.

Men and women in leather garb contorted their bodies and devoured fire, swords, and knives to the delight of the visitors. Soothsayers with crystal balls read palms and tea leaves in shops found on every corner. Minstrels accompanied bands of musicians who played wild music on platforms throughout the enormous courtyard. Exotic dancers performed to the music that inebriated the excited crowds.

Shopkeepers sold trinkets, ale, and wine. Bakers cooked over open fires, and the aroma of sweet cakes snaked into the air, charming the multitudes. Churches held special services to honor the many gods of the harvest. Disciples, dressed as spirits of the underworld, danced and sang in elaborate processions. Secret agents, hired by the king and disguised as peasants, mingled with the unsuspecting guests, looking for traitors and infidels who dared to pass out pamphlets teaching the ways of the cross.

The blast of royal horns blew, sending a shrill cry over the city. Church bells tolled from steeples in the center square, announcing an appearance by the king. The monarch's advisers ushered him outside onto his balcony that overlooked his city of E'Doom. The masses screamed and cheered; each supporter sought a glimpse of their ruler.

The wind swirled about King Apollyon's form, blowing his long dark hair around his face like raven's wings. He waved his arms in the air. The throng of worshippers fell to their knees in a sea of adoration.

"My friends," he began. "You are here as honored guests. At my expense, eat and drink from the cup of pleasure."

A band began to play music that excited the masses. They swayed and chanted to the rhythm that enticed them. Beautiful men and women sang and danced, gyrating seductively, leading the multitude to honor the king.

Apollyon's human form was tall, athletic, and agile. His competitive spirit was well-known and revered throughout his kingdom. He was idolized as an athlete and unmatched by his rivals. Many sportsmen came to challenge his skill, and he always welcomed their folly. His worshippers exalted fame, wealth, youth, and beauty above all other human qualities. The king made sure he possessed them all.

He chose his features carefully. The intention was to seduce each age group with his fake persona. For this generation, he became mysteriously haunting. His features were both feminine and masculine. He looked as if an artist had carved his face from white marble; long and oval, young and virile, with high cheekbones and sapphire-blue eyes. His body was lean and muscled. This uniquely beautiful exterior gave him a contemporary yet universal appearance.

His lips were perfectly shaped and when he smiled, he looked trustworthy and sincere. His eyes slanted upward with heavy lashes. His gaze was hypnotic and sensual. His subjects found him sympathetic and gentle. He looked at the sea of his adoring fans and delighted at the sight of sinful humanity.

The populace saw him through eyes clouded by greed. The inhabitants of Old World coveted his wealth and power, causing many to murder, cheat, and steal to acquirer what they wanted. Apollyon carefully established his lofty profile by flaunting his personal cash hoard. He loved to tempt his followers, planting seeds of covetousness within their hearts.

His subjects bowed in adoration to his charisma, and worldwide appeal. World leaders, along with commoners from many lands, journeyed for months to get a glimpse of this powerful mystic. He masterfully seduced the populace with his unnatural abilities and charm. He created a kingdom that mimicked a spiritual haven. His followers believed they could acquire a sense of well-being and spiritual awareness in his presence.

He pushed his emotions aside, hiding his hatred from the cheering crowd and suppressed a feral growl. His powers were animal-like, and he could barely control the urge to jump from the balcony and attack the multitude as they swayed to the music that seduced their souls. He hated the mortals. They were weak and vulnerable.

Yet what sickened him most were the believers in Christ. Over time, some lost the faith that made them strong and, at least, an opponent for his magnificent power. However, his keen sense of smell picked up a fragrance that whet his appetite. The blood he now smelled was that of a fallen Christian. A soiled sinner.

He felt the rift when the messengers entered his chasm. He was surprised at the power they possessed and the gifts they carried. His minions instinctively attacked them and awoke the dragon, but the time was not at hand for the beast to consume them. Timing was everything. He knew the hour was not yet at hand. There were many more to be defeated before his final battle with the King of Kings.

Shadim appeared beside the king knowing he was invisible to most humans. "Look, my king." He pointed a long hairy finger toward the gates of the city. "As I promised. It is the supreme inquisitor with prisoners from St. Regents. Infidels to use as you choose."

Apollyon smiled. He watched the procession, led by his

friends, the sanctimonious Archbishop Pietto and the easily manipulated Supreme Inquisitor, astride matching white stallions. They were followed by their entourage of fools. Priests of every rank, from every denomination, dressed in fine vestments and wearing rings and chains of gold; blind guides, each one a self-appointed judge, eager to murder in the name of righteousness.

In wooden carts, pulled by donkeys, behind this procession were the accused. Innocent prisoners locked in cages, awaiting execution.

"Congratulations, Shadim. These traitors from Safehold help to exonerate you from your prior failure." He paused. "This time."

Apollyon's thoughts distracted him. He abruptly left the balcony to the disappointment of his multitudes. His soldiers moved into the crowds and helped them peacefully disperse into the banquet halls, filling their cups with liquid passion. The king loved the praise of his worshippers. He knew how to entertain his followers to keep them coming back for more. Everyone in Old World wanted to be present for the Feast of the Blood Moon. His banquets promised debauchery and decadence of every kind. However, something more pressing had his attention.

He stormed through the triple doors into his personal chambers. His advisers and slaves buzzed around him like flies. "Get out!" He waved his hand, swatting them away.

They disappeared like smoke.

"Asmodeus." He beckoned in a mocking tone. "Come out of hiding." He pulled his sword from its sheath. The blade gleamed in the murky light within the spacious room.

Asmodeus snuck from her hiding place like a whipped dog and knelt before her king. "I swear, Your Eminence," she pleaded, "the girl from Safehold will be in the palm of your hand as soon as Ravenna set's our trap." Her voice quivered.

"In her ignorance, she will expose the entire compound to your army. You will have hundreds of Christians to murder as you choose. Their execution will be a warning people can't ignore."

He played with his sword, slicing through the air, just inches above her head. "We must not allow the infidels to continue to win converts." He kicked her in the face with a booted foot. "You do understand my predicament?"

She sprawled on the flagstone floor. "Have mercy, master."

He paced his chamber, snapping his fingers to the rhythm of Asmodeus's heartbeat. The black orb on his ring opened and closed to the vibration.

He held his hand in front of her face. "Do you know what this is?"

She cringed. The black stone, set in gold, pulsed with life.

He sighed. "It is an empty portal, a black hole, going nowhere." He admired it on his long slender finger. "Beautiful, don't you think?" He tilted his head to the side and smiled. "It is a desolate place for a spirit with your talent."

Asmodeus cringed at his feet. "Please, my father, do not place me in the void. I will not fail you again. The new plan is fail-safe."

He walked to his window and peered outside at his multitude of followers. "I will not lose any of my disciples because of your incompetence."

She crawled after him. "I have delivered to you one of the messengers." She rose to her knees and folded her hands in supplication. "Your worship, I have secured, for your pleasure, a blood-bought prize." Her azure eyes pleaded. "She is a child of righteousness, fallen from grace. A precious jewel from Safehold. The girl is a prize worthy of your collection."

He slashed her face with his sword. "Silence! You bore

me."

She fell to the floor, fighting one of the king's dogs for her severed flesh. They struggled. The dog ripped it from her hand and swallowed it whole.

"My beautiful face." She sobbed.

Asmodeus heard a stifled laugh. Looking up, she saw Shadim perched on the mantel, like a pet leopard.

Her anger boiled. "Shadim is the one who deserves exile. He missed the three infidels before they left St. Regents. This entire mess is his fault."

Shadim pounced to the floor. "She has more power than you gave me. The two sisters should have been able to stop them before they got out of control."

The king began to snap his fingers again. The portal opened and closed. "Shut up. You both annoy me with this prattle."

Asmodeus begged, "Please, your worship. Put Shadim in the void, not me. Ask my sister how well I lead our team. She will tell you how skilled I am."

Asmodeus turned at the sound of clicking heels on the flagstone floor. Aether, her sibling, entered the room, draped around a beautiful young girl.

She scrutinized this child, barely fourteen, who strutted toward her master. She had wild black hair, dark as pitch, that fell to her waist like a shawl. Braided throughout her thick tresses was a garland of red hibiscus that perfumed the air. She wore a simple white midriff top and long fitted skirt. She glided across the room like a swan over water.

Asmodeus's skin prickled. She felt unabashed evil coming from this child's presence. She looked mournfully at her sister, hoping for help. "Sister, tell my master we have this mission under control."

Aether flopped on a divan and crossed her long shapely legs. She looked elegant in a deep-blue gown that draped fluidly over her tall slender body. Her blond hair fell like waves over her shoulders. "Asmodeus, darling, you look absolutely disgusting." She stretched her arm forward, showing the sapphire and diamond bracelets on her wrist. "Gifts from the king." The expensive baubles glittered.

Asmodeus crawled toward her sister. "Tell him I am capable."

She reached out to grab her sister and watched her hand pass through Aether's body.

"I'm fading," she whispered. "Please help me, there is still time."

Aether looked past her sister's shimmering image and patted the lounge, beckoning the child to sit. "By the way," she gazed at her sibling with a look of disintrest in her eyes, "this is Kali, our new sister."

Apollyon walked with Kali toward the divan. He looked down at Asmodeus wallowing in fear on the floor. "What shall I do with her?" he asked Aether.

"The portal is a good idea," she answered. "She has failed you, Your Excellence."

Kali sat next to Aether and rested her head on her sister's shoulder. Aether closed her eyes. Something strange tickled her cheek. She heard a hissing in her ear. Her lids fluttered open to look upon Kali's youth and beauty, but the demon's face and body began to lengthen and her image shifted into a four-headed cobra.

Aether froze.

One cobra bit her neck, another her chest, the third her face, the fourth her ear. Aether's arms flayed. She tried to push away from the thick black snake that coiled around her body. Her bulging blue eyes found Apollyon's.

He grinned and snapped his fingers to the rhythm of her heartbeat. He stretched out his arm, inches from her face. The orb on his finger opened. "The portal sounds like a very good idea."

The cobra bit Aether's lips before Kali slithered back to her original form.

"Well done." He smiled.

Asmodeus watched the scene in stunned silence as Aether's form vanished into the black portal. She knew what was coming but was too weak to fight.

He pouted. "I had very high expectations for you and your sister. You both disappointed me so I will give Kali the powers I bestowed on both of you."

Looking down at her defeated posture on the floor agitated him. In a fit of anger, he stomped on her chest with his black leather boot. He held the ring in front of her face. The orb on his finger opened. "Such magnificent power," he drawled.

Asmodeus began screaming. The force of the ring pulled at her dying image. She tried to crawl away, but the power of the orb held her prisoner. She grabbed hold of the divan but her fading body passed through the piece of furniture.

"Please, Father, don't do this." She kicked her legs, thrashing around on the floor, desperate to avoid the black hole. Her glistening form was powerless against the force of the pit that ripped her from the floor and into everlasting darkness.

Apollyon turned to his new creation and slipped the ring on her finger. "A gift," he said.

Kali looked into his deep-blue eyes and saw nothing but hatred.

He abruptly pushed her aside and stalked to the balcony, hiding behind the flowing draperies while he watched the crowds. "I am greatly excited that one of the believers so easily fell into temptation." He whispered her name, "Nyla." He let the word linger in the air. *"Nyla."*

Kali joined him at the window. "Yes. Nyla. Poor naive child of righteousness. She was enticed and led astray by the power of lust." The young girl winked at her master.

He nodded his head. "Yes. You are uninhibited and highly charged." He held Kali's hand. "Asmodeus brought none of your skills to the table." He held her close. "Ravenna was merely a pawn, seduced by envy and anger." His grip on the girl's hand tightened, and his face contorted into an evil grimace. Kali tried to pull away.

"My lord, I promise you, Aza and the remnant's demise will be violent and complete."

He dragged her with him through the room. His mood constantly changing. "We need to act fast while the picking is ripe."

He moved into the throne room, his leather boots tapping the floor, his stride smooth and fluid. Thick smoke swirled beneath his feet, concealing the harvest of lost souls.

He opened the *Book of Death* that lay on the podium in front of his throne. The leather was soft and supple, the pages only slightly yellow, and the binding was solid. The huge tome was in good condition, the king kept it safe through the centuries. His human form could not lift the heavy volume. He flipped through the worn pages.

Sweat formed on his brow; his heart raced with adrenaline. "Did you know killing is my sole function?" he asked.

Kali nodded her head. "Yes, Father."

He smiled. "I care nothing for life, not even my own. I enjoy hurting others. The thought of snatching away a messenger sent from Safehold brings me pleasure I haven't felt in a long time."

He laughed a deep throaty growl and clutched Kali around the waist, pulling her to his side. "I hid the spell book." He grimaced at the girl. "I did not trust the other two with such an important maneuver." He whispered in her ear. She flinched as his breath burned her cheek. "I knew the one who was a traitor at heart would find the book and use it. It did not matter who it was, male or female, the one with the mind full of malice would do my bidding. I am well aware of the dark motives of the human heart. As predicted, the child of iniquity turned the fallen child of righteousness over for judgment."

He released his grip on Kali. "It is disturbing that these three are trying to start revival and talking about the weapons of God. If the infidels learn how powerful this arsenal will make them and if they believe they can kill the giants, it will ruin the years of careless indifference by the humans."

Kali shuddered and backed away.

"I have the inhabitants of the world where I want them," the king ranted. "I can corrupt them from the inside out, making them spiritually blind, drunk with their own self-importance, and oblivious to the spirit realm that surrounds them."

His chest heaved, and he slumped over. "I carefully and steadily attacked their minds with dark and perverted messages." His anger boiled inside him. His body twisted and his human flesh ripped.

He roared. Kali ran behind the long draperies. His anger fueled the transformation. With clawed hands, he ripped at his chest, exposing the demon within. Black leathery wings cut through the human flesh on his back. He tore away his face and ripped his scalp from the skull. He shook his massive head, tossing flesh and blood over the room. His beauty was replaced with twisted horns and an inhuman face.

He stood on thick muscular legs. Saliva dripped from his mouth. His voice was not human but demon. "I spent decades weaving a veil of compromise, indifference, and revolt into the fabric of humanity's intellect. Moral decline and spiritual decay have become the status quo in this world littered with rebellion and unbelief toward God."

Kali reached out to touch him, but his wickedness burned her flesh. She withdrew her hand in fear. "Relax, my lord," she whispered. "The human race is weak-willed and full of doubt.

The populace has bought into your lies."

The king's shoulders relaxed, and he slumped into a heavy claw-foot chair.

Kali crept from the darkness, hoping she could soothe his rage. "How cleverly you turned the masses away from the true God, luring them with ideas of self. Self-service, self-knowledge, self-indulgence are all the philosophies that consume humanity."

Apollyon jumped to his feet. "Yes. How boring and predictable these humans behave. Centuries after the fall of man in the garden, they are still eating of the forbidden fruit and reaping the same result. Still choosing to disobey and follow the path of enlightenment. How delightful," he mused, "they never learn. Or do they?"

He knocked the table over in a fit of rage. His *Book of Death* and vials of poisons careened to the ground, spreading broken glass across the floor. Dogs ran from their hiding places in the dark crevices of the throne room.

"They will see no revival. For this sedition, they will reap only torment." He turned on Kali with a new vengeance. "I want the believers to despair! My army will attack this band of renegades. They will make no more converts in Old World. I decree anyone who speaks the name of the Son of God will be killed."

He breathed out his message on parchment. Fire burned his words into the paper. He pressed it into Shadim's hairy palm. "Deliver this to my legions."

Shadim cowered at the look in Apollyon's eyes.

"Make sure my army understands the urgency of this battle. There is no room for failure."

He picked up the ancient *Book of Death*, handling the one-hundred-pound volume like it was a feather, and ripped the thick pages in two. He roared his fury while lifting Kali into the air with his tormented thoughts and tossed her into a wall.

She sprawled on the floor dazed by the impact.

He flew through the room and stood over her prostrate body. "At all costs, be certain the citizens of Old World ignore the warning signs of the age. I do not want them to turn from their wickedness and be saved from the destruction to come."

His eyes were icy and dangerous. "Do not fail me."

He lifted her hand to her face to position the ring before her eyes. Kali felt the orb on her finger pulse to life. She gazed into the inky darkness with wild eyes.

With his mind, he squeezed her throat, cutting off her air supply. "You know what I can do to you." His eyes locked on hers. "Prepare an army and destroy the remnant. Bring this Nyla to me. I want her to feel guilty to the very core of her soul. Now go!"

Kali vanished.

Once Apollyon was calm, his thoughts turned to the fallen disciple and the prisoners from St. Regents. "I will accuse Nyla in front of my jury." His cloven feet scraped the floor as he paced the room. "I will convince them of her wickedness and charge her with all her crimes against God. I will make her believe God turns his back on sinners."

He lifted his book from the floor. "I will indict her on all her weaknesses. After all, she failed in her role as a leader and ruined the lives of everyone associated with her. I will make sure she believes she is the cause of the events that will lead to the death of her own mother and the mutilation of Reverend Mother. No one in their right mind would forgive such crimes."

He stood above the flames in the pit under his feet. "I will condemn her during the Feast of the Blood Moon. How wonderful it will be to play with her guilty mind."

CHAPTER 28

Treason

Darkness fell over the mountain range of Mori. Night birds screeched in the distance, and wolves howled. Cold mountain air stirred the treetops, and the gibbous moon glowed in the dark sky.

Inside the cave, Nyla could not stop pacing the length of the private space set up for Simeon. After finding him in the garden, Alex thought it was prudent to keep him hidden and away from the patients in the regular hospice. The soldiers carried him into his room where Nyla stitched his wounds and gave him digitalis for his heart.

Alex arrived to check on the victim. She had spent the better part of the day in meetings with the commanders, generals, and elders of the tribes.

Nyla's erratic pacing rattled her frayed nerves. "Relax, Nyla. It's not like you have somewhere else to go," Alex said.

Beryl poked his head in to see how Simeon was doing. "Anything I can do?" His voice was taut with concern.

"Come in," Alex whispered. "You can take Anat to the kitchen for some food." Her brow creased. "She has not eaten all day." She held the woman's small hand. "I promised her we would look after her husband, but she needs to get some food and then rest."

Anat's eyes filled with tears. "One more moment by his side and then I will go with Beryl to eat."

Alex took her team aside and kept her voice low. "I have news. The soldiers told me they found a prisoner lost in the woods. They said she wants to speak with me. She is from Safehold."

"Who?" Beryl asked.

Alex shook her head. "The person gave no name. We have no idea if it is friend or foe. I will go to the hospice and pry as soon as Nyla gives me her report on Simeon's condition."

Nyla interrupted, "Are you sure it is not my mother?"

Alex looked down. "They didn't say. Certainly they would have recognized the queen."

Nyla let out a sigh of relief.

Alex squeezed Nyla's hand. "Maybe this woman will tell us what has been going on since we left home."

Beryl rested his hand on Alex's shoulder. "I pray, whoever it is, they have good news." He paused. "Please ask about Brother John. I've tried not to worry but…"

"I will. I promise. I will get all the information I can," Alex said.

She waited for Beryl and Anat to leave and listened to Nyla's diagnosis. "I stitched his wound. The blade cut him deeply." She gently covered him with blankets. "He is stable for the moment. I have prayed for his total recovery, but I'm afraid his heart is very weak."

Nyla fussed over Simeon's injuries, checking his pulse and wiping his brow. "We should see if Ravenna can act as a guard over him tonight. She is an excellent warrior and has a close relationship with Simeon and Anat. I saw her come back to camp a while ago." She paused, looking up from the bedside to steal a glance at Alex, hoping to see her response. "She was very upset about her actions today at the training yard. She made it clear she was horrified by the news of the attack on Simeon." She paused again and faked a cough. "I heard her tell

Aza she wanted to stay close to him so he suffers no further harm."

Simeon grabbed Nyla's hand and sat straight up in his bed. His eyes grew round and frightened. He looked pleadingly into her face. She overlooked the obvious turmoil her decision caused him. "Poor you," she whispered, ignoring his terrified look. He lay back down on the blanket, too weak to speak, and closed his eyes.

Alex wiped Simeon's wet forehead with a clean cloth. "Why is he so upset about Ravenna if she is innocent?" Alex wondered aloud. "Notify me as soon as he regains consciousness. I think you are the better choice to stay with him, in case he needs further care."

"No. I can't." She made her tone of voice hard and final. "I'm not feeling well. I have taken some willow bark for a headache. I need to rest." She rubbed her forehead. "Ravenna will be better to stay and guard him. There is nothing else I can do."

Alex slowly shook her head. "If you are feeling unwell, I suggest you don't stay alone. Before you retire to your cell, secure another warrior from the halls. Anyone but Ravenna. I don't want her anywhere near him."

Outside the compound, the entire tribe was on full alert. Everyone was jittery knowing an assassin was in their midst. Alex stationed extra guards around the perimeter of the cave, and the army was battle ready.

Her heart squeezed in her chest as she hurried through the empty cave corridors toward the infirmary. She heard the ripping of fabric the medics used as bandages and smelled the stench of bedpans and ointments as she entered the large cavern used as a hospice.

"This way, commander." A soft voice said. The medic rested her hand on Alex's elbow, guiding her to the bed with the unknown patient. Alex could hear the woman's rosary clicking as the escaped prisoner ran her fingers over the prayer beads and the rasp of her labored breathing.

"Did she tell you her name?" Alex asked the medic. She gaged at the stench of blood and manure from the patient's filthy clothing.

"Sorry, ma'am. She used her last bit of strength to get here. It was like she had been here before."

Alex dropped to her knees next to the bed. She reached out and touched the patient's hands. She could tell by the size of the beads this rosary belonged to a nun. *Mother?* The rough pudgy fingers answered her question.

The woman jumped, her eyes fluttered open. "Alex. My dear Alex. We knew you were alive. We all felt within our spirits that you had made it safely into Old World." She sucked in her breath. "How is Beryl and Nyla. Are they alive?"

Alex couldn't hold back her tears. "Yes. We made it Temperance. How did you get here? What about Reverend Mother and the others?"

The old woman clutched Alex's hand. "The Supreme Inquisitor came to St. Regents during the investigation of Joseph's death. Olga blamed you. She accused you of his death and Reverend Mother as your accomplice. They found a note, hidden in Mother's cell. The note you signed, detailing our attempts to hide your identity from the authorities."

She coughed and strained to catch her breath.

"That is enough for now," the medic said. "She is very weak. She was tortured. Mutilated. She has lost much blood."

Alex shuddered at the thought of the atrocities she endured. "I am so sorry. I never imagined the confession would come to this."

Temperance lifted a shaking hand to the young girl's cheek. "It was time the truth was told." She wiped Alex's tears with her hand. "Let me finish while I have the strength. You must know everything."

"Go on," Alex whispered.

"The inquisitor caged us like animals. He mutilated our bodies and fed us garbage. They made sure not to kill us. They were told to keep us alive until the public execution. His intention is to deliver us to the king as heretics and traitors to the crown. Archbishop Pietto came along to identify you. Olga rides by his side. They are sure they can flush you out because of those they are holding prisoner." She inhaled and coughed. "It was a miracle I got free. I hoped to find you to tell you their plan. They will be executed with or without you during the Feast of the Blood Moon."

Alex patted the woman's hand. "Rest, Temperance. You are safe...*for now.*"

"Wait," Temperance whispered. "Your sight."

Alex felt a lump form in her throat. "It is better to walk by faith."

She turned to the medic. "I will give you enough time to clean her up." She stood. "Trusted soldiers will come and move her to a more secure location."

The medic nodded. "Yes, ma'am."

Alex felt a wave of vertigo. *"Lord God,"* she silently prayed, *"strengthen us for this battle."*

Nyla was restless and walked aimlessly through the cave corridors. The dim light from the torches created shadows in the narrow halls that set her nerves on edge. Everyone she passed, seemed to be watching her and judging her after Sargo's accusations.

She stopped Frances on her way to the infirmary. "Where is the refugee from Safehold?" she asked.

Frances gave her a cold look. "They moved her to a safe location."

Nyla ignored the hostility in the girl's tone of voice. "Have you heard anything about Simeon's attacker?"

Frances shook her head and scurried away through the

dark cave.

Nyla's stomach lurched at the thought of an assassin in their camp. She smoothed her tunic with shaky hands as if she could stop the fear that churned in the pit of her belly.

Tika was on guard duty with Ravenna and noticed Nyla alone lost in thought. She waved her hand, getting the healer's attention.

"I think you should have a look at Ravenna's neck."

Nyla balked.

Tika grabbed her wrist and forced her to check Ravenna who was wet and flushed with fever. "She has a horrible wound that seems to be infected."

Both rivals glared at each other but kept their hatred hidden. Ravenna scratched the wound.

"I have something that may help with the itch," Nyla said. She laced her words with a sarcastic sweet tone.

Ravenna pulled her cloak up around her neck and over her arms. "I'm fine. Frances gave me something that helped."

"She doesn't look well," Tika said. "I'm worried about her."

Nyla shrugged her shoulders. "Where are *you* going?" she asked, trying to change the subject.

"To guard Simeon's room," Tika whispered, adjusting the sword in her belt. "Ravenna is on her way to the infirmary. What about you?"

Nyla looked at her feet. "The chatter of the tribe speculating about the identity of the traitor is unnerving." She looked at Tika but avoided her eyes. "I need a minute to clear my head."

Nyla pushed past the girl and rushed outside

It was a beautiful autumn night with a nearly full moon. The forest was washed in light. Nyla pushed the fear from her thoughts and imagined how safe she would be in Aza's arms. Fall leaves of red and yellow rained upon her, and she twirled in circles in anticipation of meeting her lover. She was so caught up in her thoughts she did not notice Beryl and Alex leaning against a tree watching her.

"So," Alex asked through clenched teeth, "out for a little stroll, all by yourself?"

"Oh! Sorry. I didn't see you both standing there." Nyla rubbed her hands together. "I was just sitting around, bored, doing not much of anything." She paused and twirled a long curl in her finger. "I, you know…decided maybe I should take a walk." She pretended to yawn, covering her mouth with her hand, hoping she was not acting the way she felt.

Alex cleared her throat. "You said you had a headache and were going to bed."

Nyla gave them an innocent look. "Willow bark works quickly."

Alex threw her arms into the air. "Enough make-believe. Are you, in fact, meeting Aza nightly after curfew?"

Nyla glared at them. "What exactly are you saying?" She stood in front of her, her head held high. "We talk, naturally, about how to handle casualties once we attack E'Doom."

"You know that is not what I'm asking," Alex said. "People are talking." She put one hand on her hip. "They say there is something going on between you and Aza."

"How dare you accuse me?"

"You are jeopardizing our mission! How dare you!" Alex pointed a finger. "We were told by some of the soldiers that you and Aza stay away from the camp for hours, hiding out somewhere in the forest and sneaking back into camp before sunrise." Alex folded her arms over her chest. "Some reports say there is a faction of soldiers that have become a cult. They are practicing the dark arts and have forsaken the faith." Alex paused, attempting to control her words. "You both have lied to the elders, the senior officers, and your team, pretending to be casual acquaintances."

Nyla smirked. "How dare you accuse a princess. I will never be your subordinate. Besides you have no proof."

"Watch yourself, Nyla. Your words can be considered sedition."

Nyla wanted to kick herself for letting her thoughts betray her feelings. "You know how these groups can get. Gossip." She rolled her eyes. "Gossip is all this nonsense amounts too. I can't believe you actually believed their rumors." She forced a tear. "I'm totally focused on our cause. God sent us. I have trained for this all my life. I would never let anything get in the way of our mission."

Nyla burst into tears. "Someone had to take your place." She tried to hide her contempt. "The soldiers needed to have a representative from Safehold to help them adjust while you recovered. I was thinking about you."

Alex stiffened. "You can't possibly expect us to believe you. Soldiers have witnessed you with him constantly." The men and women in his squadron said Aza has missed meetings that are crucial to our operation."

Nyla sobbed. "I swear to you these accusations are untrue. My focus is on our assignment and that only. I have been diligently working toward our goal of restoring these people to faith."

Alex shifted her weight from one foot to the other. "Rumors can destroy our attempts to rally the troops." She ran her hand through her hair. "I want to believe you, but," she lowered her voice, "my heart says you're lying."

Nyla wiped the tears from her face and stomped over to stand next to Beryl. "Prophet, reason with her. Tell her how dedicated I have been.

Beryl looked down at his sandaled feet.

Alex's face tightened. "I will not tolerate any more of these distractions. We must remain alert! Our duty comes before our passions."

Nyla smirked. "I guess that is what I should expect, coming from a nun. You have no idea what you're talking about."

Alex folded her arms across her chest. "This is the second time today someone criticized my chosen profession." The warrior let her arm fall to her side. "I answer to no one but God."

A group of girls walked out of the cave and waved to the messengers.

Alex lowered her voice. "Sex outside of marriage is a sin and you know it!"

Nyla took a handkerchief from her tunic and blotted her eyes. She looked squarely at Alex and Beryl with the most angelic innocent look she could conjure and lied. "I have no desire to have a sexual relationship with Aza." She leaned against the tree trunk as though she could barely stand. "I swear to God, I am not lying."

Alex looked around the perimeter of the cave. "There are heavenly angels guarding the mountain tonight. I can see them." She shivered. "This night is different from other nights" She put her hand on the hilt of her sword. "If you decide to go into the forest, outside the hedge of protection, you will be on your own." She walked away, leaving the two standing in the moonlight.

Nyla watched Alex enter the cave. "I think she lost more than just her eyesight in the Chasm."

Beryl looked around the compound. "I don't see a heavenly army, but I believe Alex does." He pulled his hood over his head. "You would be wise to heed her warning." He bid her good night and retreated into the cave.

Nyla stood alone, wishing she could make herself invisible. The loud confrontation had brought curious onlookers outside to check the commotion.

"What's going on?" Gemma asked.

Nyla remembered when she first arrived, she had prayed

for healing for this girl's boils. Holding her head high, she hoped she looked more confident than she felt. "A misunderstanding. Nothing important."

She walked to the entrance of the cave, looked over her shoulders, and watched the group whispering to each other. *Ridiculous gossips are just jealous of me.*

Aza made his way to the south entrance. The young man on duty stood straight and saluted the approaching officer.

Aza rested his hand on the guard's shoulder. "You look like you could use a break tonight. Let me take this shift for you."

The boy protested, "I'm fine. I promise you, sir. I am wide awake and ready to defend this line with my life."

Aza squeezed his shoulder, hoping the recruit understood his intent. "I appreciate your zeal, but I'm taking your shift."

The young man tried to object. "Sir. I know we face great danger tonight, but I can handle this."

Aza was adamant. "Now, soldier!"

The tone in Aza's voice left no doubt as to what he wanted.

"Yes, sir." He saluted his superior and hurried off.

Aza breathed a sigh of relief. The lingering night had brought clouds that hung low, covering the moon. He was glad for the extra cover but there was a traitor in their midst, and he had no clue who it was or why they would attack Simeon? He was sure of one thing. This assassin would turn their location over to the authorities and an attack was sure to follow. He began to think he and Nyla should change their plans. Footsteps startled him, and he drew his sword from its sheath.

Nyla walked toward him. Her beauty was unlike any woman he had ever seen in Old World. Her long curls fell loosely over her shoulders and down her slender back. A few loose tendrils framed her face, accentuating her high cheekbones and hypnotic eyes. Her full lips were seductive as were her womanly curves under her lightweight tunic.

They embraced and kissed long and passionately.

Aza pushed reason out of his mind and grabbed her hand leading her into the cover of the forest. They ran through the glade, turning now and then to make sure they were not followed. Nyla pulled back, out of breath, and pointed to the full moon that peeked at them through the clouds. Aza looked heavenward. She put her index finger to her lips, bidding the planet to keep their secret. They found a clearing in the woods that smelled of pine and damp earth and stopped to embrace again.

Nyla's head barely reached his broad shoulders. She looked into his eyes and felt her heart melt like wax. She buried her head in his chest, loving the musky scent of sun and horses. His leather-clad thigh brushed against her leg, igniting her passion. She felt herself spinning out of control.

"I've never felt like this about anyone before," Aza whispered. His voice was deep and masculine, husky with desire. He spread his cloak over the soft pine needles and pulled Nyla to the ground beneath him.

His touch was gentle yet knowing. His breath warm on her cheek and she felt tingly all over as he kissed her neck. His actions sent shock waves through her entire body. She let her emotions take control and gave herself completely to his demands.

As the night wore on, they made love, completely oblivious to the world around them. The lovers were unaware of the shift in the weather and fell asleep in each other's arms. Black clouds crept across the sky, and a wind began to rise.

Nyla stretched. Her eyes fluttered open and she gazed upward through the canopy of evergreen boughs from her bed of pine needles under a tall juniper. She dreamily gazed at the large white moon that filled the heavens, bathing the underbelly of the forest in peaceful shadows like a chapel lit with hundreds of small votive candles. It was a perfect night to lose her virginity.

A soft breeze caressed Nyla's naked body. She felt beautiful. She could not believe how wonderful it felt to be in love. Her emotions jumped inside her body like playful fauns, happy and free.

Aza's hair fell onto her shoulder. She snuggled closer into his broad chest, relishing the strength of his arms entwined about her body. He made her feel safe, loved, and protected. She could not remember ever being this content or happy. *How can our lovemaking be wrong?* she wondered. *Maybe for others who are just experimenting with sex. But between Aza and me, there is something special, sacred.*

The forest had been their secret meeting place for the past few weeks. They were free to hide in the cover of the trees, outside the protective confines of the camp, so they could get to know each other—privately. They both knew the danger of being inside enemy lines, but lust doused all their fears.

Her forehead creased as she tried to reason away her feelings. *I'm not sorry for deceiving my team about my other life or my relationship with Aza. It is none of their business. Our feelings for each other are not jeopardizing the mission. I am still capable of doing my part to help restore the remnant to a deeper relationship with God. After all, intercourse outside of marriage is an acceptable sin in the eyes of the world. I just need to be careful not to become pregnant and no one will be the wiser.*

Nyla absently twirled a long curl in her fingers. She knew her companions' stand on sex before marriage. It was absolutely forbidden! It was her opinion too before she met Aza and fell in love. She snuggled closer into his warm naked body. Her mind wrestled with her hormones.

I don't need the old rules to tell me what to do. I am sixteen, definitely old enough to make my own moral decisions.

Besides God created sex, so how could this act of passion be wrong?

She gently rested her hand on Aza's chest, feeling his heartbeat and the rise and fall of his masculine chest. The coffee color of her skin next to his pale torso made a rich contrast in the moonlight. She gently allowed her fingertips to run over his muscled abdominals. She could barely keep her hands off him, awed by his physical beauty.

Aza was everything she ever dreamed of from the time she was a child. Brave, honest, intelligent, gentle; she stifled a giggle. He was unbelievably handsome, and he belonged to her now. She was not using him to get what she wanted. Their union was not an act of infatuation fueled by their immediate feelings; they were in love, and nothing else mattered.

She stretched and rolled to her back. An icy chill caused her to look upward. She expected to see one of the constellations, perfectly represented in the heavens, but something evil caught her eye. Black claw-like clouds had scratched open the sky, scattering the stars into a new hideous assemblage.

A loud crashing in the distance alerted her that some enemy was rushing through the forest straight for them, breaking and snapping tree branches. Aza stirred in his sleep and pulled his cloak over their bodies.

Nyla gasped, sitting bolt upright. "What is that noise?" She strained her eyes, looking into the ominous black forest that had closed in around them. The wind picked up speed, taking on a life of its own. It rushed upon them, whistling, hissing, and howling like a tempest, bending and contorting the treetops.

"We must leave now, something horrific is coming!" she screamed.

Aza jumped up and began frantically looking for his trousers. He pulled them on, jumping from one foot to another. Nyla sat dumbly on the ground, looking up at him, her eyes pools of fear. He grabbed her tunic and sandals from the pile of clothing left carelessly on the ground and threw them at her. She quickly slipped the flimsy garment over her head.

Bat-like creatures came out of the air, screaming, writhing, and swooping around them. Nyla froze with her shoes still in her hand. They lifted her into the air as though she was weightless.

She kicked and punched the vapor like phantoms, but they held her in a tight grip. When they carried her above the treetops, she stopped struggling, afraid they might throw her to the ground. Looking down, she saw the entrance of the cave where the rest of the tribe hid from the enemy. She saw the guards, her friends, huddled in small groups, trying to hide from the invading army. To her astonishment, she watched as random flashes of light shot across the sky, momentarily revealing an army of angels with flaming swords, fighting the evil spirits of the air.

She saw Beryl and Alex bolt from the cave entrance. Her partners were pointing in the direction she and Aza traveled and seemed to be issuing orders to the confused and frightened soldiers.

Nyla was able to hear a word here and there before the wind carried the voices away.

"In the forest...South entrance," someone yelled.

Nyla squirmed in the phantom's arms. "Look up!" she screamed, hoping Alex would hear her over the noise. "The demon army of the air is surrounding you."

Her captor squeezed her so tight she cried out in pain. The murderer who held her captive dropped to the ground where Aza stood swinging his sword, trying to fight the phantom attackers.

The spirit spoke to her with a garbled voice. "You left the narrow path to follow the deceiver. This is your reward!"

She watched helplessly as Aza tried to use human

weapons against the spirits of hell. "Use God's Word as your sword," Nyla pleaded. She reached for him. "Your strength is powerless against them."

His eyes met hers. She saw confusion and fear.

She listened to them taunt him.

"You are a lukewarm believer and have no authority over us. Both of you have been led astray by your own desires. You look like disciples on the outside but have no spiritual life inside."

Nyla's eyes filled with tears as she watched him fall prey to their evil power.

Aza's lips curled into a snarl and the whites of his eyes gleamed under the harsh moonlight like a cornered animal.

She reached out and touched his outstretched hand. It was warm, full of life, and she could feel his pulse pumping with adrenalin through his wrist.

The demons swarmed about him and his flesh began to burn. "Your unbelief has made you weak and powerless against us."

Aza fell to the ground like a lifeless mound of ash.

Nyla could not catch her breath. Her senses seemed suspended in another time and space. Her eyes took in the reality of Aza's death, and she felt something within her spirit die. She could not feel the cold wind that flung her hair across her face or hear the inhuman laughter of her captors or smell her lover's charred flesh. Instead she felt an overpowering sense of shame. She hung within her captor's ghostly forms, suspended like a rag doll.

Within the storm clouds, Alex saw a demonic general, with pitch black hair and ebony wings, directed the army of death. The spirits of the air swooped out of the sky riding large black clouds that looked like dragons shooting lightning from their mouths.

"Stop the prayer warriors. Kill those who kneel in the

face of our onslaught."

The spirits pounced on those who prayed using their weapons to inflict wounds of doubt and fear into God's army.

Legions of warlords thundered into the camp, followed by Soul-Sifters anxious to feast on the weak.

An archangel of the heavenly army heard the songs of worship and the prayers of the faithful followers of God and appeared in the midst of the battle. His six massive wings began to beat the air. The force of his power blew the general and his army of death across the sky and cast them into space. His eyes were as lightning striking the warlords and Soul-Sifters, splitting the enemy as fine as dust.

Alex watched in awe.

The archangels arms and legs were more powerful then pillars of bronze and he crushed the horde of King Apollyon's army under his feet. He called out orders and Alex covered her ears. The sound of his voice was louder than thousands upon thousands of cheering men. The sky thundered at the sound of his command and the earth shook under her feet. Alex witnessed an army of angels advance on the demons.

Black flames hissed from enemy swords. In a desperate attempt to gain ground, they raised their weapons against God's heavenly host, but the light from the angels' swords grew brighter and swallowed the black flames, extinguishing their power. The angels of light battled the demon horde, killing many while others retreated.

Kali rode into the forest on a winged jackal and made a quick assessment of the battlefield. Her heart pumped in her chest as she realized because of prayer, God's army won the battle in the air. She dismounted and turned her attention to the healer, making sure she was unharmed. The girl was bent over her dead lover, void of all emotion.

Kali grabbed Nyla by her hair and pulled her to her feet.

The demon guards laughed at her pain.

"Get her to the castle now!" she ordered. "Make sure you take care not to harm her or you will experience your master's wrath. We have lost this battle." She looked around in horror. "Go! Before the infidels steal our prisoner."

They lifted Nyla above the grove. As she looked around, she could not believe the forest was scorched like it had been through a great fire with trees, foliage, and ground cover burned beyond recognition. She wanted to cry out to her friends as she watched them retrace her steps to the spot where she and Aza had made love; and now, he lay dead. In her heart, she desperately wanted this nightmare to be a dream and she would wake up in Safehold.

The banshees flew from the scene, clutching Nyla tightly within their ghostly forms, passing her body from one to the other. These formless ribbons of mist loved toying with her, intentionally causing her pain. The otherworldly beings were capable of taking on many shapes and sizes. Sometimes under the night sky, they looked almost human with contorted hideous faces. Their bodies looked skeletal with a thin membrane of flesh clinging to bone. Leathery wings propelled them through the air.

At other times, they were like vapor, a dark formless mist, void of human or animal limbs. The foul mist twisted and wrapped around Nyla's body. They flew across the sky like shapeless clouds tossed by the wind.

The hideout she called home for the past month began to shrink in the distance. Her apathy turned to rage, and she kicked and punched at her captors, hoping they would drop her to the ground before it was too late and she would be forever lost. Her outburst made them more vicious toward her. They controlled their desire for bloodlust while they knotted and encircled themselves about her body. They squeezed the air from her lungs, careful not to kill her.

They flew back toward Castle E'Doom.

Nyla stopped fighting her abductors. She knew she was at their mercy. The phantoms soared through the air, leaving the scene of attack far behind them. Nyla watched as mile after mile swallowed her allies, the camp, and the mountain range. Her heart sank as she witnessed everything that was familiar become small specks in the distance.

CHAPTER 29

Refining Fire

As quickly as the wind and fire had come up, it stilled. All around the camp, trees stood dead and stripped of their foliage. Grass and moss were charred and burned. The glade reeked of smoke. Silence overshadowed the dark night.

"I see something beyond the tree line," Beryl whispered to Alex.

Beryl led the warriors across the moonlit meadow. They were stunned to find a lifeless soul.

Alex bent down and rolled the body over. Her heart fluttered like a bird in a trap. She sensed it was Aza, not Nyla, who lay dead at her feet. His body was covered in ash.

"You were sent here to help us." Sargo sobbed. "Instead you brought death and destruction upon us all."

Beryl took off his cloak and covered Aza's form. "Do not weep," the prophet demanded. "God's love will not fail us."

He began to pray, laying his hands and his staff over Aza's body. Alex and the unseen host of angels circled the dead youth. Alex began to pray in unusual tongues, along with the prophet. The band of soldiers followed their lead and half-heartedly joined the prayer.

"This is crazy," Sargo said. "He's dead!"

"It will take a miracle to bring him back to life," another whispered.

An unfamiliar power surged around them. The feeling

was electric and seemed to be pumping through their veins and running into Aza's lifeless form.

A quiet sound, like the breath of heaven, whispered peace around them.

"What is that sound?" Tika asked. She looked around. "There is no wind. The forest is still."

Beryl's voice was loud and forceful as he called on Jesus the healer; his staff started to burn with a searing white light, yet he held it in his hands.

"Lord Jesus Christ, you said in your Word, where two or more are gathered in your name you will be with them…"

Aza heard Beryl's voice, but he was too far away to understand the words. Darkness surrounded him, and fear gripped his heart. He could feel his heartbeat slow down, and he couldn't get enough air in his lungs. A dark figure stood over him—waiting. He tried to fight death, but his body wouldn't move. He knew his spirit was dying.

Heavenly Father, you saved me from the soul-sifters once before. I know you are real, but I rejected you. Please forgive me for turning my back on you, over and over again. I believe that Jesus Christ is your Son who came to earth and died on the cross at Calvary so I could be forgiven and have eternal life in heaven. Father, I believe Jesus rose from the dead, and I ask right now that he would be my Lord and Savior.

The dark figure began to back away into the darkness, and a man with a white robe held out his hand. Aza reached for it, and his eyes opened. It was pitch-black, but he could hear Beryl, Alex, and the entire tribe praying for him.

"We ask you, Jesus, to restore Aza to life that he may live as a changed man, a new creation."

In the heavens, the image of the Red Dragon disappeared.

The sky opened. Swirling red clouds made random circular patterns in the black inky sky. The wild atmospheric event mixed with flashes of lightning. Fire rained from heaven like an autumn shower, yet it did not burn their flesh or the glade where they stood.

The warriors looked around in stunned amazement. Power emanated all around them which astonished, awed, and amazed them. A calm sense of peace descended on the tribe.

The sound of the wind stopped, and every eye was fixed on the two sent from Safehold. Beryl gently lifted his cape from Aza's body and placed it back on his shoulders.

Miraculously Aza's flesh was restored without a spot or blemish. Alex backed away while Beryl helped Aza to his feet. The soldiers gasped in unbelief. Many clan members fell to the ground and began to worship God. Friends of the deceased pushed forward to examine their companion who was completely restored.

Sargo weaved his way through the crowd to see what happened. "This cannot be." His voice was a murmur. "No one comes back from the dead."

Aza tried to put his arm around his brother's shoulder, but Sargo backed away in fear.

"I understand your confusion," Aza whispered in hushed awe. "Jesus took my death upon himself." He held his hands up to his face and examined them. "This gift of new life is real." His voice rushed with excitement. "Everything our ancestors and the elders told us is true. I did not understand or believe before." He laughed and walked through the stunned army.

"There really is a God who loves us." He looked into Sargo's shocked face. "He cared enough about me to send his only Son to die in my place. He died that I might live. He took the guilt and blame for my sins." He gazed at the sky in wonder.

The soldiers backed away, murmuring among themselves.

"What does this mean?" Tika asked, pointing at the red

swirling clouds.

"The dead walk and speak of God," Sargo mocked. "It is a trick created by the messengers."

Tika ran forward. Her faced was covered in ash, streaked with tears. "It can't be a trick. Aza is alive." She stumbled toward the soldier and reached out to touch him.

Baccus grabbed her tunic and pulled her back. "No…"

She twisted from his grasp and took Aza's hand. "He is flesh!" She threw her arms around him and cried.

Others came near and touched him.

"I heard about salvation, but I did not care about any of it," Aza confided. "Now I have experienced something so wonderful I could never doubt this truth again. I accepted Jesus as my Lord and Savior and he baptized me in the Holy Spirit. I am clean and free from my past as though I never sinned. I can see spiritual things now, and I can understand."

His excitement had everyone's attention. "His love for me, while I was lost in sin, is so clear I'm not sure how I missed it before. I am born anew on the inside, a new person in Christ. The old person is gone. Now I am ready to live my life to glorify God."

His voice shifted and he began to sing.

> Passed through the murky cesspool of lies
> Through fire so hot it purifies
> Ignited my tongue with a word that consumes
> I've passed through the furnace
> And come back renewed
> Filled with his Spirit my faith is rekindle
> Flickering embers stoked into flame
> Back from the dead
> Reborn again
> Passed through the murky cesspool of lies

Through fire so hot it purifies
Ignited the passion to free up my mind
From the chains of self-prison
And come back with vision
Let go of all terror, fear, and dread
Fell into the arms of God instead
Back from the dead
Reborn again
Consume us with fire
And set us aflame
With the truth of your message
And the power of your name
Tongues of fire as our weapon and a double-edged sword
To the nations that hunger for freedom
Passed through the murky cesspool of lies
Through fire so hot it purifies
Ignited my heart to surrender control
To Jesus who died to save my soul
Triumphant over death and the grave
Outpouring his Spirit on all who will pray
Moving forward in strength set on fire from above
Back from the dead
Reborn again

As Aza told them of his journey, from death to rebirth, Beryl prayed for those who were listening. A feeling, a tangible presence, surrounded the group. Some wept quietly as the Spirit of God fell upon them and they made their peace with God. Many began to speak in a new prayer language while others spoke prophetic words. A new strength and conviction spread through the camp. The outpouring of the Holy Spirit filled each believer with courage and boldness to take back from Apollyon what he stole from them.

Sargo walked away from the crowd that settled around Aza. He sat on the ground as sobs shook his body. Ravenna told him of her visit with the demon in the forest. She asked him to go with her when the promised escort arrived to take her to Castle E'Doom. He refused. He wanted revenge for the way his brother betrayed him for a secret love affair. He decided not to tell anyone what Ravenna had done or that Apollyon was sending something evil to take Nyla away. He never expected Aza's death and rebirth.

He looked up at the sound of footfalls behind him and saw his brother standing over him. He stood up and started to speak, but guilt overwhelmed him. He turned toward the forest and ran. Aza started to follow, but Beryl stopped him.

"You can't force him or anyone else to believe." Beryl rested his hand on Aza's shoulder. "Let him go. He must make his own choice as we have made ours."

Alex began to speak to the soldiers. "The Spirit of God set us free from the forces of darkness. We are filled with supernatural power. Think of yourselves as God's arsenal. No weapon the enemy tries to use against us shall triumph."

Alex continued to instruct the army. "We are ready to take our stand against the evil one who sits on the throne in Old World. With the help of God's Spirit, we are more than conquers!"

The small army cheered.

"You have the promise of a new start, a transformed life, and a new relationship with God." Her voice shook with excitement.

"I will not lie to you. This spiritual battle will be difficult and demanding. There is no room for fear or retreat. War is no time for selfish ambition and vainglory. It is a time to stand together against sin."

The army agreed.

Alex's expression was as stone. "The price of freedom

is not only vigilance but also blood. This walk of faith is challenging and not to be taken lightly. We must be on our guard constantly. Some of us may have to die for this freedom."

Her mind and body felt ancient. She forced herself to stay steady and strong while she spoke. "Beryl will organize our prayer and worship warriors. I want everyone to be ready to march out at sunrise. I'm sure our victory will not go unpunished by King Apollyon. Our hideout has been compromised and the giants will be preparing to attack us."

Her thoughts registered on her face as a stunned expression of pain. "The prophet and I will go alone to release Nyla."

Aza grabbed Alex's arm and spun her around to face him. "It is my fault she was captured. I must be the one to go and release her. I will never forgive myself if anything happens to her."

"I understand how you feel." Alex put a comforting hand on his shoulder. "The army will need your leadership more than ever. They are great warriors but new in the Spirit. They will need someone they trust to guide them through the rough territory ahead."

Aza clenched his teeth and raked his hand through his hair. "I know what you're saying is true but..." He looked away. "I feel like a knife is twisting in my heart." His eyes filled with tears.

"Let Baccus lead. He is fearless and knows what to do. Beryl can go with them and I will go with you."

"I'm sorry, Aza. I need the prophet's gifts, along with mine, to free her and to deal with whatever else we may encounter along the way."

Beryl spoke softly to his friend. "We have each been given different gifts to use in God's service. Ralf, Eldon, Tika, and the others have new abilities that will complement yours. All of you working together will accomplish what God has planned."

Aza bit back his disappointment and anger. Beryl's gentle grip on his shoulder stilled him. He hated to have to submit to Beryl's authority, but this boy had proved himself solid, strong, and wise.

"Promise me you won't let him hurt her."

"Nothing can separate us from the love of our Savior. Do not worry. We will bring her back and meet you in E'Doom, on the eve of the Blood Moon."

"Wait!" Tika argued. "Give us the lightning stick so we can have the same power as the prophet."

"You don't need the staff," Beryl said with a look of amusement in his eyes. "The power is not in the rod. That is just a prop, a symbol." He held the staff and shook it over his head. "The power is in the name of Jesus. Have faith in his authority and the authority he has given you as a child of God. That belief will produce the power to overcome every obstacle you and the army will face."

He handed the staff to the young warrior who held it cautiously. She looked it over and handed it back.

"You have been filled with the Holy Spirit, the very power of God. Each person who has been born again becomes the blazing staff of fire. As you take this message forth in boldness and courage, God will empower you to do great and mighty works in his name."

Alex stood on a scorched tree stump so all the army could see and hear her. "We are greatly outnumbered by the enemy. Victory does not depend on our small numbers or on our mere courage. Our power comes from a greater source—the highest power in the universe."

The Tribe cheered and whistled their agreement.

"The power that has been born within us will not burst forth without some effort on our part. We need to hone our skills as soldiers in the army of Christ through discipline, training, and study every day."

"We are eager for victory," a voice shouted.

Alex felt lightness and energy in her spirit. "The enemy will come against us with a new vengeance." She walked through the troops. "Your level of power will depend on your level of obedience to the words God left you in the Book of Life."

She picked up one of the enemies' discarded weapons and held it over her head. "The devil and his forces are at work and do not want us to succeed. We must stand against Satan's strategies by wearing all of our armor at all times. When we relax, we become fair game."

She threw the battle-ax on the ground and picked up her breastplate of chain mail. "As you know, this weapon protects and guards our vital organs." The silver metal glistened in her hands.

"The enemy will do everything in his power to pierce your heart with his poison." Her face glowed in the torchlight. "We must guard our hearts at all costs, for it is here," she pounded her chest with a right fist, "that we pledge our allegiance to God."

She slipped the armor over her red tunic and instructed the soldiers to do the same. The clatter of armor echoed through the camp.

"Our breastplate will deflect the blows from enemy weapons. Satan, who we call King Apollyon, and his legion will try to tempt us, create guilt, and accuse us of being weak in our walk with Christ." She folded her arms across her chest. "We are bought and paid for, servants of the Lord Jesus Christ, and washed in his blood." She pointed at the troops. "Never forget, in the heat of battle, the price Jesus paid for your redemption."

She held the next piece of armor in the air. "My friends, here is our belt of truth. This belt holds everything we believe together." She wrapped the thick bronze-studded piece of black leather around her waist. "It is a simple strip of leather to hold our other weapons." She tightened the strap, binding her tunic close to her body, then slipped her dagger into a pouch on her left hip.

"The Word of God is reliable, consistent, and unfailing. Without a firm belief in his truth, the rest of our armor is worthless." She slid her sword into the sheath. The soldiers put on the second piece of their covering.

She held her triangular-shaped shield in front of her body. "This piece of equipment is the heart of our defense. Soldiers who use their shields have a much better chance of survival on the battlefield. This weapon defends, protects, and wards off Satan's fiery arrows of lies."

She called Aza to stand by her side. "Suit up," she said. "We will spar."

She put her helmet over her thick black hair. "Never forget the helmet. It protects the most important organ of the body." She paused to align the piece of metal that ran down the middle of her forehead and rested over the bridge of her nose. "Our minds are Satan's prime targets. Whoever holds our thoughts will possess our hearts."

She pulled her sword and faced off with Aza. With weapons held high, they fought; metal clanged and scraped with each blow. "The enemy won't hit your shield intentionally, he's smarter than that. He will thrust high." She lunged at Aza. The warrior moved his shield to block the attack.

"Beware. He wants you to move the shield around to create an opening." She moved in for the kill. "He is the deceiver. He will counterattack where you least expect or are most vulnerable."

The warriors began again; this time, Alex thrust low, Aza countered the move. Their swords clashed against the shields. "There will be intense exchanges of attack and counterattack to get you to give up the good fight of faith or give in to temptation." She swung her sword high, the blade stopped on Aza's neck.

The match ended, and the warriors shook hands.

"He will attempt to kill, steal, and destroy your life through unbelief and compromise."

She pulled off her helmet; wet hair clung to her face. "Our enemy is devious. He is a formidable opponent. That is why we must rely heavily on our sword."

She held the weapon high. "Power to defeat the enemy lies within the blade of the spoken word." She held the sword reverently. "The Word of God is alive and full of power." She swung her sword in mock battle. "The word is sharper than any two-edged sword; it divides soul and spirit; and it judges the thoughts and purposes of the heart" (Hebrews 4:12).

A young warrior spoke from the crowd. "Our weapons don't look like yours. They are worn and dull."

Alex nodded. "With continual use, your armor will look just like mine. The weapons of warfare are the same for all of us."

She pointed to her feet. "Each time we engage the enemy, we must stand firm, with our feet firmly planted, to endure an oncoming charge. We march into battle every time we share our faith and rescue lives from the devil's kingdom and bring captives into God's presence."

The regiment finished suiting up and gave her their full attention. "Satan always attacks us at our weakest point of defense. If any part of your armor is missing, it creates a point of entry to a demon weapon. The enemy will come at us with every trick his black magic can conjure. He is powerful, keep that in mind and stay alert. He wants to destroy our lives and our witness." She wiped soot and sweat from her face. "Satan can only defeat us if we rely on our own power. We have received supernatural weapons to defeat the hordes of hell. The Holy Spirit lives within us. He is the fuel that keeps us on fire for God and gives us extra strength against the enemy's arsenal."

Beryl called the soldiers to order. "We must intensify our prayers and increase our guard. The elders of the tribe and the worship band will ride among you and intercede as you travel and while you are engaged in battle," he said.

Aza raised a questioning brow.

"I know this sounds unusual, but praise and prayer are powerful weapons against these evil forces." He clasped Aza around the shoulder. "We need to be prepared to fight with the correct weapons in order to win the battle."

Wind blew a piece of hair into Alex's eyes. She went stiff for a moment at the thought of Nyla and the banshees. "We will need to have our few belongings packed and on the wagons by daybreak. I want to post a double guard for the remainder of the evening. One group to pray and one group to watch for air and ground attacks. At sunrise, we need to deploy."

A hush settled over the group. The tribe went into action with a new hope of victory in their hearts.

"God will lead us away from our past failures and give us vision for our future," she said. "Tomorrow is a new day with enough danger of its own."

CHAPTER 30

Road to Destruction

The dark angels flew like a tempest through villages that dotted the region on their way to Castle E'Doom. The sleepy countryside awoke at the screeching and wailing of the banshees. Row upon row of cottages became black holes as the occupants quickly extinguished candles and oil lamps that flickered within the settlement's windows only moments before. In the dark watches of night, the loud clang of metal scraping wood could be distinguished as the villagers bolted their doors and locked their windows. The most rebellious child would not dare peek outside to watch the death angels fly past under the light of the red sky.

The landscape was washed in an odd palette of light. The autumn midnight had fallen under the eye of the red dragon. The valleys and hillsides were bathed in hues of crimson. The peasants were on edge, wondering what new tactics the enemy army may employ. This Age of Horus ushered into the land a growing poison of heart, soul, and mind.

At the sight of the village, with thin ropes of smoke trailing from chimney vents, hope began to rise within Nyla's heart. *People are home. Someone will save me.* As the phantoms swooped low along the silent streets, she began to scream.

"Help me!" she pleaded as she kicked and punched her abductors. "Please help me!"

She reached out her arms and tried to grab hold of a wooden fence post as they whirled past. She cried in pain, her arms felt like they were ripped from their socket. Her shoulders burned. "Someone help me!" To her disappointment, no one came forward. Only her own tortured cries echoed back to her ringing ears like a cruel slap in the face.

Cooking pots and campfires were left unattended and no movement from outside the huts met these evil travelers. Their high-pitched cries kept everyone locked within their respective hovels. Frightened settlers waited for the apparitions to leave their vicinity. No one cared to investigate the identity of the prisoner. They had witnessed this type of abduction before and knew interference would bring a killing spree upon the entire village.

They dragged her, on and on, sometimes lifting her high into the sky where she could see for miles, and then abruptly dropping close to the ground, forcing her to be struck and bruised by tree limbs as they whirled through the air.

Finally, Nyla spotted a jungle of trees that spread out before them for miles. Her tormentors shifted their speed and dropped low to the ground until they found a small opening. They maneuvered through the deep forest that closed leafy arms behind the specters, swallowing the unholy group inside the belly of thick tress, leaving no signs of a path. Wolves howled and snarled as they raced madly behind the spirits, following the scent of human flesh. Nyla could feel their hot breath on her dangling legs.

The heathen wilderness screamed with frightful sounds. Creaking trees with dry rustling leaves played a soulful death march. The banshees flew close to the ground and Nyla had to draw her knees to her chest when she felt the earth beneath her feet change into a wet soggy carpet. Foul-smelling slime clung to her clothes, body, and matted hair. Toppled trees, stripped of bark and bleached white, floated atop the marshy ground cover like pews in an unnatural place of worship.

Her abductors forced her further into the swamp that was home to all things that slithered. Mosquitoes and countless other insects erupted from the gloom and swarmed her body, buzzing around her in a feeding frenzy, relishing the taste of fresh blood. Nyla choked on the violent stench of decay, filth, and animal rot. She saw carnivorous plants, along with slugs as thick as her arm, feed upon spores that were incubating in this putrid cauldron.

Hollowed-out cypress trees and petrified oaks, draped with moss, welcomed her at the door of this cathedral. Her abductors lowered her into the marsh. She screamed as the cold slimy water covered her body. *Please just let me die.*

Mudbugs glided atop the murky water, and evil eyes peered at her from the muddy depths. Something slithered past her leg, caressing her flesh. "Lift me up! Something has my leg!" she screamed.

Her captors let her go.

Nyla sunk beneath the surface. She thrashed around, helplessly lost in the watery darkness.

Her abductor yanked her up by her hair. She came out of the water, sputtering and gasping for breath.

"Think of me as your priest." It laughed. "Let me baptize you in this filthy water."

The booming roar of a bull alligator sent chills through her body. Winged lizards began screeching along with night birds until their cries devolved into animal-like barks. Nyla began to scream along with them, her voice became part of some pitiless choir.

The demons lifted her from the rancid water onto the forest floor. They dragged her along, forcing her to run to keep on her feet. Patches of brier with sharp thorns dug mercilessly into her bare feet. Her blood left a tantalizing trail for all manner of unholy beings to follow.

Terror flooded her heart. Not because she was afraid of what her tormentors would do to her body, but she was ashamed to pray. Tears flooded her face, mixing with the grime that dried like plaster on her cheeks. *All my life, my Heavenly Father took care of me, protected me, and loved me. I betrayed him. I lied to my friends and ruined our mission. Aza is dead, and it is my fault.*

The banshees reveled in her sorrow and regret, and it seemed to make them stronger. They picked up the pace, forcing Nyla to fall and skin her knees, shins, and chest as they sprinted forward, dragging their prisoner over the rough terrain. She screamed in anguish. Her heart pounded and drummed in her ears. Her breath came in labored gasps, and she feared her lungs were going to explode. She felt, at any moment, she was going to pass out.

"Stop. I beg you," she whispered.

Unexpectedly they dropped her on the ground and disappeared into the air. She sat on the grass, shocked and terrified. *I don't dare open my eyes. I don't want to see where they left me.* She pulled her body into a tight ball, hoping to make her frame invisible. She tried to control her breathing that was coming in great spasms. Her gasping was loud. She covered her mouth with a filthy hand, hoping to quiet her breathing.

I need to focus. Her mind screamed. *I need to breathe slowly and with control.* She tried to force her mind to obey. Images of Aza, burned by the death angels, battered her mind. She forced her eyes open to blot out the memory of her lover's death. Looking around, she tried to take in her situation. To her surprise, she was sitting on a cobbled walkway, overrun with weeds that led to the gates of a graveyard. Old crooked trees, covered with ivy and overgrown shrubs, grew haphazardly over the entry and on the stone wall that circled the perimeter of the cemetery.

She knew it would be impossible to go back the way she

came. She wanted to take off running but needed to take stock of her injuries. Long jagged scratches and deep cuts crisscrossed her arms and legs. Something wet was dripping down her face, but under the light of the moon, she could not tell if it was muddy swamp water or blood. She used her sleeve to wipe grime from her eyes.

Her feet were sore and sticky from blood that oozed out of numerous lacerations. She tore strips of cloth from her filthy tunic and wrapped them as gently as possible around her feet before trying to find the strength to stand on shaky legs.

Nyla stood for a moment, trying to force her body to stop quivering. She held her breath and listened to the eerie sound of the night. Rustling tree limbs, the flutter of bird wings, whispers, and heavy breathing seemed to be coming from every direction. She looked around and saw something crouching in the shadows. A hysterical whimper escaped her throat. Her own voice frightened her, and she began stumbling desperately toward the entrance of the necropolis.

In her frenzy, tree limbs tangled in her hair, ripping clumps from her scalp. Branches tore at her clothing, pulling and pushing her as she fled the unseen stalker. She stumbled and fell to the ground but kept going, crawling on her hands and knees toward the iron gates. Her blood roared in her ears like rushing water. Night sounds and running footsteps were gaining on her. She reached the entrance and pulled herself to a standing position, pressing her fevered face against the cold metal door. She hung there like a moth in a spiderweb—waiting.

Particles of rust dusted her hair and face from the weather-beaten iron archway. With no effort on her part, the gate slowly inched open, guiding her into the city of the dead. A cold hand touched her from behind, and she lost all sense of reason and began running and screaming through the main street of the cemetery.

As I ran, a weird feeling of displacement came over me, and I noticed, for the first time, that my feet were no longer touching the ground. I was gliding along the path, smooth and silent. No crunching footfalls on gravel. No pounding heartbeat. No gasping breath, no breathing at all. No sensation of pain, no feeling of warmth, no icy chill touched my body. No stench of stagnant swamp water filled my nostrils. No noise. Not a sound. Only my thoughts came with me.

In this place of the deceased, there were no colors, only shades of black and white. The moon glowed with a pale misty light in the sky, casting a gray pallor of contrast over the deserted city of monuments. I tried to turn around to go back but could not control my own actions. Something outside myself was manipulating my movements. I was being ushered past stone markers where the voices of the dead were forever suspended in stone.

Cold stones, with etchings of angels, lions, gargoyles, and demons, stood side by side, guarding the resting place of their departed. The grounds on which this place of repose rested looked neglected and forgotten. Some of the stones lay on their sides like fallen soldiers. Decapitated statues and wingless beasts stood desecrated by time and weather, leaving them broken and crumbling. The crypts were tangled with wild weeds, wolfsbane and hemlock, crisscrossing the markers like choking hands.

I glanced around and saw a stone with a tormented face, peering at me with hollow vacant eyes. The face was animated and was straining and pushing forward, away from the stone that forever held it tight. It had no gender, no distinguishing marks of identification, but it seemed to know me. Its mouth was moving, trying to tell me something, but it could make no sound.

Poor you, I thought.

As I floated up to the stone, I saw, within the face, many other faces with pleading looks and moving lips. Faces of people I had paid little attention to while they were living. Faces I had looked past with little interest or sympathy when they walked in the land of the living. Now it was too late to reach out and touch them with a word of sympathy or help. It was too late to speak Words of Life and love. I wanted to linger but could not. My form was slowly gliding past the face that kept looking at me with pleading eyes and silent moving lips.

My body floated through the city of the dead toward a deep fog. The mist was dark, thick, and abnormal. Within its folds of gloom, the vapor vibrated with a malicious power and energy. The cloud parted, revealing an elegant black carriage, parked and waiting. Intricate carvings surrounded the windows and doors with spirals and spiked arches, like a miniature church. Its ornamentation was morbid and sinister. Human skulls held torches that burned with black fire.

Six skeleton horses, with tall pompous plumes on their heads, stomped the ground noiselessly. Upon their boney carcasses lay heavy black velvet blankets, decorated with the symbol of the beast. They were harnessed with fine leather bridles and straps. Tiny skulls were stitched to the lines instead of bells of bereavement.

The door to the carriage opened automatically at my approach, and I floated inside and sat on lush velvet seats. To my surprise, there sat another prisoner, looking at me with vacant lifeless eyes. I bent over, acting on someone else's authority, and put my ankle into the iron cuff that chained me to the other inmate. The door slowly closed, and the wagon began rolling soundlessly past the stone markers through the back entrance of the graveyard and into the open countryside.

I peeked at the other passenger who sat gazing blankly out the window. His long delicate hands were folded demurely on his lap. The convict's features were unusual. At first glance, I mistook him for a girl. His body was hard and chiseled like marble yet there was a fragile vulnerability about him.

However, one thing was certain, he looked no more than a child of thirteen or fourteen years. His thick blond hair was cut asymmetrically with jagged edges that shot out in every direction. It was hard to see his eyes, for his hair fell into his face.

The material of his white tunic was transparent, revealing his feminine features. He was amazingly beautiful. I looked away. His clothing distinguished his profession as a prostitute for the temple clergy.

The carriage sped on, attempting to outrun the sunrise that would soon creep over the horizon. We lumbered past huts that were outlined against the surrounding forest like a wall of mountain peaks in the blackness. The buggy floated down a narrow dirt road that wound its way past many farming homesteads where serfs would soon awaken and begin another day of servitude.

The carriage stopped behind a cabin that had a homey wooden fence enclosing an impressive herb garden. I recognized many of the plant species from my studies in Safehold. A strange mixture of wormwood, madwort, black hell bone, and motherwort grew side by side with sage, mint, and rosemary. Oddly there were other insidious species like nightshade, ergot, and belladonna.

A young woman floated toward the carriage. She wore the usual tawdry dress of a peasant. Mud-brown tendrils, spiked with silver, hung from beneath her white cap. She stopped and placed flowers on a grave in a concealed area that hid numerous dirt mounds. A look of regret momentarily clouded her eyes. I could tell many secrets were laid to rest beneath the cold earth in this garden of scandal.

I perceived this peasant was a midwife. Some saw her as a witch, a practitioner of medicine and magic. The herbs in her garden were used to bring on miscarriages so the young village girls could go about their lives without reproach.

The woman approached the waiting carriage, and the door opened automatically. She submissively cuffed herself to me, obeying the same unseen jailer, and then sat quietly, awaiting her fate.

As the carriage sprinted forward, I spotted Castle E'Doom. The elaborate palace sat on a rocky summit, high above the countryside. It was so high, storm clouds obscured the bottom of the precipice, making the palace look suspended in the air. The citadel filled the sky with flying buttresses, rounded turrets, and numerous towers. It was a strong and foreboding fortress, built for war and defense. The moon hung overhead, like a beacon, illuminating the mysterious structure with an eerie glow. Large shadows crawled across the face of the keep and billowing mist swirled about the stockade like a dragon guarding its lair.

I looked at the two inmates sitting in the hearse along with me. Their faces were pale and ashen. The reality of my situation stung my brain like the bite of a poisonous snake. I was a healer, sent into Old World as a special messenger, equipped and qualified to go into the front lines of this war with honor, bringing hope and promise of a great future to the floundering troops. Now I sit in a seat with the sinners, on our way to meet King Apollyon at his very epicenter. The prince of darkness who rules this world has the power to send me into hell for eternity.

Her fluttering heart banged inside her chest. She realized she could feel it beating again and could hear the carriage wheels turning on the cobbled street. *I thought I was dead.* Her eyes shot open. *Death would have been better than capture.*

Nyla looked at the castle that held the secret of her fate and tried to wipe the filth from her clothing. She raised her eyes to see the other inmates staring at her and knew she was sitting among the condemned. One question kept repeating itself and battled for possession of her mind. *Are we beyond salvation?*

CHAPTER 31

Rise from the Ashes

Sunrise extended an orange glow across the black sky. Heavy smoke from the war fires gripped the forest floor. A veil of gray smog stretched upward, concealing visibility into the burned-out glade, beyond the soldiers' headquarters. Footsteps alerted Aza that someone was coming. He quickly stood up from his kneeling position and wiped the tears from his eyes. It surprised him that just yesterday he was running away from God and today he couldn't get enough of his presence. Believing in God, let alone talking to him, was new and a little scary but his spiritual resurrection left him transformed. He looked like himself physically and his thoughts were his, yet he had a new reverence for sacred things. He felt the power and presence of God and knew in his heart that he would never be the same again.

Beryl rattled through charred tree branches. "Aza, are you there?" He crawled behind a boulder and found the hiding soldier. "We've been looking for you." He stumbled over a root covered in ash. Aza's stallion reared up and bolted away.

They watched the animal kick up soot that thickened the air. Aza coughed as he breathed in the particles, and Beryl wiped his face, spreading grey dust over his lily-white skin. The acrid scent of cinders clung to their hair and clothing.

Beryl dusted himself off. "The officers are ready to deploy. We are just waiting for you." He pulled his river rock from his pocket and rolled it over his fingers.

Aza tried to quiet the anxiety that was creeping into his spirit. He had just prayed and felt the peace that passes understanding, and now, just looking at his friend made him want to punch him. His emotions were all over the place. He ignored his urge to lash out and whistled for his horse that pranced back to his master, snorting and bucking.

Aza shut his eyes and inhaled. "I'm ready," he said. "I just needed a little time to myself to seek the Lord's presence."

Beryl looked at him and felt a twinge of guilt. "I'm sorry, Aza. I didn't mean to barge in on your time with God."

Aza nodded. "This is new to me, and I have a lot to learn. Thankfully I don't have to do it alone or all at once." He rubbed his eyes, hoping to conceal the tears that kept coming from the inner turmoil he was feeling.

Beryl took a leather-bound Bible from his backpack and handed it to his friend. "Everything you need to live a victorious life is written within the pages of this book." He put a reassuring hand on Aza's shoulder. "In time you will learn to wield God's Word with confidence."

Aza sighed. "I believe what you say. I witnessed it for myself. I have to let go of control and trust God. I feel empowered but a little mixed up." He rubbed his neck. "I'm worried about Nyla," he confided. "I'm grateful God spared my life, but my heart is overwhelmed with fear that the beast will do something unspeakable with…" His voice broke and he sobbed.

Beryl lowered his eyes, trying to hide his own fear. "We need to leave soon in order to find her before the Feast of the Blood Moon." His voice was soft, almost a whisper.

Aza hung his head. "Sargo," he whispered. "I pray he will find his way in this unbelieving wilderness." *Please protect him, Jesus.*

Beryl remained silent, sensing Aza had more he needed

to say.

"I cannot ask God to help Ravenna. She is a traitor. She brought the enemy into our camp. She set us up. She staged this attack, knowing the danger she put us in." He shook his head. "She wanted to punish me and Nyla. She tried to kill Simeon." He clenched his fists. "I can find no forgiveness in my heat for her."

Beryl rubbed his hands together. "Simeon is awake, and Anat was able to get a little broth into him."

Aza snorted. "I am glad he is going to fully recover, but the fact remains, Ravenna tried to kill an innocent man and she sent Nyla to face the executioner."

Beryl looked away. "I understand how you feel. I am fighting the same feelings." He paused. "Forgiveness is hard to swallow, very hard to digest, but we must forgive others so our savior can forgive us. We do this to obey."

Aza shook his head. "Never."

"As you grow in Christ, 'never' will become just a word from your past."

Both men walked back to the camp, lost in their thoughts. When they arrived, the encampment was buzzing with activity. Young and old worked together, loading wagons with food and extra blankets. Soldiers harnessed and saddled the horses. Women loaded last-minute rations while men folded tents, counted spikes, and checked ropes for fraying. The emergency of their time of departure electrified the air with energy.

Alex paced around the campsite, waiting for the medics to finish placing the injured into wagon beds. Both Temperance and Simeon would be together in the care of handpicked guards. She had no intention of letting another traitor cause them further harm.

The thought of Temperance made her mind reel back to St Regents. Her emotions burned in the pit of her stomach. Her feelings of distrust toward her mentors in Safehold had changed. She realized they were her tribe. None of them were perfect, but they were still family. She smiled inwardly, wondering what Mother would think of being part of a tribe.

Tears filled her eyes. Her loved ones were headed to Castle E'Doom to face execution for treason. Temperance was mutilated and tortured for her faith. Nyla was taken prisoner. Her heart dropped in her chest, thinking about the demons that were sent to take Nyla to stand trial as a fallen saint. *Lord God, am I strong enough to handle a real rescue?*

While she mentally talked to God, a soft voice spoke words of comfort to her thoughts. *My strength is sufficient for you.*

Her heart slowed down and her racing emotions settled.

Beryl stood by her side. "What are you thinking?" he asked

Alex put her hand on the hilt of her sword. "Do you think Nyla knows we will come for her? Does she realize God is with her?" She swallowed back her emotions. "I remember how oppressive and frightening it felt when I faced the demons in the ziggurat. If you don't remain alert, they will attack your mind, causing you to doubt God's love and faithfulness."

Beryl reached down and took her hand in his. "Your army is ready."

"Fall in!" Aza gave the command and the soldiers got in formation. Infantry leaders collected banners that had been locked away and held them, proudly displaying the righteous names of the Lord. The worship band and the elders carefully prepared the scrolls with the sacred Words of Life, along with their musical instruments, and climbed on a flatbed wagon.

Tika stood on the flatbed, holding the flag that read "Jehovah Nissi," (God is our banner). "The sacred weapons are ready to be carried into battle, ma'am."

Alex stood proudly in front of her army. "Eyes front."

Beryl began to pray. "Hear and listen to the prophetic

word." A soft breeze blew, stirring the treetops, and a hushed peace descended upon the army.

"Take courage because I have a plan for my people. There will be obstacles in your path as you engage in warfare, but these obstacles will not stop what I have ordained. My Spirit is the banner that flies high within you. Let it soar in your heart as on the wings of an eagle. Strength is on your side, an inner strength that comes from pure faith, a faith born of a clean and forgiven heart. Carry my words forth in courage and boldness. I will never leave you or forsake you."

The soldiers and refugees stood silently as the words of encouragement took root in their hearts. The band began to play a marching song.

"Onward soldiers," Alex commanded.

The small army moved into Old World bringing a message of hope to a beaten generation. The banners floated freely in the breeze, and a new song filled the air, a song of bravery, valor, and triumph.

The sound of hoofbeats and wagon wheels brought a smile to Alex's spirit as the army proceeded down the mountainside.

"I hope they can keep this attitude," Alex said pensively. "You know Apollyon will not go down easily, especially while he is holding Nyla and other believers hostage."

Beryl wiped his brow on his sleeve. "Yes. I agree."

Alex nervously tossed a charred stick back and forth from hand to hand. "What do you see in your spirit?"

Beryl looked up at the sky. It was bright blue and cloud free. "An unthinking mind and an untrained eye might think the world is free of wickedness." He sighed and absently rubbed his head. "I see war. The ruler of this world is not defeated… yet." He tried to shake his feeling of foreboding. "We must hurry if we are going to find Nyla alive. I'm afraid the evil one will come down on the remnant harder than ever because he knows his time is short."

Alex tightened her belt and secured her sword.

Beryl put his lion skin cape and the staff away and picked up his suit of chain mail and slipped it over his tunic. He positioned his breastplate over his heart and his belt around his waist. The shoes he now wore were not the sandals of his younger days of freedom in the desert, they were the boots of a soldier, a warrior, fashioned to carry him and the word of truth into a hostile nation.

His eyes scanned the twisting road that led to Castle E'Doom. A shiver of fear crept up his spine as he fixed his eyes southward toward the lush countryside that belonged to the king of Old World. He knew in his spirit that something had been unleashed within the inner recesses of the earth. Something the remnant had not yet experienced.

When he finally spoke to answer her question, he willed his voice to sound courageous. "I do not know what lies ahead." His stomach flip-flopped. "I do know the Lord is faithful, and he will strengthen us and protect us from the evil one." He picked up his sword and shield and climbed into the seat of the donkey cart.

Alex mounted Malak and they rode toward E'Doom to free Nyla and the captives during the Feast of the Blood Moon.

About the Author

Lynare Pipitone is a wife, mother, successful businesswoman and real estate investor with a desire to share her Christian faith. She became an author and blogger eight years ago to encourage other believers to finish the race God set before them with passion, purpose, and conviction. Her work appeared in *Grandparenting through Obstacles*, a collage of true stories about the changing role of grandparenting in today's society. She hosts an inspirational blog, *Voices from the Wilderness*, and finished her first novel.

Rise from the Ashes is book 1 of the New Inquisition.

CPSIA information can be obtained
at www.ICGtesting.com
Printed in the USA
LVHW082048030420
652151LV00007B/414